ON ROMFORD ROAD

Andrew Sanger was born in London in 1948. He attended the Lycée Français Charles de Gaulle in London and Colchester Royal Grammar School. He dropped out of University College London to spend most of 1967 and 1968 in and around San Francisco, followed by a continuous journey of several years through the US, Europe, the Middle East and India. He settled in the Languedoc region of southern France, where he worked as a truck driver.

In 1978 Andrew Sanger returned to the UK and became a freelance travel journalist contributing to a wide spectrum of British national press and popular magazines. For ten years he was editor of French Railways' travel magazine, *Top Rail*. Several of his travel features have won media awards.

Andrew Sanger is the author of more than forty travel guides and four other novels, *The J-Word* (2009), *The Slave* (2013), *Love* (2015) and *The Unknown Mrs Rosen* (2020). He lives in the New Forest, on England's south coast.

For reviews and comment see www.andrewsanger.com.

Find him on X/Twitter at @andrewsanger.

Other Novels by Andrew Sanger

The J-Word
The Slave
Love
The Unknown Mrs Rosen

ON ROMFORD ROAD

A novel in four parts

HARRIET, MAUD, ELIZABETH, ALEX

_____

Andrew Sanger

FOCUS BOOKS

London, England

www.focus-books.co.uk

ON ROMFORD ROAD
Published by Focus Books, 2025
Print ISBN: 9780955820182
Digital ISBN: 9780955820199
Copyright © Andrew Sanger 2025
All rights reserved worldwide
www.andrewsanger.com

The right of Andrew Sanger to be identified as the author
of this work has been asserted by him in accordance with
the Copyright, Designs and Patents Act 1988.

Cover design © Andrew Sanger 2025
incorporating detail from
'A Lady Playing the Piano' by Carl Holsøe (1900).

CIP data: A catalogue record for this book
is available from the British Library.

FOR GERRY AND JOSH

. . .

THANK YOU

I am grateful to all whose knowledge and recollections were freely given to help me write this story, especially HHJ Sarah Plaschkes KC, Linda Strudwick, Linda Toynbee and Chloë Wennersten. Thank you Rory Isserow for helping me with the cover. Above all, thank you Gerry, for memories, advice, patience and love.

GEOGRAPHICAL NOTE

An undistinguished thoroughfare, wide, busy and without charm, runs across East London from the City into Essex. Among the oldest paved roads in Britain, it leaves the City of London at Aldgate, eastern gateway of the Roman wall. At the start it passes Whitechapel, after one mile reaching Mile End. It fords the spreading river Lea and its backwaters at Stratford ("paved ford"), the Roding at Ilford ("stream ford") and the Beam at Romford ("wide ford"), making altogether a march of fifteen Roman miles. On the way it serves as a high street for a succession of working-class neighbourhoods.

From Romford the Roman march continued across the flat landscapes of Essex to the garrison at Colchester. Like us today, Romans numbered rather than named most of their highways; the names were given later. From Aldgate to Colchester was Iter IX and Iter V – Routes 9 and 5 – known in later ages, along parts of its length, as Aldgatestrete, the Great Road, the Romford Road, Great Essex Road and Pye Road. Today it is numbered A11 and A118 to Romford, then A12.

East of London's Roman wall lay cemeteries. From the fall of Rome to the Middle Ages, more burial grounds were founded outside the eastern wall, and charitable hospices and hospitals, and religious houses. The poor and needy gathered here, and those seeking refuge from the law, those making a living from the river, and harried refugees disembarking at the nearby docks, as well as great numbers of craftsmen and tradesmen serving the needs of the City.

"The East End" historically and culturally refers to the districts from the City to the River Lea. It began to be built up in the 16th century, embracing rural and riverside settlements, Bethnal Green, Bow, Mile End, Poplar, Limehouse, Wapping. All were within the medieval manor and parish of Stepney, in the county of Middlesex. Its people and their speech became known as Cockney. By the 18th century the area was crowded with the artisan, labouring and servant classes and with Huguenot refugees, a century later followed by thousands of Jews fleeing Russian pogroms. By the early 20th century the East End was synonymous with immigrants, poverty, crime, crowding and deprivation.

"East London", although sometimes including the East End, refers to the districts from the River Lea to Romford that once were all in the county of Essex. From the 1860s, estates of terraced streets for London's expanding working class were spreading along Romford Road as new industries and transportation developed. By WW1 East London had reached the River Roding. After the war, London County Council purchased tracts of countryside beyond the river, at Becontree and Dagenham, to create modern housing estates for East Enders. After WW2, developers and local councils pushed further into Essex to rehouse overcrowded and bombed-out East Londoners. The new estates and new districts have themselves become part of East London. Romford Road remains its main thoroughfare, the network of terraced streets to either side now home to new generations of immigrants.

"There ain't half been some clever bastards.

Lucky bleeders, lucky bleeders."

– Ian Dury & Russell Hardy

HARRIET

Born June 1878, East Ham Levels, Essex

1

A sound woke her. Not music – she could sleep through that, slept through it every night. She could hear it now, the piano and a wild rollicking chorus. This was quite different, something in the street. She slipped from the bed and hurried to the window, feet cool on the floorboards, fingertips wiping condensation from the glass.

Ogres, giants and looming demons she saw out there, monstrous limbs waving high upon walls and gables. Among them tiny hobgoblins and bogeymen swarmed upon the ground in the glare of blazing batons, menacing as hornets, surging this way and that in fury, restless, eager, approaching. Their shrieks became loud as she watched. One of the creatures hurled a big stone, then a cobblestone flew through the air, and another, and shards tumbled like hail onto the pavement. Booming roars and howls echoed around the terraced street. At the sight of glass crashing down, some cheered. But those were human cheers, surely?

She understood then that the monsters were real people, the terrifying giants mere shadows on the brick. The flames were held aloft in the hands of men and women. She became more awake. The cobblestones had been thrown at the windows above the sweetshop where Mr Zuckerman lived with his family. Painted wooden shutters covered the shop windows and the door. Men began to rip down the shutters with a fantastic tearing sound.

Sometimes she was taken to the sweetshop to buy a gobstopper, dolly mixtures, licorice strip or marshmallow, or other sweets of Mr Zuckerman's own invention made in mysterious rooms behind the shop. He wore a brown overall, and was very little, and had to climb a step ladder to reach the jars. He scooped the sweets into a brown paper bag and she would give him her farthing. But these people, she sensed, were not looking for sweets. They were looking for Mr Zuckerman. A great, brilliant point of fire like a dragon's tongue shot out from the shop, greeted by long, ecstatic screams that reminded her of the seagulls scavenging by the river. And they whirled like the gulls too, the flock turning as one to continue their hunt, towards the public house.

As it happened Maud knew exactly where the sweetshop man and his wife (whose belly was huge like a football under her dress) and their little boy Yitzy were at this moment. They were hiding fearfully in the attic right above her bedroom and she was not to tell anyone, not anyone at all, ever.

Mum had always said it would be very naughty to go downstairs after she'd been put to bed. Dad said if she ever did go down he'd give her what for. She knew, though, that now she *must* go down. In hasty steps, with no time to put on shoes, she dashed across the landing and descended unlit stairs towards the music and voices, nearly slipping, almost falling. At the foot of the stairs, a golden glow from beneath the forbidden door beckoned along the corridor.

The din inside struck her like a physical object. It consumed her as if she had been flung into the ooze of Barking Creek. She floundered unable to understand or see or breathe. The air was thick with cigarette smoke and the smell of beer. The long aprons of barmen and barmaids pushed past indifferently. At last she spied Dad, and he spied her standing in her flannel nightdress, frail and small, brown curls hanging loose, overwhelmed and barefoot among the kegs, crates and pails of dishwater. He was gesturing at her furiously – 'Bad girl! Back to bed!' He had to finish pulling a customer's pint before he could deal with her. His wife Harriet could not leave the piano. To a barmaid he hissed: 'Oi, quick, take the kid back up.'

'What is it, duck – something wrong?' The barmaid had once been Maud's nursemaid, and still shared her bedroom. Her firm arms raised the little girl from the floor in a single movement. At last Maud could see. On the other side of the bar was revealed the whole fantastic spectacle of adulthood at leisure, a crowd of loud, laughing men and just a few women, bright lamps lit all around the walls. There in the midst of it sat Mum, slight and little, full of life, so pretty and with such poise, awe-inspiring with a black ribbon and white pearls around her neck, her waves of dark hair piled high and the long train of her creamy dress pulled to one side, playing and playing and playing the piano in front of everyone!

'The Sweet Man,' Maud struggled to find the correct words, 'his shop, the sweetshop, they set it on fire.'

'Who did?' The barmaid readily grasped what she was saying. 'When – now?'

Maud nodded vigorously. 'They're coming here.' It was already too late. A gang burst yelling through the street door. Armed with glowing sticks, they could hardly look less like monsters and ogres; more like mangy dogs, snarling, wretched and enraged.

Maud's mother stopped playing at once, her hands poised oddly motionless above the keys in the midst of a ragtime piece. Conversation and laughter came to an abrupt halt. From the street pounded an uncouth chant, *Lu-si-ta-ni-a* and *Set them alight, set them alight.* The cruise liner *RMS Lusitania* had been sunk by a German u-boat one week before, drowning twelve hundred civilians. Revenge parties were on the march. Inside the pub everyone was silent, waiting and fearful.

The head of the mob shouted, 'You hiding that bloody Hun in here, Ted Cotter?'

'Get those brands out of here, Charlie Sleet,' retorted Maud's father from behind the bar. 'Zuckerman's no Hun, is he? They're from Russia, those people – they're on *our* side. Clear off out of it.'

'Don't be a mug, Cotter. That Yid is no Russki. Him an' his missus jabber in German. A Yid's same as a Hun or worse. Hand him over or we'll find him ourselves,' threatened Sleet. He took a step as if to make good his word.

For Edwin Cotter, landlord of the Well Smack inn, breaking up fistfights, knife fights and glassings and chucking out rowdies had been part of the job ever since he started twenty-two years ago as a potboy carrying beer mugs and clay pipes out to navvies in the street. It was a long time since there had been any serious trouble, but he remembered how to deal with it. He and his pair of sturdy young barmen vaulted over the counter. In their hands each held the customary billy-club, a sturdy, flexible cosh of finely twisted leather with a weighty lead-filled head. With those lethal tools strapped to their wrists, the three men set about Charlie Sleet and the intruders.

Most of Sleet's companions made a quick retreat, but some stood their ground. Sleet himself was no ordinary drunk to be tossed out of a bar. On this occasion he happened to be sober; he was powerfully built, fearless and quick, he hated Germans, hated Jews, hated Edwin Cotter and everyone like him, and was himself armed with a length of wood smouldering at the tip. Things did not go as Cotter and his barmen expected.

Charlie Sleet, a large, bear-like creature, slouching and shabby, his suit filthy from an evening of destruction, his shaved head and face stubble-covered, was much fitter than he looked. Edwin Cotter, a clean, handsome, upright man of good height in a decent suit and cravat, was strong and well-formed, with a full twirled moustache and neatly trimmed light brown hair. Both men were in their late thirties, Cotter only a couple of years the older, but lately Cotter felt constantly weary from long hours, heavy cellarwork and worries about wartime licensing laws, while Sleet passed his time as a roughneck street-thief and bare-knuckle boxer.

Dodging the cosh with ease, Charlie Sleet struck Edwin Cotter across the head and chest with the smouldering stick. Cotter fell back hurt at once, blood trickling from his scalp and gathering in his hair. A voice shouted, 'Get a policeman!' Most of the pub's customers recoiled in horror and began a frantic push through a door to the saloon bar, from which they would be able to flee into the street. Those who stayed to join the fight seemed mainly to be on Sleet's side. A pint glass was thrown and smashed.

For a second Edwin lay stunned. As Harriet desperately struggled to raise her husband onto his feet, only then did she notice Maud in the barmaid's arms. 'What the hell is she doing in here?' she shrieked. 'Mind that child, mind that child! Take her out.'

The barmaid said, 'Poor mite's come down to warn us.'

Maud had seen everything. She had watched her father fight and fall and grasp helplessly at the wall for support, his head cut, his beautiful jacket and cravat scorched. She would never forget the sight. Even Sleet seemed abashed that the brawl had been witnessed by a little girl in a nightdress. He lowered his weapon. 'Come on,' he spoke to his supporters, 'leave it for now;' and to Edwin, 'I'll be back to finish you off, Cotter, an' that Yid o' yours.'

*

By the time Edwin Cotter landed the job as manager of the old Well Smack inn in Barking, the local fleet of well smacks and cutters with their famous 'short blue' flag – once the largest fishing fleet in the world – had long ago faded from memory. Barking had given up fishing and was becoming part of east London. Street after street was under construction, shallow foundations dug into every remaining scrap of field or marsh. Small two-storey terraces were laid out for the labouring class, with bay windows for the more genteel. Quays and wharves alive for centuries beside the river Roding, which winds down into the mighty Thames estuary, were dead at last and forgotten. Most of Barking's population never so much as glimpsed the sea now. They worked in sweatshops, workshops and warehouses; in factories, not fishing boats. Nor did the sea come into their thoughts; only the oily, lapping tide of London docks. The last reminder of fishing was in the names of Barking's rowdy public houses.

The Well Smack's large public bar opened onto a busy street corner. The two saloon bars smart with rugs, a cosy snug with a coal fire, and a sedate lounge bar could all be entered from the side street. Pressing against the rear of the pub were overcrowded lanes where an alley door opened into a rough tap-room with no seats. To celebrate the coronation of King Edward VII, under Edwin's direction the Well Smack had been given a handsome new façade of glazed red brick and tile, and inside, a glorious display of modern cut glass, polished brass, colourful mosaic and carved wood in the latest Art Nouveau designs, new zinc on the bar, and new windows and partitions all leaded, etched and glazed with stained glass. A new sign, still depicting a fishing smack in full sail, hung from the outside wall.

In his years of living and working in the Well Smack, Edwin Cotter had never seen the place looking so grand.

It was a giant step up the social ladder for Edwin to take over the licence and become a pub landlord. He had himself grown up in one of the narrow lanes at the back, his father a sorter in a tobacco warehouse, his mother a machine operator at the jute works. His parents were immensely proud of his rise in the world. Unlike the thousands drifting in from Essex farms, it was from the worst dockside squalor of Limehouse that they had come searching for a better life. Edwin's success justified all their privations and efforts. As soon as he was installed as manager of the pub, he started sending them a quart jug of stout every evening for supper and five shillings a week so they could retire from work.

And this was the perfect moment to propose to the petite, graceful, half-starved Harriet Beryl Hayes. He had so far snatched only the barest conversation with her on the way in and out of the old parish church, beside the ruins of Barking Abbey, nearly opposite the pub. His greatest longing was to save this woman from the wretched life she was wasting as maid-of-all-work for a vicious black-and-whitesmith and his family. There, at twenty-six years of age, she toiled alone from five in the morning until ten at night, was insulted, beaten and barely fed. Sometimes in pain and weakened by her heavy, erratic monthly periods she was further chastised as her work fell short. Harriet's uncouth 'master' enjoyed thrashing her. It was a form of intimacy. Her living quarters, Edwin knew, were in the space beneath the stairs. Yet Harriet considered – she told him – that even this was not a bad situation, when you thought about it, compared to some.

In those glances and brief exchanges at the church Edwin perceived in Harriet what others may not have noticed, a resilient grace and beauty and unquenchable strength, determination and vivacity. Harriet Hayes, he learned, was one of a large family of unskilled, uneducated labourers and skivvies, a veritable tribe in the ragged eastern edges of the capital. Many worked at the Beckton Gas Works and were housed in the company's terraces in Barking, Harriet's disreputable father among them, raising there a dozen or so children and burying three or four others. To Edwin's parents, Harriet Hayes was unspeakably common, even more than they were themselves, and they did not approve of her or the match. On the other hand they felt it no bad thing for Edwin to have a wife accustomed to hard work and obedience. She was good-natured and polite, and deft with a darning needle.

Harriet and Edwin married in that old church beside abbey ruins. She moved into his rooms above the bar and felt that truly she had ascended bodily into some kind of heaven. An actual bed! Real bedlinen! A coal fire! Even a place to wash! She explored the unfamiliar delights of normal rooms, normal furniture. A moment of puzzlement about a mouth organ in a drawer revealed to their astonishment that she was musical. Harriet could hear a tune and play it from memory, just like that! She had never realised she had a skill or talent of any kind. Edwin bought a second-hand piano and installed it in the public bar, to call her very own.

She was to play and sing any popular song customers asked for. The sauciest music hall favourites, though, Edwin insisted she may play but not sing. Her audience readily and raucously supplied the words. Harriet loved the ragtime sound and could turn any tune into ragtime. Edwin said that sort of thing would be just the job.

To pick up new tunes was a good excuse for a weekly outing to the East Ham variety theatre. This was the good life indeed! The gloriously ornate palace of entertainment, with its marble and velvet, its carpets and panelling, seating two thousand twice every evening, was the main attraction for miles around and surpassed all Harriet's dreams of modernity, luxury and pleasure. Having heard a song there the drinkers of Barking were only too glad to hear it again free of charge at the Well Smack inn, performed by the talented Mrs Cotter.

In fancy florid walnut with a German name in gold lettering, an inlaid pattern on the front and winged candle sconces, the piano was by far the grandest and most wonderful thing she had ever owned. A music holder folded away into the lid. Pulled out, it fanned open with struts, a narrow ledge and swivelling prongs to hold printed music sheets. However, Harriet did not use the holder because she could not read music sheets. Indeed nor could she understand the concept of sound made soundless on paper. She need only say, 'Hum it for me' to play a piece straight away and forever after. She had never heard of music lessons. Even now she did not think of them.

During her pregnancy, as decency required, Harriet did not appear in public. She practised hard at her playing in the smoky bar-room when the pub was closed until she was too large to reach the keyboard. Maud was born in the room above the bar on June 13th 1908, as a procession of suffragists with banners marched by in the street outside.

*

After the blow from Sleet's baton, with Harriet's help Edwin rose to his feet unsteady and breathless. He felt faint, even queasy, and understood that something had changed about him; more was wrong than merely being knocked about. He felt with his fingertips: the blood on his head amounted to very little, yet his head was pounding. He stared about in bewildered despair at the damage caused by Sleet's men to the new fittings in the public bar. 'Get this mess cleaned up,' he muttered to Harriet and the staff.

Harriet refused. 'No, Ted, we'll deal with it tomorrow,' she said. To the barmen and barmaids she shook her head, negating his order, 'That's it for tonight, thank you. You can go off now. Good night.' She took a damp cloth from behind the bar to wipe his face and cool a livid mark on his scalp. 'You're goin'a have an almighty bruise.' She dabbed blood out of his hair.

'First thing I must do,' Edwin said, 'is get Zuckerman an' his wife an' kid to a place o' safety.'

'Where, though, Ted?'

'Somewhere they can lie low. Among their own kind, their own people. If I borrer an 'orse an' cart I can take 'em.'

'No, you can't. You're hurt. Your coat is burnt.'

'I'm well enough. It's not safe for 'em here.'

'Well, wherever it is, they can make their own way, can't they?'

'What, out there with a kid, the woman eight months gone, an' gangs roaming?' He shook his head. 'No!' As he spoke, the sound of wild yelling in the street could be heard not far away, and the clamouring bell of a fire engine.

Harriet warned, 'Well then, wait till morning. Rest now an' get your wind back.'

'No, Hattie, they'll be worse off in daytime. They'll be noticed. They look so foreign, don't they? Even in the dark we might have to hide 'em. One of our regulars'll lend me an 'orse an' cart.'

'At this hour? No, you can't drag customers into this, Ted.'

'I'll go with 'em on foot. Maybe find a cart for hire on the way.'

Edwin sent Harriet upstairs to tell the Zuckermans to be ready to move during the night. She came back to say they were already packed and decided upon getting to Spitalfields, in Whitechapel. 'They know someone there. He's told me an address. Reckons they can walk it.'

'Not likely, duck, not on their own.'

'I've got a cousin,' Harriet mused, 'lives by the Ilford Bridge. His name's Will. Ain't seen him in years but we always got on. Scrap dealer in the markets. He uses a little barrer, a handcart. He'd lend it for nothing, I expect, but give him a drink. You an' Zuckerman push the barrer. His missis an' kid can ride aboard wi' their bags.'

'That'd be good, Hattie, if he'll lend it. We can stick on Romford Road straight down to Whitechapel.'

Another doubt struck Harriet: 'What about coming back? You'll be on your own. Will you be all right?'

'The cart'll be empty on the way back. I'll manage.'

'Take your pistol. I want you back here safe an' sound.' She gave a short laugh.

'No, no, better not, love. Don't want to end up on a murder charge.'

Emerging at midnight from the attic where they had been hiding, the Zuckermans came cautiously down into the public bar, a young couple with small bundles of luggage. They too stared, horrified by the damage. Aaron and Lieba Zuckerman were foreign-looking to be sure, strong-featured, Aaron much shorter than Edwin, Lieba even shorter than Harriet, their faces defiant and resolute, hard-bitten. Despite living above a sweetshop, Yitzhak – Yitzy – was the thinnest of them, suspicious, giving Harriet a glare, then a fearful smile. Lieba's belly was rounded and stretched, not eight months pregnant as Edwin had supposed, but at least eight and a half.

Harriet shook Aaron's and Lieba's hands, wished them well, and in case they should need something on their night walk gave each man a wrap of newspaper around some bread and sausage and a bottle of ale, and for Lieba and the boy, a jar of boiled milk and some dry biscuits. They thanked her in a way that Harriet considered excessive and embarrassing, even invoking blessings, in elaborate, accented English, slightly incomprehensible. 'If we can for you do something, dear, if one day, God forbid...,' murmured Lieba, with a gesture as if to suggest every unspeakable mischance that might lie in wait for any of us, 'when, who knows, for you, for your daughter, come to us...'

Aaron knew he would not touch the goyish sausage, nor probably the ale. He expected he would share the milk and biscuits with his wife and child and give the sausage and ale back to this brave Englishman who had helped them so much and was now willing to do even more.

In the chill air outside, a black dust hung; and an acrid smell of burning from the Zuckermans' own home and shop. Led by Edwin, they took the dark riverside footpath on the other side of the Roding, hardly frequented at night, which ran from an abandoned quayside mill, over the railway tracks, to Romford Road.

Harriet's cousin Will rented an end-of-terrace and a side yard in one of the newly built back-to-back streets, close together as a comb's teeth, seemingly intended to become a slum as fast as possible. Unconcerned by being woken, happy to do anything for his cousin Harriet, he willingly rolled out the barrow and warned the two men not to let anyone steal it from them as they walked.

Lieba and the boy settled themselves between sheets of sacking; Aaron and Edwin began pushing. Edwin already felt exhausted and his headache had not gone away. But as Harriet had said, the cart was easy even for one man to manage, and they had only seven or eight miles to travel. Aaron kept his face wrapped in a muffler, while Edwin's more evidently English features were exposed to view. Soon after the start of the journey a crowd on the lookout for Germans raced past crying for blood but took no notice of two cloth-capped working men pushing a barrow.

Edwin and Aaron passed shops that had been invaded, Krenz and Sons, watchmakers, completely emptied; Streitberger, a pork butchers, everything taken; Bachmeyer's hairdressing salon, smashed to pieces; Bornheim, furrier, pillaged and destroyed; and others with German names, burned, looted, stripped bare. Edwin asked, 'Are they, you know – like you, Russians?'

'No, these are not Jews, these are German. But they are not your enemy. These came to open a shop, not fight.'

Further on, the area was calm, with no sign of disorder. Eventually the distant yelling had died away. The main highway, Romford Road, became broad and well cobbled, the wide pavements lined with fine, solid houses now asleep. The street lamps were unlit.

There were tram lines, but there would be no more trams until tomorrow. An occasional horse-drawn carriage was the only traffic. Public houses, locked and dark, appeared as landmarks along the way. In many Edwin had taken a drink over the years, the William the Conqueror, the Earl of Essex, the Waggon and Horses, the Three Rabbits, the Rising Sun; some he knew by reputation, the Freemason's Arms, the Princess Alice. Along the side roads were others he remembered. Even to think of them increased his longing for rest.

Edwin's wandering mind turned to picturing running a pub in a tranquil, better-off neighbourhood like these, weighing up how they compared to Barking. He wondered how they were faring with the wartime regulations that he was finding so onerous. Of course, most of these establishments were smaller than the Well Smack. They passed the handsome arched brick and ironwork of the Live and Let Live – "the Live", they called it – just visible in shadow.

The problem, Edwin decided, was the smell. He supposed you get used to it. From tall factory chimneys vapours rose in the dark. The air passed from one odour to the next, more or less raw on the eyes, nostrils and lips. Escaping the bitter gases of chemical works they walked into the sweet fumes of brewery and bakery, confectionery, the gagging smell of the glue factory, a rubber works, the nauseating stink of a tannery.

The cart rattled forward, Lieba lost in fears and memories; Yitzhak asleep against her. The two men, side by side, kept a steady pace. Rising ahead in the middle of the road stood the old church at Bow. 'About half way,' Edwin announced. 'Time for a break?' He yearned for even a short pause.

Aaron shook his head. 'No! Not here!' He was perhaps right. Within minutes the atmosphere changed. To either side groups hurried on the pavement in the dark. By the church a house had the words *Votes For Women* painted across the front in large letters. Policemen stood watching.

Here debris lay in the roadway. Aaron and Edwin hurried past wrecked shops and houses. Aaron's wary eye darted knowingly around. He murmured, 'Trouble will start again in the morning.' The area became more populous, dwellings more tightly packed, taverns more numerous. Edwin could see plainly that these were mere rough drinking houses and common lodgings. At Mile End Waste an incomprehensible chaos of abandoned stalls and stands surrounded by litter could be made out in the shadowy light of dying lanterns. A weather-boarded pub with figures gathered in its doorways stood on a paved island in the midst of the highway.

Aaron pointed out the first shop signs in Yiddish and, soon after, a pair of strangely attired men walking quickly, orthodox Jews. Off the main road were small factories lit up and busy. Clusters of such men stood on guard outside synagogues and damaged shops with the plea *We are Russians* chalked across broken shutters. Cobbles and stones that must earlier have been thrown at them were scattered about. Edwin despaired – he was taking Mr and Mrs Zuckerman and their son into what looked like a battleground!

Aaron called out to a couple of ragged men, asking them the way in a tongue that Edwin thought was undoubtedly German. Following their directions, they wheeled the cart away from the main road into stinking courts and filth-strewn lanes of a type Edwin had never seen, pressed between looming tenements. He glimpsed unwashed women and little girls on the corner of an alley, offering themselves for rent, even calling out their price in pennies. Whole families were encamped on the grimy pavements, squatting against the walls. Ragged, barefoot boys darted about like flies in the dark.

Turning to right and left and right again, they entered quite a different labyrinth, the narrow alleys like tunnels crowded with countless workshops packed into high terraced houses, foreign names above every front door, and unreadable lettering, and people hurrying, all of them thin, quick and strange in the way of the Zuckermans, or something more outlandish by far.

At last Aaron called a halt. He and Edwin lowered the handcart legs outside a lofty dwelling of crumbling brick facing a sweatshop teeming in the night with workers and machines. It was here that the two men wished each other farewell. Aaron remembered to give back the sausage, bread and ale, grasping Edwin's hand. 'Mr Cotter, there is nothing we won't do for the people who helped us,' he promised gravely. Sleepily understanding that the journey was over, Yitzhak sat up. 'Here we are safe,' said Lieba.

*

He could hardly face pushing the empty handcart miles back along Whitechapel Road, the Mile End Road, Romford Road. Edwin was exhausted and a pain thudded within his forehead. He felt gloomily that he had been too generous to the Zuckermans! What had they ever done for him, what *could* they ever do for anyone, people in such straits? He recalled though that young Aaron, little foreigner though he was, was a good sort, a decent family man, a hard worker, and had always been kind to Maud, and pleasant to everyone. Such people should not fall victim to dissolute brutes like Charlie Sleet. All the same, he thought, he *had* done too much for them. Wearily he pressed forward. His next task this morning would be to clear up and repair the public bar, and in a few hours he must open the pub as usual and get on with his work.

First intimations of dawn in the sky ahead gave him new vigour. Above the crowded rooftops of Mile End majestic cloud mounted to the airy heavens. Roadside trees every few hundred yards, newly leafed, stood in silhouette. A damp haze in the air was refreshing, his face and brow gently moistened. In Forest Gate and Manor Park the trams had started their day's work and now great numbers of costers and tradesmen were pushing carts and barrows or passing by on horse-drawn wagons. In the half-light streams of men and women made their way along the pavement. Outside small yards and workshops some loitered, talking loudly about the night's disturbances. The road curved a little, the rising sun shone more brightly towards him and he tilted his hat to shield his eyes.

At last Edwin reached the home of Harriet's cousin Will to return the pushcart. He found the man already up and busy. He gave him the sausages, beer and bread, which he had not eaten after all.

Pacing the last mile unencumbered Edwin felt exalted by the sense that his ordeal was nearly over and that he had 'done the right thing.' As he approached the Well Smack, there seemed to be some commotion in front of the pub. Harriet and Maud were standing in the street. Maud was crying. Suddenly fatigue left him and everything else was forgotten. He broke into a trot. Maud rushed to meet him with a wail while Harriet stood staring, perfectly still like a bird in shock. Maud cried, 'They came looking for the Sweetshop Man.'

All the pub's new stained glass windows had been smashed. Across the glazed red tiles of the façade a word was roughly painted in large white letters – TRAITOR.

Edwin stood gazing at the shameful word and at his wife and the gathering of curious neighbours. Then a shocking, terrible pain lashed across his chest and arm. The exhaustion he had been fighting all night chose this instant to consume him utterly. He tried to remain standing, and grasped at the air. But his knees failed him. Without haste his body lowered itself to the pavement and stretched itself on the ground. There was screaming, but he heard nothing.

2

With straight back and pleasant smile Harriet carried in a tray of filled glasses for the police officers. It had been a regular thing, every Thursday evening, that six CID officers based at Barking police station would come to the Well Smack inn for a drink "on the house".

They always sat in the snug, a small private saloon which they had to themselves. It started years ago, when Barking police station was only a few paces from the pub. After the new, modern police station opened a little further away, the officers continued enjoying this favour. For the inn's landlords of old as for Edwin today, entertaining the police was in part insurance and in part gambling, and he could not in any case risk refusing. He could only hope that in an emergency, if ever, for example, the pub experienced a brawl that got out of hand, or a robbery, there would be a quid pro quo from the police.

Harriet didn't like the arrangement because apart from the expense and the fact that she didn't believe there *would* be a quid pro quo, Thursday became the one night of the week when Edwin drank too much. Every other evening her husband liked a drink as much as most men, but on Thursdays he felt obliged to join the CID officers for a while, share a joke and some banter, chat amiably with them about local goings on, and most importantly, in this secluded room with the doors closed, let them know everything he had seen, been told or overheard that might be useful to know. For in the Well Smack as in other big, busy pubs, *objets trouvés* were bought and sold with no questions asked, schemes and ideas quietly discussed, rendezvous kept, matters arranged, bets taken.

The officers were free to order as much as they liked of whatever they wanted, with Edwin's compliments. Round after round was brought to the low table surrounded by armchairs. The CID officers liked it that the landlord's wife served them herself. It was a privilege, it showed respect and she made a pretty sight coming in with a tray of drinks. One in particular, a stout older man with a habit of constantly wiping beads of sweat from his scalp with a folded handkerchief, took a shine to Harriet. The name was Detective Inspector Fisk. Sucking on his billowing pipe Fisk would give her the eye even when Edwin was sitting beside him. Neither Edwin nor Harriet liked this insolence but there was really nothing they could do or say about it.

Edwin became so drunk sometimes on a Thursday evening that Harriet took the loaded revolver he kept in their bedroom and hid it. She was afraid he might shoot DI Fisk. Certainly she would like to.

'I'm sorry, gents.' As Harriet stepped into the warm, smoke-filled snug she apologised at once that Edwin could not join them. 'Mr Cotter's very, very poorly,' she said, 'after what happened. It's taken him very bad. You seen the winders [windows] boarded-up, an' we had to have some writing cleaned off the front. He'll be with you in a couple o' weeks as usual. He's asked me to take care o' you in the meantime.' She smiled again, closely watched by the men as she leaned forward to put the glasses on the table. 'But between you an' me, gents,' in sombre tone, 'the doctor says he'll never be the same. All because of – well, you know this ruffian Sleet?'

'We know him,' responded an officer. 'What happened, exactly?'

Harriet's account suited her purpose and reflected her true belief. She had insisted to the doctor that Edwin collapsed because of the whack from Charlie Sleet, but the doctor had disagreed. 'Forgive me, but what's happened to your husband is nothing to do with being hit on the head,' he said. 'It's a myocardial infarction – a heart attack. A bad one, I'm afraid, probably been brewing for some time. I daresay getting involved in fights didn't help, but your husband may have had heart disease for years. Did he drink a great deal, go short of sleep and have a lot of worry and strain?'

'He didn't get involved in no fights!' she had protested. 'Mr Cotter always tried to prevent fights!'

'Yes, well, that might amount to the same thing. I'm sorry Mrs Cotter, a large area of your husband's heart has been damaged beyond repair. You must expect him to remain very weak and need nursing. At least he is still alive though, eh, Mrs Cotter, at least he is still alive! We must give thanks for that.'

'How long will he be very weak? That's no good! He's got his work to attend to.'

'Oh, he won't be able to continue as an innkeeper. He should seek some other occupation.'

'Say what you like, doctor, Charlie Sleet did this. If it wasn't for him none of it would've happened.'

Explaining to the CID officers, Harriet again insisted, 'It's because of that man Sleet.' She set the facts before them, the mob bursting in with firebrands, the blow to the head, not forgetting to mention that no one came from the police station when they were called. 'Then when Edwin saw the broken winders an' the terrible word written, the shock was too much. He's fell down senseless then an' there.'

'Well, that *is* bad, very bad! I'm truly sorry how things turned out, Mrs Cotter,' responded the Detective Chief Superintendent 'We was so busy Tuesday night wi' this disorder we didn't have no one to send round. We'll make it up to him. You tell him that – your husband – tell him we'll make it up to him.'

'Well then, if I *could* mention,' said Harriet, 'if you can get this feller Sleet put away – sent down for something, anything, for a good long time – you know how much me an' my husband would appreciate it.'

Detective Inspector Fisk exchanged a nod of confirmation with his senior officer. 'I think we can do that for you,' he said. 'Tell me, what about when they set light to the sweetshop – did you actually see that?'

'My little girl Maud saw the whole thing from upstairs.'

'Ah, I see. I'll need to ask her about it, to be quite sure.'

'We ain't so fond of Germans ourselves,' admitted another officer, 'but setting fires an' smashing winders ain't the way. People should enlist if they feel like that.'

'Ah well, you see, a lot that wants to enlist,' one of his colleagues pointed out, 'gets turned down. Not fit enough to be soldiers, so they turn to this sort of thing.' Another officer added, 'A lot of the looting is done by women, an' they can't enlist.'

'Anyway Zuckerman ain't no German,' retorted Harriet. 'Those people, them Jews, my husband told me, they come from Russia, not Germany.'

'Maybe. Maybe not. Got German names an' talk German, so…'

'Anyway,' said Harriet lightly, anxious not to argue with police officers, 'let's pray it comes right in the end, eh? All for King an'

Country. Well, must get back to my joanna. Cheers, gents. I'll send a man in to make sure you've everything you need.'

The six CID officers raised their glasses: 'Thank you, Mrs Cotter. Cheers. All the best.'

'But,' she had a further thought, 'me an' Mr Cotter don't want to be no witnesses or nothing like that. We don't want Sleet putting two an' two together.'

'You leave it to us.'

*

It was a month rather than a fortnight before Edwin was able to sit again in the snug with the police officers and offer whatever they wanted. He himself would take no more than a single glass of ruby port.

Harriet tended to Edwin, cared for him as his nurse and maid, and helped him descend the stairs in the mornings dressed and brushed as sprucely as ever. He served in the saloon bar during the brief permitted hours of the wartime regulations, struggling to wear a face as affable as before. Customers gazed over their pints, fascinated by how very ill he seemed, the 'affable' face a bloodless pale. In the evening Harriet played patriotic songs and old favourites on the piano as if all was well. Then came the "No Treating" law, prohibiting the practice of buying rounds. That proved the last straw for some of the rival neighbouring pubs, mercifully driving a few of their customers into the Well Smack.

Without debate or discussion about her father's weak heart, Maud took on the role of a cleaning and serving girl in the saloon bar. A regular clientele of local men with their wives, together with a few closed-faced men on leave from the front, came in to enjoy Harriet's plain "British Supper and Ale" costing hardly more than eating at home. Despite Edwin's fears, the accounts still showed a profit.

And the seven years hard labour to which Charlie Sleet was sentenced for riot, arson, larceny, threats to murder and wounding persons unknown – all witnessed in person, according to his sworn testimony, by plain-clothes police officer Detective Inspector Fisk – was certainly gratifying.

But Charlie Sleet was not alone in the world. In the flat, marshy borderlands stretching from Barking Levels to Wanstead Flats, from London's Essex fringes to the foreshore of the Thames, generations of Sleets had toiled as farmhands and stable lads, or porters, hawkers, even footpads, mudlarks and pickpockets, itinerant hop and pea pickers as the seasons turned, and kitchen maids, washerwomen and wet nurses, generally managing to stay clear of workhouses. Now in the narrow streets spreading over this low terrain an army of Sleet's uncles and aunts, brothers, sisters and cousins were feeling outrage at his long sentence and his treatment at the hands of the Law.

Charlie Sleet had, too, a wife, Emmeline, and six tough-minded young sons, in a decrepit old cottage beside a track on the East Ham side of the Roding, rough ground not yet built upon. There they lived in close proximity to insects, cold and dirt, each other, and their snarling dogs.

Emmeline was a sturdy, strong woman just past thirty, not tall and not slender, but discernibly shapely, with wide blue eyes, full lips and coarse light blonde hair always tightly covered by a scarf knotted at the forehead. Her attractions were disguised by carpet slippers, a shabby housecoat and a cigarette with a length of ash periodically falling onto her bust and her nursing baby. (So far she had spent most of her married life with a baby on the way and another at the breast.) Emmeline's people were not like the tribe of Sleet. Her father had been an itinerant cobbler, and others in her line were tanners, glovers, smiths, farriers and ostlers. Unlike her husband, Em was used to the idea of jobs requiring a certain skill. She was disappointed that Charlie had not applied himself more.

To different degrees, all the Sleet boys took after their father in size, strength and temperament, and their mother in looks and intelligence. The tough, quick-witted firstborn, Micky, his hair as fair as cotton, twelve years old and already as tall as Em, had left school with no intention of looking for anything useful to do. Alternating an unpredictable, menacing friendliness with casual bullying, Micky was feared by local children; admired by them also for his strange pale colouring and a remarkable shoplifting talent. His brothers George and Ronnie were wilder, fouler-mouthed tow-headed scrappers of ten and nine.

Billy Sleet, sweet and gentle exception, slightest and quickest to smile, but with the same flaxen hair, at seven and a half was the same age as Maud Cotter, the publican's daughter, and at the same school as her. Billy and Maud this year left the mixed infants, so had to cease being playmates. Henceforth they must enter the school through separate Girls and Boys doors and sit in different rooms to be taught different things. Em's 'youngest living' (she had lost her baby girl) were Terry and Arthur, just five and four years old when Charlie was sent down.

Before Charlie was imprisoned, he and Em daily raised their voices in temper to one another and to the boys; fists too, and a birch switch. Even Em described her man as a brute, especially when in drink. The boys depended on her for protection from their unruly father. Yet she and the boys were distraught that he must be taken from them for so long and suffer so much. From morning to night Micky burned with anger at losing his father's savage guidance.

After sentence was passed, for the first time Em's sons saw her in tears, though of rage rather than sorrow. Em and her sons became even more tightly bound together. At night Em lay in bed and made calculations. She would be pushing forty when her husband returned so she could forget her dream of having a daughter while there was still time. Always she had hoped to have a grown-up girl to talk to and understand her. Instead she was in this too-masculine house. She pictured the non-existent daughter, imagined conversations with her. She would have named her Flora, or maybe Belle.

And with Charlie gone there would be money problems. The Sleet cottage had an unpaved yard at the back with a toolshed, a chicken shed with some chickens, and a privy; and at the side, a ramshackle stable for a pony and trap and a derelict outbuilding once used as a workshop. Em had an idea to patch up the old workshop as a small livery yard so she and the boys might earn a few pence grooming and feeding horses or maybe even repairing carts.

Micky had a different idea: 'Go into motor repairs, Ma,' – it sounded like a flight of fancy rather than a real proposition – 'an' sell motor spirit an' that.'

'Why, Micky – we don't know how. Most people round here has even seen a motor car, never mind drove one.'

'Yeah, but in the future, Ma,' Micky reasoned, 'there a be more motors, not less. I'll learn it, how it's done.'

'No one's goin'a come all the way down here looking for repairs or, you know, spirit.'

'Well, then, we need a place up on the Romford Road.'

'Oh come on, Micky, we ain't got no money! Specially wi' Pa gone.'

'Well, we must get some, Ma.'

Private motor vehicles had only recently been sighted this far along Romford Road. In his idle, quick-eyed wanderings Micky had spotted one outside the Women's Suffrage campaign office at Bow. He took a close look at it, then discovered a small workshop nearby for repairing and maintaining them. In fact this was a bicycle repair shop that, like him, had glimpsed the future. Indeed it had previously been a blacksmiths. He walked boldly into the yard and asked if he could do odd jobs. His urchin appearance, overwhelming uncouthness and poor diction had gone against him and the answer was – 'Scram. Go on, scarper!'

When he reported this to his mother, she said, 'You didn't ask right. Wash your face, smarten yourself. Let's go there together.' She put on a clean frock and brushed her hair and his. She re-tied her headscarf. At the garage Micky stood quietly as she asked a man in oily overalls if she could speak to the boss of the place. 'That's me,' he said.

'My boy's int'rested in motors an' would like to make hisself useful if you can find something for him. He's not fussed about wages, whatever is reasonable. He's a good lad – hardworking an' honest, an' a right quick learner.'

The boss looked at Micky quite differently from last time. He looked Em up and down, too.

'Why have *you* brought him – where's his father?'

'His father enlisted an' is fighting for his country in France.'

The man nodded with grim admiration. 'A'right, I'll find something for the boy to do. Can he start in the morning at seven?' He turned to Micky. 'Can you, lad?'

'Course he can,' said Em.

*

After seeing a Zeppelin swimming between the clouds and sending down bombs onto the terraced houses of working people, scores of men and boys went at once to enlist. Maud sat with the sickly Edwin in his little office space. She put down the tray and poured him a cup of tea. 'Dad, did you see that Zepp?'

'Yeah, I saw it. Did you?'

The girl nodded. 'Yeah. Did it kill anyone?'

'Yeah, it did. It blew up an house full of people in Plaistow, an' some more people in Forest Gate an' Manor Park. Then it went back to Germany.'

'So, they got away with it, then?'

'Sorry to say, duck, they did. But in the end they won't.'

'People shouldn't get away with things like that.'

'No, duck, they shouldn't.'

The mood among drinkers at the Smack was of furious indignation, and their opinion was that the Hun had embarked on a path never before conceived of in warfare, something uniquely evil – armed forces targeting unarmed civilians. Attacking women and children in their own homes, from high in the sky where no one could strike back – it was unmanly and despicable! *Typical Huns.*

Edwin felt he ought to *do* something to fight such vileness. It was so cowardly his mind could hardly take it in. Yet he could do nothing! His heart began rapping hard against his ribs and even drummed in his head, and an ache pressed on his lungs so he could hardly take a breath.

'Dad,' Maud asked lightly, 'why do people say you're a traitor? What *is* a traitor – what does it mean?'

'Is that what they say? It's someone what helps the enemy. They thought the Sweetshop Man was German, which he ain't. Even if he had'a been, Mr an' Mrs Zuckerman ain't our enemy. Attacking *them* is near as bad as dropping bombs on innocent folk from a Zeppelin.'

Maud agreed doubtfully, 'Well, don't worry Dad, me an' Mum don't think you're a traitor.'

To be called a traitor wounded him. His own daughter had heard it. People had seen the word painted on his pub, and must have wondered what he did to deserve it. No smoke without fire, they'd have said. No doubt people thought Aaron Zuckerman *was* German, after all.

In his emotion Edwin raised himself from his chair and paced to the window, holding the sill and gazing out. From this side of the building he looked on all the clamour and passers-by of Barking and could make out the ruins of its millennial nunnery – Barking Abbey – rising behind, and the peaceful old church where he and Harriet were married in hope and happiness. It was familiar territory. He'd seen it all his life. Again he felt the ache in his chest that at first he mistook for poignant melancholy. The ache became sharp, growing as though it were something he could see approaching from afar. The pain was rushing towards him. It was arriving too quickly to prepare himself. This would be quite a bad attack, he feared, half turning as if to implore Maud for help; but his voice made no sound and his eyes could not see. This is like the first time, he thought, only worse, a breathtaking agony. It seemed to strike diagonally across his torso. And he was gone.

*

The Zeppelin that Maud and Edwin saw from Barking had also been seen by Micky Sleet as he cycled along Romford Road after work. He was awestruck by its size, its ambition and audacity. Moving slowly above the slate rooftops of Forest Gate the silver leviathan blotted out moon and stars.

As he stared a bomb emerged like a tiny egg from a huge hen. Micky stood entranced as it descended. The thought that there was about to be an explosion made him smile. The shell struck an old workshop on the corner of a side street. With a single, deep, resounding drumbeat the whole building instantly became myriad small fragments and splinters flying in every direction from a thrilling pillar of fire and dust. The air quaked, but Micky did not die. He was thrown together with his bike onto the pavement, where he lay for a moment, all sight and sound replaced by a dizzying high-pitched screech. When the sound stopped, he stood again. Neither he nor the machine had suffered the slightest harm. At that instant, Micky became inspired as if by a majestic vision. There was a war on – who won would be nothing to do with people prattling about right and wrong or king and country. With dazzling clarity he suddenly understood the power and purpose of violence.

The pathetic cuffs and blows of family life, the fists of angry men, were not to be compared with this. He hurried home. There was something he needed to discuss. 'Ma, d'you see that Zepp?'

'I heard shells go off. You a'right?'

'I saw a place blowed up, an old works in Forest Gate. It's a good spot for our motor repairs shop. We can build it again how we want. We'll tell the lan'lord to let us have it.'

'Why would he – how can we pay for it?'

'All we have to do is say we'll burn his house down if he don't.'

Em laughed aloud. 'Oh, yes, Mick, an' what if he goes to the Old Bill – eh?'

'Thing is, Ma, he'll understand that won't help, cause we'll burn his house down whether he goes to 'em or not.'

'He might burn *our* place down! Micky. He'll tell you to clear off. He won't be afraid of you.'

With the certainty that had come upon him, Micky exclaimed, 'No, but Ma, don't you see, none o' that makes no difference when you *mean* it!'

'You'd be done for arson, son. You'd end up in the nick like your poor father! This lan'lord – we don't even know the man! He might be a nice feller, or someone that might be of use to us one day.'

'Point is, Ma, it don't matter *who* he is, or who *anyone* is, if they're scared of you. By the by, I found out motor spirit is called petrol. It makes stuff burn like hell. There's gallons an' gallons of it at work. We could go in one night an' help ourselves. There's a strongbox in there an' all, with the week's takings. We could have that, too.'

Em chuckled. 'You'll be nicked, done for arson an' thieving, *and* out of a job.'

'Ma, stop saying I'll be nicked. I'm serious. They won't know who done it. I'll turn up for work as normal.'

Em gazed fascinated at her tall, handsome son. Despite her mocking laughter, in truth she was impressed by his resolve and determination.

*

Especially in the distasteful circumstances of his death, Harriet understood that every propriety was essential to preserve Edwin's respectability – and, therefore, her own. In addition to the hearse with its four 'mutes' in top hats, she asked the undertaker for three coaches. With the dress, crepe and veil, closing the business and providing black kid gloves for every man, it amounted to ruinous expense just as she faced being given notice to quit the pub.

Inspected and judged by murmuring gossips on the opposite pavement, the cortège departed with solemnity towards Woodgrange Park cemetery, a private burial ground in Romford Road that offered taste and respectability at a very reasonable price. Edwin Cotter's funeral was conducted by the vicar who had conducted his wedding a few years before. Owing to the absence of men due to the war, it was decided to allow womenfolk to attend. Present were Edwin's parents and Harriet in deep mourning dress, his aunts and sisters whom Harriet had never met, together with the staff of the Well Smack wearing second mourning. His brothers and others who might have been expected to attend were either away at the Front or could not take time off work. The publican was buried at ten feet in the pre-paid economy double-depth plot where Harriet was expected to join him in due course.

Harriet loved and admired Edwin while he was alive and felt lucky to have been his wife, and would miss him for the rest of her days, but her sole thought during the interment and brief eulogy was that unless she could run the pub by herself or quickly find an under-manager to run it for her, she would soon be destitute and homeless. There would be an immediate loss of business from the mourning. It seemed only decent to close the premises for a month. A month was less than the usual, but mourning had been relaxed lately with all the war dead.

When the Well Smack eventually reopened, a framed photographic portrait of Edwin bordered with black hung in every bar room. Away from home Harriet kept to full mourning dress, but inside the pub she wore half-mourning, with a little black crepe on a closely fitted black costume of silk and lace. She could not respectably play the piano for the time being. However, Maud was allowed to play it, which surprisingly proved nearly as good and just as popular.

The next Thursday evening after reopening Harriet welcomed the CID officers back into the snug, offering them drinks and accepting their condolences. 'Is there anything we can do for you, Mrs Cotter?' asked the Detective Chief Superintendent kindly.

'Well, there is something, a favour.' She greatly feared they must refuse, and suspected it might be considered impudent, a request too far. She asked anyway.

'What favour would that be, Mrs Cotter?'

'Well, gents, it's that Charlie Sleet. It's 'cause o' Sleet that my husband has passed away. I'm sure you remember as how no one come from the police station to protect my husband despite all he done for you. I think you know what I'd like you to do.'

It took a moment for the policemen to understand. This time the Detective Chief Superintendent shook his head. 'No, I don't think so, Missis. Not that. Sorry.'

Detective Inspector Fisk saw an opportunity. He expressed his most profound sympathy, but counselled Harriet against feelings of vengeance. He wondered aloud, with tender solicitude, how she should manage now. What was to become of her? She said it was too early to decide. 'I'll keep the pub, though.'

The other officers nodded. 'You'll be a'right,' they said, 'course you will.'

Fisk shook his head sadly, 'Difficult life for a lady! Especially a big place like this. How'll you cope wi' ruffians? The brewery might not like it, a lady on her own.'

'I'll see how I get on,' she said.

The next day at lunchtime officer Fisk dropped in by himself. She offered him a drink on the house but he refused, saying he would pay his way. He tapped his pipe and mopped his brow. 'Mrs Cotter – or Harriet, may I?'

'Oh! I don't –,' she certainly did not want Detective Inspector Fisk to call her Harriet.

'Quite right, quite right, Mrs Cotter, early days,' he agreed. 'Now, let's talk about that favour you want done.'

3

I n the gloom of an unlit passage a warder and prisoner walked quickly towards the cells. The warder held in his grip a length of plaited hemp from the prison workshop. At one end a loop had already been tied with a slip-knot.

The warder turned a key. Inside, faint half-light came through the bars of a narrow unglazed window high on the wall. At the far end of the bare chamber their target lay dozing on a bed of three wooden boards. He began to wake as they stepped inside, but had no time even to make a sound. The two moved so fast and knew so well how to perform their task that in an instant the noose of plaited hemp encircled Charlie's Sleet's neck and was being tightened.

*

Dear Madam. Emmeline Sleet received news of her husband's death in a letter folded into a small brown envelope. *We regret following a thorough investigation we must inform you that Mr Charles Sleet hanged himself in his cell with a rope of plaited hemp smuggled from the prison workshop.* The governor sent his sincere condolences.

Em was not good at emotion, and her reading was poor too. The letter was from the prison, so it would be important. She sat down at the kitchen table to look at it carefully. She had trouble making sense of the words. On first reading she felt indignation and disbelief. How dare they tell her Charlie was dead!

As it dawned on her that they were actually informing her that he really was dead, she tried to picture the scene – that great strong body of her husband had been found hanging from a home-made rope. Her feeling changed to anger and pity for the lonely, wretched life that had ended. In horror Em struggled to read and re-read the words to extract more understanding from them, but none came, and at last a few tears ran from her eyes.

How would she tell the boys? To have a husband and father in prison is one kind of shame. A husband and father who commits suicide in prison while other women's husbands and fathers of other sons die fighting for their country is another, and much worse.

Yet somehow this didn't seem like Charlie. It required cool planning, resolve and effort, which wasn't his nature. It also meant he must have been suffering from melancholia and black moods and couldn't face the future, which was not the kind of man she had married. Nothing ever touched him in that way, no matter how bad. He was the type that always carried on fighting. Em sensed there was more to his death than the prison would let on. Perhaps he had fallen out with someone and been killed in a fight. Maybe a fight with warders. That would be like him.

'At work, tell 'em we had bad news,' she advised Micky, 'that Pa was killed in a battle at Flanders. Say you'd 'preciate a day off to respect his memory. They won't give it you but it's the right thing to ask.'

'What really happened – Pa never hanged hisself, did he?'

'I don't know what to think,' replied Em truthfully.

If she failed to collect the body, the letter went on, the prison would bury her husband in its own graveyard under the auspices of the Church of England without a funeral service. That sounded like a good option to Em. So long as she knew where he was buried, what difference did it make? It would be a considerable expense to bring his body back to East Ham.

She was never one for graves anyway. It was the living man she loved, not a dead one. She fought back any misgivings about him. Charlie had his faults – of course! Who doesn't? – but to have her man taken from her like this! And be left unprotected in the world! Charlie would never have done that to her and the boys. She would not believe he killed himself. And somehow she would make the boys proud of their father, no matter what. And she would pay back whoever was responsible for his death.

*

When officer Fisk next turned up, he had made quite an effort over his appearance. The shoes were shining, he wore a better suit, was immaculately shaved and the grey hair to either side of his moist fleshy crown had been neatly oiled.

'That favour of yours, Harriet. I took care of it.'

'You mean...?'

'It's done.'

She stared and stared at him, turning over the dreadful information in her mind. That she had willed such an enormity and it actually had come to pass suddenly became incredible to her, something miraculous, beyond comprehension. She was thrilled and relieved – and alarmed that this time the police officer had not even bothered to ask before using her name. At last, feeling almost that she could hug the man, yet fearful of him, she clasped her hands tightly together in glee.

'Well, well, well, a world without that ruffian – there's justice for Ted. Thank you, Mr Fisk, thank you.'

'Roland, please!'

'This time, it *is* on the house. What'll you have?'

With the glass placed before him, he spoke deliberately and carefully. 'Another thing I'd like to say, Harriet, now that – forgive me for mentioning it – you've no husband to care for you, if this pub ever seems like it's too much for you, always ask me for help. I retire soon from the police force with a tidy pension and, God willing, a good few years still ahead of me. Running a pub like this would be right up my street.'

She laughed. 'Well, that is kind! But, ah, Mr Fisk –' She must be careful not to offend the man or fall out with him.

'Do please call me Roland.'

She smiled sweetly. 'Well, as I say, for the moment I shall try to manage it myself.'

'Quite so, of course, Harriet. But call on me as soon as you need help.'

*

Micky Sleet proved his point beyond doubt (to himself) that the way forward in life was to act decisively with force and without restraint, doubt or fear. He was right that he would not be arrested for the burglary at his place of work. They never did find out who was behind it.

He was wrong, though, that he would have to threaten a man with fire to make him hand over the tenancy of a bombed-out warehouse. In her good frock, a little bit of make-up and her best hat and shoes, Em simply called on the owner and put it to him that the premises were worth nothing in their present state. He agreed with her.

'What about, sir,' she proposed, 'me an' my son rebuild it for you an' open a little workshop there – it'll be worth a damn sight more'n it is now, what with these bombs. We can start paying rent after the end of the war. What do you think? It'll give my boys a chance in life.'

The owner of the premises pondered the unexpected offer. He was taken with the idea. 'So you're saying, I sit back and do nothing, while you repair the place without charge – and then pay rent on it,' he laughed quietly. 'Well, I can't argue with that! And it's to help a lady whose husband died fighting for his country!' One difficulty occurred to him: 'What about when I want the premises back?'

'Oh, you know – that will be a'right. That's a separate matter, ain' it, sir, to be settled in due course?'

On reflection, he supposed it was. They smiled at each other and he offered her a cup of tea, but she said unfortunately she had to leave. 'Well then, we'll shake on it,' said he.

'Nah, let's put it in writing,' Em replied. 'I ain't much good wi' that sort of thing, so my son has writ this for me.'

Badly worded, misspelled and in a poor hand but perfectly understandable, the plain and simple contract set out in half a page Mrs Charles Sleet's proposal exactly as she had explained it, for an indefinite loan of land property in Romford Road, London E7, in exchange for rebuilding the premises, payment of rent to commence not less than a twelvemonth after the end of the war in an amount to be agreed at that time. 'Is there anyone can witness it?' asked Em.

The man chuckled at this formality and called in his daughter and a maid. Grinning benignly all the while, he watched as they signed. Afterwards, he told himself he was a silly fool. Still, he thought, it was only a casual arrangement after all. She seemed a reasonable woman, a war widow, so there would be no problems.

Afterwards, Em and Micky met for a closer look around their rent-free corner site. 'We know people, don't we, Ma, in the family, that can make what we want here?'

'Well, yeah, my brothers – your uncles – brickies, joiners, plumbers an' that, them what ain't been called up. They'll help us out now Pa's gone.'

'Go on an' ask 'em, then. I've got ideas.'

One of Micky Sleet's ideas was properly planned break-ins at small commercial premises. The burglary at the garage where he worked had been a great inspiration, yielding more cash than he had dreamed of, as well as the petrol. Now he turned his thoughts to the food shortages and rationed produce. He asked his brother George to join him. All you need for this job, he explained to George, is will power and muscle. 'You mustn't mind using a blade on anyone who gets in your way. Don't hold back.'

At night Micky and George targeted family dairies, butchers' storerooms and importers' warehouses for chests of preserved meats and flour, sugar and tea, cases of eggs, barrels of cheese and salted butter, and of course petty cash tins and office safes. They bought a horse and cart to move goods around. Em quickly sold everything edible to women locally or further away. The greatest trick was to steal from one shop and sell to another. Taking care of the cash was also part of Em's role, as well as having the final say on what jobs to do. She was still their mother, after all.

One of the out-of-town customers asked Em about a product she had never heard of, called fertilizer, apparently urgently needed by farmers. She learned that it was stored under lock and key at the docks. The other thing Em learned was that this substance must be handled carefully as it can explode. 'I think we're in the money wi' this one,' she said.

The fertilizer lock-up they chose looked tougher to break into than anything they had tried before, behind iron gates guarded by a night-watchman. Micky decided to leave it until they knew more. Tireless and determined, he studied the area, noted the policeman on his beat, timed the watchman's routine. He waited till the man finished work in the morning and followed him home.

The next night Micky and George arrived at the chemicals store. George was in cocky mood, while Micky as usual kept an opaque calm. 'Let us in or we'll burn your house down an' your family with it. We know where you live.'

'Ha ha! Oh yeah, is that right? Where do I live then, son?'

George pulled out a knife and Micky gave the address, at which the watchman swiftly opened the gate and invited them to take as many tubs of nitrate fertilizer as they wanted. 'Sorry lads, didn't mean to be rude.' He even advised them to be careful with it in case they blew themselves and him 'to kingdom come'.

As Em expected, nitrate fertilizer was worth a lot more to Essex farmers than sugar and tea to the housewives of East Ham. For the sake of his *amour propre* the night watchman did not tell the police that the robbers were two children, saying instead they were a gang of armed foreigners wearing masks.

Nonetheless, Micky's luck ran out. When he next went with George on a raid the police were there to catch them in the act, perhaps by chance. George ran off, lively and agile, disappearing into the dark night over fences and walls. Micky, although as hard to handle as a writhing rattlesnake, was firmly handcuffed before he could slip away.

*

Maud was a good pupil. Girls, like boys, were taught everything they needed to know. Maud was learning to cook and sew, how to wash and mend, read and write and master the everyday arithmetic she would face as a housewife or housekeeper, as well as physical fitness and proper conduct. After school she hurried home to change out of her pinafore, eat her tea and get to work cleaning the pub before its doors were unlocked. Then she helped in the kitchen.

Harriet had not had the schooling Maud was having, and had not been such a good pupil. Educated to the age of ten, passable at letters but weak on numbers, praised for her cross-stitch, and having done only skivvying between leaving school and getting married, she found Edwin's account books beautiful but baffling. She was not familiar with his routines of ordering and payment or keeping cash aside for wages, and she was not clear what the overheads amounted to, or even what the word encompassed. She readily understood the cost of food, but not the cost of cooking.

If the customers were happy, that surely was enough, she told herself. She felt it was proper to play the piano again now, but nothing gay or raucous. The mood had changed. Too many men were dying at the Front – the local paper listed hundreds in every edition. It was being said that Britain had lost a million men.

All the same, she reasoned, people still enjoy a drink. However, the price of a pint had gone up so much. She was hopeful that ordering beer, selling it with a tasty, simple plate of food, and paying a barman, barmaid and housemaid out of the takings should be enough to keep the business afloat.

Detective Inspector Fisk, a regular lunchtime customer, was watching her and waiting, ever helpful.

Fisk took his old seat in the snug, having the little room to himself when she brought in his tray. He was a daily visitor now. 'I see this Reform Act has passed,' said he, tamping his pipe.

'Honestly,' Harriet replied, 'I don't know nothing about it, politics an' that.'

He chuckled. 'You better find out, dear. You ladies'll be able to vote for the town hall, you know.'

'Well, well, well, so they've gave in to the suffragists then, did they? Good show!' She set down a meat pie and a pint of ale for him. 'There was a Votes For Women procession right outside just as my daughter come into the world.' It was a favourite tale of hers, and true. Suffrage Society women on the march in red, white and green sashes were singing below the window as Maud uttered her first cry.

'When this war is over,' Fisk predicted, 'I reckon with the workingman having a say in things, an' even more if their wives vote with 'em, licensing laws will go back to normal. The pub trade will pick up again. That's what I think.'

'I pray to God you're right,' she said. 'I don't know how I can carry on like this, I really don't, in a mess wi' the books an' no cellarman for the heavy work.'

'I've said a hundred times, I can take care of that. Nothing I'd like more than to run a good old inn like this.'

'No, I can't let the pub go – I can't. I've nothing else. I can't leave this place.'

'You misunderstand me, dear. You'd be here too, obviously.'

Icy fear crept over her skin. She had been too familiar with the man, and it was true he had got rid of Sleet for her. The trouble was, as Harriet knew too well, favours have to be repaid.

She affected a dismissive laugh. 'Ha ha! Well, well, Mr Fisk!

Anyway, I must get on – work to do.' She turned away. But he stood and reached out to grasp her arm.

'For God's sake, call me Roland! We could be partners,' he declared, 'think of it, dear!' As she tried to move away, he gripped more firmly.

'Now, now, Mr Fisk – let go! Come to your senses!'

'Partners, dear! You know how I feel about you, Harriet. So graceful, so good at your work. Your lovely hair, your pretty face. Wi' my pension –' He went to put his arms around her, but she pushed hard against him. Not in the least deterred he leaned forward to kiss her lips. Her push caused his mouth to land instead on the side of her head, amidst the dark ringlets he found intensely alluring.

His arm lunged urgently around her waist, his first embrace of the desperately longed-for female form since his wife died of consumption twenty-one years ago. 'Harriet, be kind to me as I have been to you.' An edge of insistence in his wheedling tone frightened her. 'Harriet, dear, I mean to have you for my own. The only alternative for you and little Maudie is the workhouse.'

He made another attempt to kiss her, clutching her body with both arms, drawing it close to him. This time to Harriet's disgust the man's wet lips landed full on her cheek, the tip of his moustache brushing into her nostril, together with a stinging scent of pipe tobacco. His hands moved downward from her waist, holding and caressing her, pulling her against his body.

Workhouse or no workhouse, she realised in her revulsion, she had to get away.

*

Micky Sleet gave his name as Jack Frost, which the police officers could not disprove, and his age as fifteen, too young to be sent to Borstal but too old for the orphanage. He explained he knew stealing was a sin, and was mortal sorry about it only he was half-starved and his father dead in Flanders and his mother passed away from flu. The magistrate felt such pity for poor Jack Frost he sentenced the lad to just two months in a men's prison.

There Micky thrived. He shared a cell with an older convict, learned a lot of useful tricks from him, made friends in the workshop, and could be suddenly violent and cruel to a degree that won everyone's respect. Micky's teasing, bullying manner appealed to many of the inmates. They admired and envied his youthful vigour and menacing charm. The name he used was considered a good joke. The others called him Frostie. One day in the workshop the man beside him murmured, 'A man topped hisself last night. Or the screws topped him.'

Micky whispered, 'My pa died in this prison. Ma reckons someone did him in.'

'What was his name?' – 'Sleet.'

'You Sleet's boy?' – 'Don't say nuffin or you're a dead man.'

'Don't worry about that, Frostie, I believe you. They say your dad killed a publican in Barking wi' just one punch, an' the publican's widder persuaded her copper fancy man to have your dad done away with. Eye for an eye, like.'

'Silence!' A warder had noticed the whispering amid the clatter of tools and work. 'No talking!'

Killed a man with one punch! Micky did feel proud of his father. In the next days he found out as much as he could. That the murder of Charlie Sleet was indeed arranged by a police officer with connections in the prison. A screw and a lifer carried out the hanging together. The felled publican was the landlord of the Well Smack in Barking, a traitor who helped the Huns, according to Charlie Sleet's own boast to fellow prisoners.

His companion in the workshop murmured, 'Tell you more when I get out o' this place, if I get out alive.' – 'Tell me now.' – 'More 'n my life's worth, Frostie, if someone found out I talked.' – 'When d'you get out?' – 'Not for a while yet.' – 'I can wait. Where will I find you?'

Micky simmered with impatient rage. He did not attach blame to the life-sentence convict coerced into taking part. To give his father justice, he must identify and deal with three people – the prison warder, the police officer and the publican's widow.

When Micky's sentence had been served, he was welcomed home. Em listened tight-lipped as Micky told her what he had found out. She agreed with him that they must do whatever it took to avenge her husband.

*

Harriet shook Maud awake. 'Get dressed, we're goin' out.' – 'Why?' – 'To see someone.' – 'In the night? Who we goin'a see?' Her mother helped her pull on thick stockings and a thick woollen dress. – 'Just someone.' – 'What about school?' – 'No school today.' – 'Why not?' – 'Shush!'

Harriet was anxious to get clear of Detective Inspector Fisk's territory as quickly as possible. It had occurred to her to call on Cousin Will, who lent Ted his handcart, but she feared he was too near home. She packed her bag the evening before, making sure to include Edwin's old pistol and bullets, a full set of the pub's many keys, all the money on the premises and his cosh too. After slipping out of a back door into the dank autumn dawn, Harriet hurried Maud in the direction of East Ham. Their outfits were plain and dark, Harriet in an old coat and her hair tightly pinned within a cheap hat draped with a veil.

When Detective Inspector Fisk arrived at the Well Smack inn for his lunchtime drink and, he hoped, a further talk with Harriet about their future together, he found the place locked. Together with other customers he read a note fixed to the door. It was written in a neat, childlike hand. *CLOSED owing to influenza. Signed: Mrs Edwin Cotter, licensee.*

It was not completely impossible, he supposed, that Harriet had indeed become ill since yesterday. Many local pubs and shops had similar notices. The "Spanish flu" was springing up everywhere, creeping along streets like a fungus, reaching from house to house. It was said that this amazing virus could kill within a day, starting with a chill in the morning, a fever at lunchtime, turning blue by evening as the lungs flood with liquid. Dead the same night. Scores had succumbed in and around Barking and East Ham.

Fisk went at once to the family's private entrance at the side of the building, and there spoke to Harriet's young maid-of-all-work. 'Hello, Lucy. Is Mrs Cotter in – has she got the flu?'

Lucy recognised the corpulent, haughty figure. 'Madam ain't home, sir. No, she ain't got the flu, far as I can tell.'

'Oh! Any idea why the pub is closed today, then?'

'I'm sure I don't know, sir,' said the girl. 'Madam up an' left wi'

Miss Maud first thing. Miss Maud weren't in school clothes. Madam never said where they was going nor nothing about when they'll be back.'

'Did she take any luggage?'

'Only a carpet bag, sir. That's all. I made an early breakfast an' off they went afore first light.'

'Oh! Before first light! She didn't seem unwell?'

'Can't really say, sir. Not very, at any rate.'

'Well then, may I step inside, Lucy, to check for myself?' Fisk knew the request was impudent, since he had been told the lady of the house had gone away. But he was not sure he believed this tale. It was so inexplicable and strange. He made a move to pass the girl. As a CID officer he was used to entering people's homes without permission, and not used to being defied.

The maid stood her ground and bravely barred his way. 'Sorry, sir, madam told me absolutely no one was to be admitted during her absence. I can give her a message when she comes back.'

Fisk could hardly barge past without any justification. He stepped back onto the pavement. 'Is she inside?'

'No, sir, like I said, she's gone away. When she returns, was I to tell her you called?'

'All right. Tell her I called. Tell her there's no point in running away. Tell her I'll find her. You tell her that.'

Fisk strode to Edwin's elderly parents, a few minutes away. Harriet had anticipated that would be his next move. She had told them nothing. She would not have told them her plans in any case, and would not dream of asking them for help. After Edwin's funeral she had stopped their five shillings a week and nightly jug of stout. They had never liked her and never done anything for her, and nor would they, especially now their son was dead.

Fisk discovered both of them seriously ill. The mother was nursing the father, who she said was likely to pass away within hours. Fisk introduced himself as a police officer on official business. He did not accept an invitation to step inside, instead covering his mouth and nose with a handkerchief at the door. 'Where might she have gone?'

The old woman shook her head. 'Don't know an' can't concern myself.'

'She's got the little girl with her, your grand-daughter Maud. Aren't you concerned about that?'

'She's probably gone to one of her sisters. Or her brothers, if they ain't been sent abroad to fight.'

'Who exactly do you mean – where do they live?'

To get rid of the man, she did tell him a few addresses, as far as she could remember them.

Among the passers-by and would-be customers who paused at the door of the Smack that day to read Harriet's note was young Micky Sleet. Eager as always to press forward with his plans, he was keen to confront, or at least see with his own eyes, the publican's widow who caused the death of his father.

Micky too knocked at the family's private door at the side of the pub, and again the servant girl Lucy opened it. She gazed warily at the swaggering fair-haired youth, a precocious sneering ruffian no more than her own age.

'Mrs Edwin Cotter here?' he asked.

'Who wants to know?'

'Well, is she or ain't she?'

'She's packed up an' left this very day wi' no word where she's gone nor when she's coming back.'

'Don't believe you, Miss. It only says on the door she's ill, so I reckon she must be here.'

'Well, she ain't ill an' she ain't here. Don't mind if you believe me or not.'

4

Harriet could not think of a single friend outside this part of London. Nor could she go to her sisters or brothers down in Beckton and Barkingside. They, surely, were where Fisk would continue his hunt. She compared herself to the Zuckermans, who fled into the bottomless squalor of Spitalfields. At least they were armed with an address on a scrap of paper. She had not even that.

The day's stream of motor buses started up along Barking Road towards the City. Harriet and Maud boarded the first that came along. As the bus moved from stop to stop, filling with cigarette smoke and men in work clothes, it took her further and further from familiar ground. Passing through Plaistow and Canning Town and reaching the docks, Harriet became terrified of her own recklessness. Peering out, she recognised nothing. She argued with herself that she must go back, and responded that she would not. Hearing the conductor cry out *Chrisp Street*, in haste she pressed the bell and tugged Maud to the platform. They stepped off by the market.

There was bomb damage everywhere. It was obvious this area had taken some bad hits. As if Zeppelins were not enough, the Germans had lately been dropping bombs from aeroplanes high in the sky. At an infants' school somewhere near here, she had heard, eighteen little ones had been killed by a bomb, and dozens maimed. The good news was, there had been no bombs lately. People were even saying the Huns were in retreat.

Having once told Ted it would be wrong to call on the pub's customers for help, that is what Harriet now found herself doing. She had always got on well with Mary Cass, the two of them being sometimes the only women in the public bar. Harriet knew that Mary and her husband Ray sold pots and pans in the markets. Mary had said Chrisp Street Market in Poplar was one of their regular haunts. Harriet walked between stalls as the day's early bargain-hunters arrived.

She spotted Mary Cass stacking a barrow with cans, saucepans, kettles and metal kitchenware. Ray was setting a bag of feed onto their pony's neck. Harriet approached close before speaking quietly. 'Mrs Cass – hello there!' She raised her veil.

'Why, it's Mrs Cotter! What on earth... don't tell me you come in search o' pots an' pans!' she laughed.

'No, Mary, I need help an' got no one to turn to.' Harriet reddened, horribly aware that she had gone beyond the limits of what is normal. Ray looked up in great puzzlement. 'Morning, Mrs Cotter...' It was clear that the stallholder and his wife were astounded by these words from a woman they hardly knew beyond a few exchanges at the bar.

Harriet sent Maud to sit by the pony. To Ray and Mary Cass she began to explain. She made no mention of the regular CID evenings in the snug, and no mention of the dreadful favour Fisk had done her. Only that a senior police inspector was harassing her and would not leave her alone. Just yesterday he forcibly embraced her and kissed her and insisted she marry him and let him run the pub. 'I'm scared of the man. Being as he's a copper it's hard to do anything about it. I'm looking for somewhere me and Maud can stay a while.' The pair listened attentively. They were horrified and sympathetic; they had liked Edwin, disliked the police and were sorry how things had turned out.

'But Harriet, dear, if I may,' said Mary Cass, 'you're on a hiding to nothing running off. Far better to go back to this copper. He's a godsend, really.'

'He makes me sick. Edwin never liked him neither.'

'All the same,' said Ray, 'it's a hard life for a woman on her own.'

'I feel for you,' Mary assured her, 'I really do, but we ain't got no place to put you up. I know a lady as might be worth a try, name of Atkins, over Stratford way.' She wrote the address. 'If there's anything more we can do...'

'There is something though, Mary. Can you take Maud? Hopefully just for today.'

'Course we can.' Mary was clearly not pleased.

'She won't be no trouble,' Harriet promised. 'Give her something to do. She's a good worker.'

Mrs Violet Atkins had a room near the Stratford railway sidings. She said Harriet was lucky to catch her in. She was doing her husband's job as a train driver while he was at the Front, the shift this week starting at two o'clock. Making space to sit, she pushed aside stacks of political pamphlets, tracts and rolled-up posters. They talked over a lunch of bread and jam. 'It's nice to have company.'

Like Mary, Violet was not clear what Harriet objected to about officer Fisk. 'He sounds quite a catch.'

'I married Edwin Cotter, I loved Edwin Cotter. I mean to be true to my vows.'

'Wedding vows only last till death parts you.'

'This copper sweats like a pig an' he's nearly old enough to be my father.' She hated his moist corpulence. She did not want to be touched by his fleshy fingers. The thought of bodily intimacy with any man other than Ted disgusted her. She could not even contemplate the repulsive details. It was hard to say why. She was not religious. Perhaps it was prudery. She tried to understand her feelings, but could not. It was horrible, that was all.

Violet did not share her view. 'Listen, though. You need a partner to run the pub, he needs a partner to share his bed. A woman always has to give something, don't she?' She half laughed. 'It's the way of the world.'

'No, no, no, a business partner is one thing, a bedroom partner is something else.'

'No, Mrs Cotter – Harriet, it's the same thing. Grit your teeth an' make compromises.'

'Being on the trains, Vi, you must o' been in the women's transport strike for equal pay, back in summer. Was *you* happy to compromise on equal pay?'

'We had to compromise, happy or not, see? They give us part o' what we want. Something's better'n nothing, ain' it, Harriet? Right now, looks like you got nothing. No home, no husband, nothing to live on. You ain't a young girl no more – sorry, just being honest. You're lucky, really, there's a man who wants you. Give ground an' get part o' what you want.'

'Well, the other thing is, Vi, I'm scared of this feller. He's had men killed. I know that for a fact.' She did not explain how she knew.

Violet stopped smiling. 'Ah, now that's different. I didn't realise *that*. Look, if you don't find nowhere, come back and stop wi' me. We'll all share the same bed, mind, unless you're happy on the floorboards! My shift ends at midnight. The door key is on a string in the letterbox. Help yourself to what you want.'

Harriet put on her hat and coat, pulled the veil over her face and left Violet's digs. The weather was perking up; the cloud cover thinner in places and through it slanted a few gleams of cool brightness. She decided to call on Cousin Will after all. The tram rattled along Romford Road. Approaching from this direction she hoped she was less likely to be seen.

'Why, hello there, duck!' Wearing a thick, unravelling pullover and trousers that were almost rags, her sturdy Cousin Will was in his yard busily sorting pieces of worthless-looking metal scrap. 'Long time no see!' he exclaimed, cheerfully leading her indoors. His place really was very meagre, and quite filthy, she thought – a man on his own can get into a terrible state.

He made a pot of tea as she told him about Fisk. 'We're talking about a copper, Will.' She said Fisk was pursuing and harassing her, and was a nasty piece of work who had had men killed. This did not sway Will as it had Violet.

'I don't suppose he'll want to kill *you*, Hattie. The nub of it is, you got a choice. On one hand, you can have a comfortable life as Mrs Fisk. It's perfectly respectable for a widder to marry again. Nobody'd think the worse of you. On the other hand, take your chances on your own an' good luck to you. Even if you can't make a go of the pub, I doubt you'd end in the workhouse. There's plenty of decent jobs for women these days.'

'Fisk ain't give me that choice, Will. He's determined to have me, married or not. He's out looking for me right now.'

Will nodded as he understood. 'No, Hat, he's not out looking for you. He's using his loaf, working out where you've gone. What you done with your nipper?'

'I left her in Poplar market with a couple, Cass by name. They're regulars in the pub.'

'Oh, I reckon I know Ray Cass. He's in the same line as me. I seen him in the markets. Sells metalware from a cart.' He pondered. 'Well then, you know our Aunt Gina?'

'Not really.'

'No, you prob'ly don't. She's not on terms with the rest of the family, cut herself off. Her boys won't be coming back from the Front, sorry to say, and her husband, our uncle, he's been dead for years. So you see, she's a widder too and got a room free, the back bedroom, till it's let to someone else. She's only a lodger, but worth a try.'

'Where's she live?'

He gestured. 'Not ten minutes' walk. I'll square it with her.' He put on a muffler and cap and an old woollen coat. 'You go an' get your kid. Be careful.'

'Look, I've got this,' Harriet felt inside her bag and produced Edwin's revolver.

'Ruddy hell! Not planning to shoot him, are you?'

'That depends.'

Daylight faded on the journey, a smoky fog descending. It was altogether dark when Harriet and Maud reached the street of neat two-up two-downs. Harriet warned her daughter to be quiet and say nothing. They stood in a tiny porch banging the knocker. There was no light within and none in the porch, but footsteps could be heard. When the door swung open Harriet had to peer intently to discern a slight, wiry woman, middle-aged, hair tied in a scarf, with no trace of a smile, who with equal uncertainty was trying to scrutinise her. Into the dark hallway and up a flight of uncarpeted stairs they followed.

Aunt Gina had told Will she would take Harriet and 'the girl' for a day or two to see how it went. She mounted the steps quickly. In the usual way of such arrangements, Aunt Gina's home was not private; she simply rented the two upstairs rooms. Her doors had no locks.

In the back bedroom Gina turned on a dim light. Harriet saw now that the unwelcoming aunt was no older than herself, a prim, sour-looking woman in a shapeless brown housedress, tight-lipped with dissatisfaction. No doubt she had cause to be dissatisfied. Cousin Will had prepared Harriet: Aunt Gina's husband had been a boilerman who died of his injuries after a works explosion. Their two sons had both been killed fighting in France. So Gina lived alone.

'This was their room – the boys,' she said. Her steady expression revealed nothing, with an unblinking stoniness that in itself spoke of the unspeakable. 'It can be yours, if you want, for a share of the rent.' It was small and bare, containing only two narrow single beds, a chair and a stand for a washbasin. There was a small fireplace, an unexpected luxury. A window looked into the yards and back windows of houses in the next street, pressing close.

Gina sat on one bed, Harriet chose the chair, Maud the floor at her mother's feet.

Aunt Gina offered a cigarette. Harriet took one and lit it from Gina's. 'What has Will told you, aunt?'

'He's told me you're my niece on the Hayes side,' said Gina. 'Tell you the truth, I don't remember you. I never knew my husband's sisters,' she admitted bluntly. 'He's told me you've took over a pub in Barking after your husband passed away. An' he's told me you've a feller pestering you so bad you've shut up shop just to get away from him.'

'He's a dangerous man to cross. He's a copper, a tec from the local nick. I'm real scared of him.'

'Why?'

Harriet continued, 'He tried it on in the pub, he's grabbed hold o' me, kissed me an' – you know what I mean?' She flicked a glance at Maud as if to protect the girl's innocent ears. 'He said he won't rest till he's had me, hook or crook.' This was not true – DI Fisk had not said that or anything like it. But she had correctly divined his feelings.

Maud looked up astonished at her mother. This was the first glimmer of explanation cast on their peculiar day.

'Stay clear of him then,' advised Gina sharply. 'All a woman's got in this ruddy world is her good name. Her reputation. Don't give it away to no one. Use your maiden name to throw him off the scent. Hayes, I s'pose?'

'Miss Harriet Beryl Hayes. Won't that look like I'm single? It'd make me look available.'

'No, I mean call yourself *Mrs* Hayes, same as me. We can make out we're sisters-in-law, couple of widders. Your girl will need to change schools. There's one at the end of the road, very handy. She needs to go on the register as Miss Hayes. Has *she* got middle names?' They spoke about Maud as though she were not present or not sentient.

'She's Maud Doris, but you can't expect a little kid to –'

'Course you can.'

Now Maud did speak up: 'But what about Dad? He was Mr Cotter an' you was Mrs Cotter an' I was Miss Cotter. We don't want to forget about Dad.'

The women stared amazed at the talking child. Aunt Gina glared, but Harriet stroked her daughter's hair tenderly, 'Don't you worry, love, we're doing as Dad would o' wanted.' Maud resumed her unhappy silence.

To her aunt, Harriet said, 'Who's downstairs?'

'A docker an' his missus. Sam an' Phyl an' six nippers. They're only tenants, not 'llowed to sub-let, so it's cash in hand an' they can chuck us out anytime. You can't have tea till they've had theirs. If you want to make a cup between meals you must ask. The lav is off their scullery, no need to go outside, but you got to ask first before going.'

'Me an' Maud can stay here, then?'

'You'll have to pay your way,' her aunt cautioned. 'Something for rent every week, a bit for heat an' light, a bob or two to keep downstairs sweet, what with using their kitchen an' privy.'

'I'll be skint in a fortnight at that rate. I've bills to pay at the pub even when it's closed. I've staff to pay.'

'Well, you better find something quick,' her aunt responded tartly. She meant, an income. 'If I was you, I'd get shot of the pub. Face it, you ain't never going back there. We'll talk tomorrer. I have to turn in – I start work early.'

'What work d'you do?'

Aunt Gina answered that she worked as a buttonhole-maker in a factory. 'Dresses, mostly. Some shirts. The place is called Egbert's Garments. I'm forewoman on my bench, being the oldest.'

'Can you get me a job there, seeing as you're the forewoman? I'm good at sewing.'

'Are you? I can put in a word, I s'pose.'

*

Inspector Fisk had been a police detective for many years. Several things occurred to him immediately. As her family was local and she had no experience of travel and limited spending money, it was likely that Harriet's hiding place would be not far away in the home of a close friend or relative. She might be using her maiden name. Fisk well remembered the very day Edwin Cotter died so it was a simple matter to obtain the death certificate. It gave a date of birth which Fisk used to find Cotter's marriage certificate, also conveniently local. This gave the maiden name of Cotter's bride as Harriet Beryl Hayes, and her parents' details. He noted it down along with everything else about her that could be useful.

It also occurred to Fisk to check the borough's school board registers for a newly enrolled girl with the name Hayes or Cotter. He could follow Maud home from school if necessary.

He would check the Town Hall records for borough residents with the surname Hayes or Cotter. There was a remote possibility that she had travelled further afield, perhaps even outside London. He would find her eventually, of course, he was sure of that. He did not mean to be thwarted. He intended to have this woman as his own, whatever it took. He reasoned that she was bound to see sense in the end.

Unfortunately for Detective Inspector Fisk, the woman he was pursuing guessed every step he would take. Harriet did not register Maud at a different school, instead notifying her usual school by letter – posted from Romford Market by Cousin Will – that her daughter was gravely ill with flu. Gina did find Harriet a job at Mr Egbert's garment workshop. Harriet asked Mr Egbert if he could employ her "off the books", no questions asked. He readily agreed as this reduced his own overheads. Each morning except Sunday the two women hurried to work together on side streets, Harriet always in her old coat and veiled hat. Maud was put on the payroll too, at 'young learner' rates. It was explained to Mr Egbert that Maud turned twelve early this year, just before the leaving age was raised. Despite this being obviously not true, Maud having every appearance of being only ten years old, Mr Egbert accepted it as a fact. It would take him time to prove otherwise and serve no purpose. He was not minded to question anything his employees said about themselves. Nobody objected to a pretence that put bread on the table of a poor widow. Nor did Maud mind, as work was more interesting than school and there were several other girls who really were twelve years old. Her special friend was called Effie.

*

Cousin Will called on Harriet. They stood together in the bedroom. 'You all right here, Hat?'

'All's well for now, thank you, Will.' – 'No one round about knows Fisk, do they?'

She assured him no one she had met at Aunt Gina's was likely to know Detective Inspector Fisk, 'nor ever gone so far as Barking in their lives,' she added, though it was not two miles away.

'What you doing about the pub, Hattie? You can't leave it closed, losing money. They'll take the licence off you.'

'I ain't decided.' – 'Well, you better.'

Will said he had concocted a ruse to have Ray Cass visit the Well Smack pub to find out whether Fisk had been asking after her.

Harriet approved. 'Can he give Lucy her wages while he's there?'

In the darkness of evening Ray Cass knocked on the side door at the Smack. 'Lucy, is it? I've been sent to ask if there's been messages left for Mrs Cotter.'

'Yes, sir, there is messages, an' there's a young man what never left no message, been a couple of times, an' is sometimes stood watching from across the road.'

'I wonder what *he* wants. Mrs Cotter asked me to give you this.' It was six week's wages and some extra for her keep. The young servant made a movement almost like a curtsey as she took the money.

'What did this young man look like? Was there no name at all?'

'No, nothing.' She described the burly, blond youth. 'Sir, can you ask Madam if I'm to do all the same jobs an' hours as usual while she's away?' He said she probably was.

Ray Cass reported to Will and Will reported to Harriet, but none of them knew the identity of the young man who had been asking for her.

Harriet especially was perplexed. 'D'you s'pose it might be a constable sent by Fisk?' she said.

'Don't sound like it,' said Cousin Will.

'Maybe if he comes again Lucy can insist on knowing his name.'

5

In the moments before the hour, in the last seconds, work continued in a hush, all talk subdued. Eyes were glancing up at the clock. At eleven o'clock in the morning, as the minute hand jerked forward and began to click into place, deafening explosions of 'maroons' on every side signalled that across the Channel the fighting had come to an end.

The whole workshop broke into cheers. Sirens and horns began to sound outside and the clamour of church bells, and more maroon rockets and fireworks. The sewing rooms were full of excitement and talk until, at three o'clock in the afternoon a jovial Mr Egbert, arriving red-faced from a celebration lunch, let his staff quit their benches to join hectic crowds gathering in the wet, darkening streets.

The rain had eased to a murky scotch mist. 'What d'you want to do, where shall we go? We can't sit at home!' Harriet cried out to Gina in the throng. She could not hear the answer. Effie pulled Maud away. 'Come on, there's a party in our street.' Effie – Ethel – was a precocious, saucy girl about whom Harriet had doubts as a companion for Maud. She called out, 'Maud, go to Auntie Gina's after.' Effie called back, 'She can stay over at ours, Mrs Hayes.'

Now Gina's voice was right beside her. 'Cheering an' clapping! Pah!' she spat. 'I lost my boys to the bleeding war, two fine lads. I ain't cheering nothing. What've *I* got to wave a flag for?'

Harriet linked arms with her aunt and saw that water running down Gina's face was tears, not rain. There were no cries, no sobs. She pulled her close. 'No one's cheering the war, Auntie. We're just glad it's over. No more boys shot an' gassed or limbs blown off, mothers an' wives an' sweethearts waiting for news. Peace deserves a drink, don' it, eh?'

'This ain't about peace, it's about vict'ry,' returned Gina curtly. 'All very well, but at what cost? My sons buried in foreign mud.'

'At least we *won* the war! You bet those ruddy Huns ain't too cheerful about it, thanks to your two, an' the other poor fellers that copped it. Tonight's for being glad we won, Auntie, tomorrer for counting the cost an' thinking about them we lost.'

Yet the crowds seemed unable to achieve the happiness they sought, becoming more and more wild and frenzied in their efforts, screaming, chanting, bellowing, shrieking. In the midst of the din the thought slipped quietly into Harriet's mind that Ted too died because of the war, because if he hadn't protected the Zuckermans he'd be alive today. It was not comparable to Gina's loss, so she did not mention it.

Whatever Gina's bitterness, the two women continued among the thousands surging westward in sopping coats and battered hats. Friends and strangers were embracing, running, walking, hanging onto bus platforms, crowding into trams, many shouting drunkenly or singing, even dancing, waving Union Jacks in the drizzle.

'Did I hear someone say they're going to the Palace?' yelled Gina. 'Seems like the King is goin'a make a speech. You ever been to Buckingham Palace?'

'No, I never seen the Palace.'

'Well, then.'

Buses abandoned all attempt to drive forward, passengers instead streaming off into the ecstatic crush laughing madly and soaked through. Grasping one another for fear of being parted, Harriet and Gina were pushed with the crowd along Fleet Street. Beside Clement Danes church it became impossible to move further. To shouts of joy and amazement, the streetlights were lit for the first time in years. From where they stood the two women could see the whole length of the Strand completely filled. Gina said they would all catch their deaths standing about in this weather. 'The King is speaking!' cried someone, but if he was, not a word would reach them from as far away as the Palace. There were roars of 'God Save the King!' Clinging on to each other, aunt and niece squeezed past others, edging along the Aldwych to be a few yards nearer to His Majesty.

A long note of song swept eerily through the crowd towards them, the vast volume growing rapidly as it approached like a great rolling breaker in the sea. As it broke upon them the frantic, restless mass became utterly stilled and like a holy congregation burst into one voice, in relief, pride and sorrow, hundreds of thousands – Harriet pictured them from Buckingham Palace to the Houses of Parliament to

St Paul's Cathedral, though she had only the vaguest notion of where these places were – singing *God Save the King* together in November rain.

Harriet raised her veil to join in. That was when she saw a face in the crowd looking directly at her from only twenty yards away. 'Gina, Aunt Gina! That's him, him there, the man staring at us – it's Fisk.'

Fisk stood still until the anthem ended, his eyes fixed upon her.

At once the crowd was in motion again, loosening a little as some turned to leave, shouting, weeping and waving their flags. Rowdy singing came chaotically from different directions, *Tipperary* one way, *Auld Lang Syne* the other, *Land of Hope and Glory* from further off, somewhere a drum and a marching band. With his height and bulk and a skill that perhaps he had been taught, Fisk plunged one arm after another into the sea of backs and shoulders as if swimming, pushing others aside, moving towards her. Harriet and Gina, small and slight, urgently slipped through the crush.

Gina pulled Harriet into a stinking passage between buildings. Along here they ran into a web of paths and alleys, emerging into a deserted lane. Downhill towards the river they again saw a narrow path to one side. Harriet saw that they had not lost Fisk. Despite his age and ungainly size he trailed only a little behind. Across another street they hurried down steep steps. At the foot an unbolted iron gate swung open into manicured gardens.

'We can't go in here,' warned Gina, 'it's private. This is the Temple, the lawyers' place. We'll get in terrible trouble if we're caught in here.' Yet they ran fearfully across the gardens into a confusion of paved courts and yards, across another lane, only an occasional gas lamp casting a glow. To either side were barristers' chambers, next to each one a wooden board listing the names of its residents. Into such an entrance they darted, hiding behind the door as footsteps approached and passed.

Gina wanted to know, 'What's the worse could happen if he ketches you? Can't do nothing, can he?'

Harriet herself could not say. 'He'll drag me away, force me to go with him. I don't want to find out,' she replied lamely, adding, 'he could even arrest me – he's a copper.'

They listened. Gina murmured, 'All quiet.' Emerging cautiously, they saw or heard no sign of Fisk or anyone else. They walked through courtyards handsomely paved and found themselves beside a strange little circular fortress.

'What's that place, is it a church?' said Harriet.

'If it's a church, let's go inside an' dry off.'

'Not the Temple itself, is it?' The door creaked into an eerie space, domed, with painted walls and stained glass, and stone effigies lying like corpses dead in battle. A vaulted circle of arches opened into another space more recognisable as a church. They straightened their coats and dresses, took off their hats and shook rainwater onto the floor.

Behind them the door made its noisy creak. 'Evening, ladies.' Detective Inspector Fisk stood across the entrance with his arms folded. He was panting slightly. 'Hello, Harriet. Seeking sanctuary or praying for salvation?'

'Not going with you, Mr Fisk,' replied Harriet.

'Blimey, I ain't run so much in years. Not as fit as I used to be. Come now, Harriet. Be sensible.'

'What do you want?' asked Gina boldly.

'To give my friend Mrs Cotter a friendly warning.'

'What warning?' retorted Harriet. 'I'm very sorry, Mr Fisk, but I ain't goin'a marry you, no matter what.'

'Let's sit. Pull up a pew, as they say. I could do with a rest.' He shook water from his hat and coat and ran a handkerchief over his brow.

The Armistice rejoicing was inaudible in the quiet of the church. 'Who are you, sir, may I ask?' asked Gina politely. There was hardly a trace of East London in her tone or bearing.

'Ah, so Mrs Cotter has not explained?'

'Only that you're too persistent in an offer of marriage and unwilling to accept a refusal.'

Fisk grinned at her pretensions. 'Well, Missis, I don't have to answer no questions from you nor nobody else. But since you ask, my name is Fisk. I'm an old friend of Mr Cotter's. Him an' me done many a service for one another over the years. At his untimely end he asked if I would be willing to watch over his widow an' his daughter, take them under my wing an' ensure the very best for them. I promised him I would.'

'Why, that's a brazen flipping lie, that is!' exclaimed Harriet. 'What a load of poppycock! You never promised no such thing!'

Fisk ignored her. 'And, Missis,' he enquired of Gina, 'may I ask who *you* are?'

'Mrs Dorothea Amber at your service, a long-standing friend of Mrs Cotter,' Gina answered with cool, dignified politesse, 'housekeeper of a family in Kensington. My mistress has kindly allowed Mrs Cotter to live and work in the household. She's took in the little girl as well, and is providing her with a tutor.'

Fisk observed Harriet's open-mouthed astonishment and responded with an arch 'Well I never,' adding, 'What you doing all the way over here, then? It's quite a walk from Kensington.'

'We came in a hansom to see the King at St Paul's this afternoon,' retorted Gina.

'Did you now?' chuckled Fisk. 'Well, whether you did or not, Harriet, you can't leave the Well Smack shut as it is.' His voice became serious and imploring. 'Look, I retire next month, dear. Now's the time to let me help you with the business. It would be a crying shame if we was to throw away this opportunity, the two of us.'

'For what it's worth, Mr Fisk,' said Harriet, 'what I will do for you, if you'll leave me alone ever after, is make over the Well Smack licence to you.'

She regretted the words – it committed her – she should have thought more. Was she, in fact, now willing to give up the pub, having sworn that she never would? What alternative did she have, other than to let this fleshy, sweating man fondle her with his big, moist hands, lie on top of her, use her and be her master? What would Ted have wanted, what would he say? If only she could ask him!

'That's not up to you,' Fisk retorted gently. 'It's between the brewery an' the licensing authority. When I become your husband, the licence will transfer to me.'

'You ain't goin'a be my husband, but I'll write to the brewers. I'll say you're already managing the pub for me.'

He paused in surprise. 'That actually is a very good suggestion, Harriet.'

'If you want, in the meantime you can open the pub doors again an' run it for me. If you'll only leave me be.'

'Bless me, now that *is* an idea! But Harriet, I must speak to you about something important, to warn you. Do you know someone's been calling for you at the pub an' keeping watch on the place?'

'So I heard. I thought it was some man of yours.'

'Not at all. Frankly, I don't know who it is. I'm worried. I wondered if it might be to do with Charlie Sleet.'

Harriet grimaced in dismay and covered her ears. 'I thought you sorted that out!'

Gina listened mystified. She perceived there was more to Harriet's problems than she knew.

'So I did. But Charlie Sleet had friends and family. Be on your guard, Harriet.' From his breast pocket he produced a calling card and offered it to Harriet. 'My home address. Come to me the instant anyone threatens you. May I know *your* address?'

Harriet stared in blank refusal. From her purse Gina drew out a calling card, florid and tinted. 'Here's *my* card, Mr Fisk. Mrs Cotter will be remaining with us for the foreseeable future.'

Again taken by surprise, Fisk took the card from her hand and read aloud, '*Mrs Dorothea Amber. Rutland Gate, Knightsbridge.*' He looked at Gina with new eyes. Impressed and delighted, he exclaimed, 'Well, well, that's excellent. Dear Harriet, I'll be in touch very soon.'

'You can have the pub. Even so, I won't be marrying you.'

'You will, Harriet. You're goin'a need all the protection you can get.' He pushed the church door and peered out. Remarking that the rain had nearly stopped, he left.

Harriet turned to Gina. 'Blimey, you ain't half a good fibber! Dorothea Amber, ha ha! He's gone an' left us in peace! What was that card?'

'That come in for an order at work this morning. Mrs Amber wants two dozen boys' shirts.' Her voice and manner had reverted to normal.

'You ain't half clever, Aunt!'

'Who's this Charlie Sleet – what's that about?'

Harriet had not told her, and nor did she mean to now. She replied, 'It's nothing, just a local troublemaker who fell out with Ted.' *If Gina knew the whole story she wouldn't let us stay in her rooms.*

'Anyway, we've thrown your suitor right off the scent.'

'Suitor! He ain't my suitor! I'll be more careful he can't find me in future.'

It was Gina's opinion that Fisk would give up his hopes of

marriage. 'After all, he'll have the pub.'

Harriet shook her head. 'No, no, no, he won't give up. He's got a fixation.'

*

The Well Smack public house was vibrant once more, the mahogany and brass polished and lamps cleaned, floors scrubbed, glass and mirrors sparkling. Heaped coals smouldered bright in the fireplaces. A bluff, pipe-smoking new landlord offered a hearty greeting to each arriving customer. The pictures of the rather prim Victorian-looking former landlord, Edwin Cotter, had gone from the walls.

Public bar, saloon bars and lounge alike, and even the tap-room at the back, were loud with debate. Roland Fisk had been right that the pub trade would pick up with the end of the war. He conceded he had been wrong that letting the working man vote would lead to a Socialist takeover. Instead, Lloyd George's coalition of Conservatives and Liberals had been swept back into office in a triumphant landslide.

Still, the picture was complicated, as the bar-room pundits discovered. Most of East London *had* voted for Socialists. At the count in Barking Town, nearly every vote had gone to Labour. However, as part of Romford constituency Barking ended up with a Liberal MP. In the public bar, this was declared unfair. In the saloon, perfectly reasonable.

The election had brought forth fascinating new divisions. The House of Commons had been remade. Seated on the opposition benches now were rows of tough-minded labourers, scrubbed-up coal miners and factory workers, leaders of marches, strikes and protests, ardent soapbox orators, night-school men and self-taught men. Somehow even Tories and Liberals had been transformed, landed gentry in high starched collars replaced by relaxed modern professional men and manufacturers. A new politics was in view. Glass after cheery glass was raised to the King, the future, the people, the women's vote, the victory, the peace, to a merry Christmas, to longer drinking hours and to the reopening of the Well Smack inn.

In another public bar a few miles away, young Micky Sleet was buying a drink for his newly released prison workshop comrade. Only now, away from the jail, would the man tell "Frostie" what he knew about the fate of his beloved Pa.

When a warder from the prison was found hanged in his own home, it was widely believed that Frostie had gone to the house and personally strung up the very man who killed his father. It appeared that his victim had first been cut and beaten. They said old Charlie would have been proud of him. That was what Micky wanted to hear.

The warder himself, as he pleaded for pity and poured blamed upon others, gave Micky the next piece of information he needed.

From the bar Fisk noticed three people step into the saloon, showy types, a heavily made-up woman and two obvious spivs. They might be, he guessed, a mother and her two grown-up sons. (Emmeline Sleet these days wore a winter coat with generous rolls of fur around the cuffs and collar. Her thick blonde hair was piled in a luxuriant pompadour. Micky and George, with clipped moustaches and trilby hats pushed back, were powerfully muscled young men in well-cut check suits and winter driving jackets).

They remained standing, lit cigarettes and surveyed the room. Fisk stood awaiting their order. One of the young men approached.

'Why, hello there,' said Micky, 'is it Mr Fisk?'

'At your service,' replied Fisk, unnerved, 'have we met?'

'We ain't met, pal, but I know you well enough. Port an' lemon for the lady an' two halves o' pale. Have one y'self.'

To be spoken to in this way, and by a youngster, was galling, but Fisk understood that as a pub landlord he must learn to endure such slights. 'Good of you, sir, but when I'm working…'

'No, Inspector, I told you to have one,' insisted Micky, 'an' make time to sit with us.'

By a wary intuition Fisk had an inkling who they were. 'Yes, I will have a half, why not? Thank you.' He poured the small port, filled three half-pint glasses. He did not want a scene in the pub. 'Let's go in the snug. It's more private.'

The snug was as comfortable as always, with lamps lit on this dreary day, a red patterned rug, framed prints hanging, wallpaper of red and cream. Micky took off his coat, removed his hat from short hair neatly oiled and settled himself into an armchair drawn close to the glowing hearth. The others lowered themselves into chairs to either side. In a long pause Em sipped her drink while her sons studied Fisk.

'I can't spend too long,' said Fisk.

'A'right Fisk, let's get on,' Micky announced. 'They call me Frostie, son of Charlie Sleet. This here is my mother an' brother. We won't beat about the bush. We've spoke to people an' we've put two an' two together.'

Roland Fisk was conscious of an emotion; he was afraid. He feared this extremely composed young man. 'Meaning?'

Em answered, 'Meaning we had a word wi' former colleagues o' yours down the cop shop, an' former staff o' this pub, an' former prison screws an' former people what served time wi' Charlie before you had him bumped off.'

'I promise you, that was nothing to do with me. God's truth.'

'All them people we spoke to, they say different. Look, Fisk, your name was on the charge sheet against my husband as the key witness. We been watching you. You're sweet on Cotter's widder, we know that much, an' now you've took over her husband's gaff. Fact is, you done away wi' Charlie an' we've come here to do away wi' you.'

'Oh yes?' Fisk chuckled slightly. 'How do you propose to do that?'

Micky sat up and leaned towards him. 'Like this, Inspector: first off, we razor noughts an' crosses on your fucking moosh till your own mum don't know you. We make chopped mince o' your horrible flesh an' shove it down your gob. Then we call on your brother in Chelmsford an' do the same to him an' his lady wife an' his three kids. Then we set fire to this fucking place an' destroy it an' you with it. See? That's how.'

Long experience had made Fisk sceptical of wild threats. He was a big, capable man used to handing it out to fools and hotheads. Despite which, on hearing Micky's savage formula, his stomach, bladder and testicles contracted sharply. It annoyed him too that the others were scrutinising him so intently, as if fascinated by a beetle before treading on it. Fisk took out a handkerchief and ran it over his sweating scalp. The mention of his brother's family unsettled him most – the Sleets had done some homework. It crossed his mind that he might have to dispose of Widow Sleet and her boys, which he did not readily know how to do for the moment, nor did he want to think about it. He could try to have this older lad put in the frame for some serious offence, get him sent down for a long stretch. That would not be enough. The others would come after him.

He picked up his glass, drained the contents and rose to his feet. 'Right-o, sorry, but I've work to do. Our little chat is over. Nice meeting you.' He mustered some confidence. 'I think you ought to leave now an' forget what you've said. If I was you, Missis,' he counselled Em, 'I'd put the past behind you or you an' your lads will be the worse off. You'll end up in Holloway prison, madam, not a place any lady wants to be.'

Em said, 'Sit down, friend, I ain't finished my drink.'

'Don't you worry about us, Fisk,' said Micky, 'think about yourself. Even if we was to be hung, drawn an' quartered, you an' your brother an' his wife an' kids are still goin'a get carved, an' this pub is still getting burnt down.'

'So what you doing here, then? Get on with it an' see where it gets you.'

To his amazement, George and Micky now stood up with open razors in hand and calmly moved towards him. 'Let's make a start then,' said George. The Sleets watched Fisk's unflappability evaporate before their eyes.

Had it been one alone, Fisk told himself uncertainly, he would have tackled him. Both at once was impossible.

'Only,' Em said, 'there is an alternative, if you play ball, mister. Nothing'll happen to you, nor your brother, nor his family, nor the pub. You can even make a bob or two out of it.'

Almost any alternative would be welcome. He ran his teeth over his lips nervously, thoughtfully bit the inside of his mouth. He sat down again. 'What you suggesting?'

6

The alternative to being slashed and burned that Widow Sleet offered was as he feared. 'You got contacts at Barking nick, obviously,' she said. 'You got contacts from here to Scotland Yard. Stands to reason, being a Detective Inspector, you know people all over.'

'I don't know people all over. My work was local. I've never spoke to Scotland Yard.'

'Well, we think you have,' said Micky.

'Anyway, I retired last month,' protested Fisk. He knew he could not altogether refuse to help them.

'We think a retired bogey is more use than a working one.'

'How so?'

'No job to lose, see? Persuade your old mates to drop charges, get rid of evidence, turn a blind eye, see? You know who's open to a deal. You know who to speak to. You can meet 'em right here in this room, same as always.'

Fisk smiled nervously. 'No, that sort of thing, it's not possible. I don't know how to persuade anyone.'

'Really, don't you know?' mocked Em. 'Why, Inspector Fisk, it's no different from how we just persuaded you. The good old carrot an' stick. I bet there's bogeys could do with a little bit more...' she rubbed her thumb and forefinger together, 'an' bogeys with a lovely wife an' kids to protect.'

Fisk did indeed know what she meant. He said, 'Apart from being left in peace, you mentioned a bob or two.'

'Ah, that's the way, Inspector!' Em nodded, 'Be nice to us an' we'll be nice to you. There's coin in it for them as cooperate. You tell 'em that. Now then, this lady, Cotter's widder. Where you keeping her?'

Worse and worse for Roland Fisk. Certainly he had no wish to see Harriet fall into the Sleets' hands. 'I been looking for her. Truly, I have. I don't know where she's got to. She told me she was working in Knightsbridge, gave me an address, but when I went there, it wasn't true. That's all I know.' He wiped his scalp and the back of his neck with the damp handkerchief.

'Don't sweat, pal,' said Micky, 'we believe you. Only find her soon, a'right?'

Fisk was put to work helping the Sleet family to bribe, threaten and bludgeon their way to more and better jobs. Everything was carried on under the cover of the motor business on Romford Road. They gave him a generous percentage. Despite his initial denials, he did know plenty of police officers happy to take a share in their success.

Fisk wondered how Harriet would ever be able to live with him unless the Sleets were got rid of. He realised he was thoroughly in their grasp. He was enmeshed in what he had already done for them and fearful of the terrifying madness of Micky Sleet. To save his skin he dare not defy them.

He fell into a constant fantasy that he and his lovely Harriet would flee together to some paradise far from East London, far from the Sleet family, and run a different pub, a pretty country inn, in perfect peace and happiness. It was impossible, he understood that. The Sleets would hunt her down, and him, wherever they were.

Consumed by his longings for a blissful escape with Harriet on his arm, he carried out his duties for the Sleet family and his tasks as cheerful landlord of the Smack public house, where CID officers still met for a drink and a private talk with him every Thursday evening.

As weeks passed from wet winter to cold spring, the subject of Mrs Cotter came up less frequently. It seemed for a spell that there was no urgency. The Sleets were busy. Fisk gave them occasional misleading snippets, false trails: Mrs Cotter was seen with a lady in Kensington, with a gentleman in Pall Mall, employed as a housekeeper in Mayfair, a nanny in Belgravia. 'Believe me, if I knew where to get hold of her, I would,' he pleaded.

Roland Fisk was torn. While he dreamed of finding Harriet and carrying her to safety, he knew being found was the worst thing that could happen to her. He devoted his energies both to searching for her and keeping her hidden.

One by one, after being discharged from the forces Harriet's brothers came to look her up at the Well Smack. That they did not know where she was convinced Fisk that Harriet had successfully gone to ground. He passed it on to the Sleets that even her own family did not know where to find Mrs Cotter. 'I'll keep looking. I expect she'll turn up in the end.'

Somehow these words infuriated Micky. In a savage change of mood, Micky said he had run out of patience. 'In the end? *In the end? How long you think we'll wait? This joke has gone on long enough,'* he announced. 'If you know where she is an' ain't telling us, it'll be the worse for you. If you *don't* know where she is, you better start looking. We're taking measures. We're offering a reward. Put it about. First person to give us Harriet Cotter alive gets a hundred quid, no questions asked.'

*

Harriet and Gina reckoned Mr Egbert a not-especially-bad boss. Besides, Harriet regarded the job as a godsend. Six days a week they arrived with Maud at the little factory in time for a seven o'clock start, buttoned their overalls and set to work in rooms densely crowded with local women and girls. A haze of cloth dust drifted above the closely packed sewing benches. Smoking was not allowed, except for Mr Egbert himself. It was not quiet – sewing machines clattered all day long, and despite the ceaseless toil there was plenty of chat, jesting and gossip. Harriet and Gina worked on fine needlework and buttonholes. When a bell rang at the front counter, forewoman Gina went to take new orders, soon returning to allocate the tasks. In another room Maud snipped excess thread from sewn collars and carried lengths of cotton to a row of other girls stitching hems and pleats. Effie sat sewing buttons and sequins. The girls were sometimes put to folding finished dresses and shirts, tying shirts into bundles of a dozen, Effie happily showing her young friend how things were done.

When the clock hands finally jerked to six in the evening, all rose from their benches. Women hurried away, fleeing in groups, in pairs or alone, lighting cigarettes. Some were weary, others not. Many went directly to their chores at home, for there was washing to be done and tea to make before husbands arrived. Some met with friends and neighbours. The youngest girls reverted to childhood, playing hopscotch or skipping on the pavement. Some preferred more mischievous fun, taunting rivals. Not wanted at home, others wandered aimless, cadging cigarettes, teasing boys, stealing sweets from stalls and shops. A few, like Effie and her friends, set their sights on fancier goods, cheap finery, small luxuries for themselves or to sell. It was a grown-up thing to have a bit of money, Effie said.

Maud had none at all. Every Saturday evening Mr Egbert's workers lined up for their wages, each of them handed a small brown envelope. It usually contained one pound two and six for the women, and six shillings for girls. Neither Harriet nor Maud considered the six shillings to be Maud's own money. Maud handed it to her mother. Their view was that since Maud belonged to Harriet, her wages belonged to Harriet. Harriet gave the money straight to Gina, who handed some of it back. From what remained Harriet put a penny aside for funeral insurance and a penny into the Friendly Society 'savings club' Ted had joined, and gave Maud a penny to spend as she wished.

'A penny,' complained Maud, 'ain't enough. By rights I ought to be on the women's wage now. *You* know why.' She meant, because she had lately started having her 'monthlies'. Harriet had shown her how to fold absorbent rags into place, which urgent and secretive inconvenience Harriet had described as 'being a woman'. She hinted at the perils to come: a woman's body, she told her daughter, is always a burden to her. By some unconscious process the idea then lodged in Maud's mind that it was this misfortune that entitled women to higher wages than girls.

However Mr Egbert did not know or wish to know the difference between a girl and a woman. His invariable rule was that workers under fourteen years of age receive the children's wage.

'Oi, what's this?' demanded Harriet. She held up an exquisite ladies' evening bag. The soft sides were of a delicate enamelled mesh in pink, green and white. It had an intricately worked silver clasp and hung on a slender silver chain. It was, in fact, as lovely an object as she had ever handled in her life.

'That's mine,' said Maud, truculent and embarrassed. The bag had been concealed under folded clothes, but now was pulled out and exposed to view.

'Where d'you get it?' – 'It's mine. I bought it.'

Harriet gave a mocking laugh. 'Bought it? This cost more than you'll earn in your whole life. How much was it?'

'Well, I didn't actually buy it. I… found it.'

'Found it? Where?' – 'On the pa'ment, at Mile End.'

'*Mile End?* What the heck was you doing over there?' – 'Me an' Effie went to look at the fair on the Waste.'

'Did Effie "find" something an' all?' – 'No, well, I didn't exactly find it. Effie found it an' she give it me.'

Harriet examined the pretty object, opened it, ran her finger over the ice-smooth enamel mesh. Inside was the copper penny Harriet had given Maud as pocket money. 'Did she steal it, Maud? Tell the truth. From a person, or from a shop?'

'How do I know! Anyway, it's mine now.'

'No, it ain't, love. It belongs to someone else. That's thieving. The last thing we need is trouble.'

'I was goin'a give it you for a present.'

Harriet was still holding the bag between her fingers. 'Oh, duck! Was you? With a penny inside that I gave you?' She shook her head in sorrow at this touching little untruth. 'You little darling. Promise me right now you won't have no more to do with nicking stuff.'

'All right,' Maud pouted. 'Anyway, *I* never nicked it.'

Harriet ran an anxious hand over her face, murmuring, 'Dear God, I really must do something about you.' She did not know what she meant, and did nothing. Nor did she know what to do with the beautiful bag, how to dispose of it honestly without suspicion. She decided after all to keep it. She buried it in a drawer among her clean underwear, her stays and garter belt and sanitary cloths. It was taken out occasionally to be admired for a moment and hidden away again. Inside it she kept whatever pennies and shillings still remained from the week's wages.

*

Harriet took off her overall and put on her coat and cloche hat. Whenever going into the street she obscured her face with the black mesh of a half-veil which, besides, gave her an air of old-fashioned respectability and dignity. Tonight at clocking-off time, an earnest young woman stood outside the factory gate of Egbert's Garments. Beside her was an older man. The woman spoke like a street preacher, eloquently extolling the trade union movement. The man was a recruiter for the Garment Workers' Union, hailing workers as they passed and urging them to join 'your union'. The pay at Egbert's, the woman cried out passionately, was below the level agreed by the trade board, and it was also against the law to employ children of school age during school hours.

A small crowd gathered to listen. Some murmured in agreement, some listened thoughtfully, some jeered. There was playful, foolish heckling. Trade boards and trades unions had not reached Egbert's Garments. Somehow Mr Egbert had managed to avoid their notice.

As Harriet emerged from the gate the speaker paused and looked at her squarely. Despite the veil, the two recognised each other at once. 'Harriet?'

'Why, hello Vi! What a surprise.'

The young woman was Violet Atkins, the train driver from Stratford who had said the key of her door was hanging inside the letterbox.

'Fancy seeing you, Harriet! Found somewhere good to stay?'

It was slightly embarrassing. Everyone could hear. 'Oh, I did, Vi, thank you ever so much.'

'Blimey though, surely you're don't work in *this* place?' Violet whistled with incredulity.

Harriet laughed, made light of it. 'You have to do something to make ends meet, don't you? You done your hair different, Vi.' Violet had her hair short in the neat new style. 'Suits you. What you doing over this way?'

'I go all over, tryin'a get people to join a union.'

Harriet caught sight of Maud with Gina. She called out to them, 'You go on, I'll catch you up.'

Violet politely introduced Harriet to the union recruiter: 'Mrs Cotter, wasn' it, Harriet? Mrs Cotter, Mr Pick.'

Harriet squirmed: she had not told anyone at work her real name.

'Nice to meet you,' said he. He handed her a leaflet about the Garment Workers' Union. 'Join the union, Mrs Cotter. Oh,' with sudden recognition, 'it's Mrs *Cotter* from the Well Smack! Well I never! I'm from Barking myself. What you doing *here*, Mrs Cotter? You know the Smack has a new lan'lord? He's always saying he'd like to know where you got to! Wait till I tell him I bumped into you. He won't half be surprised! We miss your pianer playing, by the way.'

Harriet suddenly 'remembered' she had left something in the workshop. To Violet she said, 'See y'again, Vi,' and gave the union man a polite 'Nice to meet you, Mr Pick.'

All too vividly Harriet could picture the scene later that night: *Mr Pick, at the bar of the Smack, says to the genial new landlord, 'Remember you was asking about the lady who had this place before you? Guess what, I bumped into her in East Ham. Never believe it but she's working in a sweatshop over there, Egbert's Garments.'*

She hurried to Mr Egbert's office before he left for the night. She asked if she could change to homeworking, starting tonight. She would prefer to do piecework at home. Urgent family reasons.

Mr Egbert, working quietly at his desk, barely looked up. He was perfectly agreeable and had no interest in her reasons. He said piecework rates were roughly equivalent to tuppence three-farthings an hour if she could stick at it all day and keep up a good speed. Was she happy with that? Harriet said she was.

'If you don't mind, sir, the work for tomorrow, can I take it now, save time in the morning?'

'Well, why not? What about your girl – she want to work at home?'

'No, sir, sorry, but I been told by the, ah, officer, she's got to stop working. I must send her to school straight away on 'count of her age. It's the law.'

'Well, that's fine.' Egbert led her to the pile of sewing for the next day's homeworkers, dozens of sleeves to be attached to dresses.

She lugged them back to the house and up the stairs. To Gina she explained what had happened. 'I reckon Fisk will turn up at Egbert's tomorrow asking for Mrs Hayes or Mrs Cotter. You're Mrs Hayes. Stick to it that I live up West somewhere. He might ask what I was doing at Egbert's yesterday. Invent something, say anything.'

'Like what though?'

'Just stick to it, Aunt. Don't tell Fisk where I am.'

Gina agreed, and warned, 'But you do know being an homeworker is hard, don't you? More work, less money.'

'Not much choice, is there?' Poor at arithmetic though she was, Harriet understood well enough that her earnings would fall sharply. It meant losing Maud's six shillings a week as well. 'I've known for a while it would come to this. There's no other way.'

As Harriet expected, the very next morning Fisk stood outside the gate of Egbert's Garments. He recognised Gina as she approached. 'Remember me? Mrs Dorothea Amber my eye! Housekeeper, wasn' it?'

'I lost that job. What d'you want now?' She made no further attempt at fake gentility.

'Is Mrs Cotter coming in to work today? I need to tell her something. It's important.'

'She don't work here, that's the truth. What "something"?'

'I need to tell her personally.'

Gina snickered contemptuously. 'Yeah, I bet you do.'

'This is serious, Missis. It's about the Sleet mob. They're putting it about that they'll give a hundred pound to anyone finds Harriet for 'em. For the time being they don't even know what she looks like, which is all to the good. They only say she was the landlady of the Well Smack in Barking, which will jog a lot of memories for a hundred quid.'

'Why they doing that?'

'Can't say, but they're not to be trifled with.'

'How do *you* know about it – you mixed up with them?'

'I got it from my old colleagues on the force. I'm not looking for her anymore, I don't even want to know where she is in case the Sleets find it out from me. I want her to stay hid.'

Gina scrutinised the man's troubled face. 'I'll get the message to her.'

Gina knocked on the door of the back bedroom. Harriet sat sewing. Maud too was working on a share of the stitching.

'Busy?' – 'Yeah, an' always will be, I reckon. Leave that fag outside, will you. Got to be careful wi' this fabric.'

In a low, troubled voice, Gina gave her Fisk's message. 'D'you believe it about the hundred quid or is Fisk playing some sort o' trick? Why pay a hundred nicker to find you?'

Still Harriet dare not explain what shameful grievance the Sleets held against her. 'I don't know nothing about that. It's Fisk worries me,' she replied boldly, 'not them. I don't trust him.'

'Well, he seems serious. He says he ain't looking for you no more, an' he's only worried they'll find you first.'

'I don't believe it, not a word. Either way I'll keep out o' sight, just in case. Not that I can go out even if I wanted to, not with these ruddy sleeves to finish.'

Gina said, 'That's another thing, Harriet. You didn't ought to waste your time sewing sleeves for Egbert. Any woman can sew. They can't do fine needlework like you. You should be a proper dressmaker. Don't sell yourself short, Harriet. You make lovely frocks. You'd earn more.'

'Not being funny, Aunt, but how can I work as a dressmaker in this little space? I'd need a table to lay out an' cut fabrics. Dressmaking ain't like the stitching we do for Egbert!'

'No, well, I've spoke to Sam an' Phyl downstairs about that, if you're interested,' Gina declared.

Harriet listened as her aunt explained.

'They'll let you use their front room table nine to four each day. You got to make sure everything's cleared away by four, when she's back to make the kids' tea. You can do the hand-finishing later, can't you, in your room?'

'What'll it cost?'

'Nothing, but you've to play their joanna for 'em of an evening an' make a pretty frock for Phyl each year, an' do repairs on the kids' hand-me-downs to make them look nice. What d'you think?'

'I think it's a bloody miracle. I'll do it.'

*

Maud lay awake, looking at patterns in the darkness, listening to the music downstairs. Her mother was playing Sam and Phyl's piano, singing *Way down 'pon the Swanee River*. Raucous laughter, men's and women's, accompanied a suggestive version of *When I Take My Morning Promenade*. Then, as heartrending as a hymn, *Keep Right On Till the End of the Road* was sung by every voice together. Maud could play those tunes too, knew every note in her head. In a low voice, she joined in the words...

A final jest and a farewell. She heard the front door close, footsteps upon the stairs. Harriet didn't put on the light when she came into the room. Maud watched in the dark as her mother sat on the side of the bed and took off her shoes and stockings. How old she looked, worn out and thin. Harriet washed her face at the bowl, dried herself, took off her cotton frock and pulled on a long white flannel nightdress. She stood looking at the picture of Edwin for a long, long time before getting under her covers.

Harriet too lay awake, thinking, the evening ringing in her head. It seemed to Harriet that she had given Roland Fisk the slip. She went so far as to give thanks for the way things had turned out. Living on black tea by day and a decent little meal when Gina came in from work, she had 'no complaints.' The dress clients were local women with well-paid jobs of their own, or the wives of men with good wages. To be on the safe side, she went to see them only after dark.

It pleased her immensely that her girl walked to and from school. Having missed the chance to leave at twelve years old she must now stay on until fourteen, the new leaving age. Harriet considered that a great stroke of luck. Ted would have been glad, she thought.

Several times a day Harriet praised Ted and praised him again every night before bed. Ted had rescued her and for a few years they had been happy. What had befallen her since – widowhood and trouble – was but the normal lot of women; it had happened to Gina as well, and to women up and down the street and all over the land, always. And what had befallen Ted, hard work and worry, his struggles all in vain, dead in his prime, was normal too, no different from what happened to so many men.

She must not repine: Ted lived on in Maud. Harriet's dearest wish now was for Maud to get on in life; and do much, much better than herself. She wanted nothing more than that. And should the need arise, under the bed she still had Ted's old revolver and his cosh.

MAUD

Born June 1908, Barking Town, Essex

1

Droplets of starry light flew from a revolving mirror ball like handfuls of confetti. *I can be good, I can be bad, it all depends on you, it all depends on yoo-oo,* crooned a smart young man with a glistening smile. Saxophone, trombone and cornet, banjo and fiddle, piano and drums, rattled out a swinging foxtrot. Couples clung in swift steps about the crowded dancehall, men and women, or pairs of women. The rustle of satin and of talk, the slide and clack of shoes on the floor, added to the delightful all-enveloping sound. On plush seats against the walls others sat chain-smoking, watching and waiting, everyone primped and polished, the whole ballroom redolent with hair oil, scent and cigarettes.

Such glamour and joy as this Maud had never known. She was half mad with it. A woman in a lovely gown played piano, glancing around with a broad smile. The slick band leader with twirling moustaches was exotically foreign. She studied with interest a group of Jewish boys and girls dancing. Loud, extrovert and exuberant, they too appeared foreign to her. She scrutinised three 'coloured' men playing drums, trombone and cornet, so strange were they to her eyes – the hair, the features, the dark skin. Until now she had danced only with neighbours in the downstairs living room.

Effie had said it was time she went to a proper dance. Harriet's best efforts to steer her daughter clear of Effie these last few years had failed. The two girls remained friends, and Maud tagged along with Effie's gang, though a year or two younger than the rest. Harriet knew Maud must live her own life; it was inevitable. She envied her going to a dance. She helped her daughter prepare herself, and cautioned, 'Don't let a boy kiss you. Watch out where he's putting his hands. Don't let them take advantage.' Maud did not know what this meant. She joined Effie and the others at Manor Park Broadway and they walked down the High Street to East Ham Palais.

Maud and Effie joined in a foxtrot three times, putting their arms round each other and taking it in turns to play the man. The foxtrot was the easiest of dances, quick and fun to do. Effie took the opportunity to explain some of what Maud had not understood about the difference between men and women (Effie used the more familiar difference between a stallion and a mare to help Maud understand), which she felt it might be useful for her young friend to know before a strange man asked her to dance. She explained the enigmatic remark about the putting of hands.

'A girl needs to know what's what,' said Effie. 'Men have got this urge, see – *the* urge. You ever seen how cock pigeons carry on? It's like that. They can't stop. You know when you miss your dinner, an' can't stop thinking about having something to eat? That's how blokes are about *it*. When a geezer says you've got a nice frock, that means he fancies what's inside it. It's the sex urge. They don't talk about it. They keep it hid,' she explained. 'You might not like it, but that's what makes the world go round. Lady pigeons don't like it neither. It's the way of the world. Otherwise there'd be no baby pigeons born, then where would we be?'

Effie knew several older boys, who to Maud all seemed perfectly amiable and polite and not visibly in the thrall of any particular urge. Effie assured her that they were.

One of them asked casually, 'Feel like dancing then, Ef?' – 'Oh, all right,' she said. While Effie danced, Maud stood shyly. Another boy came by with a 'Hello' and a charming smile. Well-built, in a pale blue woollen suit, striped tie and spectator brogues, like his brothers he had remarkably blond hair. He looked posh but sounded common, a combination that appealed to her.

'That's a nice frock,' said he. Maud had on a shift dress, perfectly fitted, of fine cotton and tulle in delicate jade green, touching the knee in the new short style. 'It's classy.' He nodded with approval, and she was pleased.

'My mum made it. She's a dressmaker,' she explained simply.

'You ain't the only dressmaker's daughter but you look the most t'rrific of anyone,' he smiled, 'prettiest.'

'Oh! Thanks.' She flushed and was stumped for any idea what else to say.

He cast his gaze around then returned it to her eyes. 'Good band tonight. You come here a lot?'

'Not often.' She did not want to admit she had never been before.

'Me neither. Hey, I know you!' he realised. 'You're Maud Cotter, ain't you? Don't remember me, do you?'

Disconcerted, she replied frankly, 'Why, what's your name?'

'I'm Billy Sleet. We was friends at infants' school. Remember? In Barking.'

'Oh, you're Billy! I remember you! Blimey, *you've* changed,' she grinned.

'Long time ago! We was just little, wasn't we, Maud? So, d'you go out to work now?' he asked above the din.

'Only half-days, in a haberdashers.'

'Oh, that'd be a good job if it was full time.'

'Think so? The old baggage I work for treats me like dirt. I can't say nothing or I'll be chucked out. The wages ain't much neither. You have to know all the stock, an' make no slip up giving change. You're on your feet the whole time. You have to be so blooming polite to the ruddy customers, only they ain't polite back. To be perfec'ly honest with you, I'm glad it's only part time.'

'Well, it's a clean job, behind a counter.'

'I want to be a milliner only my Mum can't afford the premium. What about you?'

'I'm a motor mechanic. You know Sleet Motors in Forest Gate? That's us.'

She confessed that she hardly ever went to Forest Gate and had not noticed the garage.

'Yeah, well, we buy an' sell cars, do repairs an' that.'

'*Do* you? Blimey, that's good!'

He smiled happily. 'Let's dance, sha' we?'

'Yeah, come on then.'

Billy and Maud were the two youngest on the dance floor. They could hardly fail to be noticed. In any case Billy was being closely watched. The East Ham Palais was a big, popular dance hall, renowned for the resident band and resplendent ballroom. Billy had arrived with his brothers George and Ronnie, who danced with any girls they could pick up while looking out for each other. All the Sleet boys looked out for each other. There was 'never any trouble' but as a precaution George and Ronnie were armed with razors.

After a couple more dances, Billy led Maud away from the dance floor. He held her in his arms and lowered his face to hers. Their kiss was barely a touch of lips, fleeting and nervous, but thrilling for both of them. A second attempt was no better than the first, and again they found it exciting and intimate. She said, 'That was nice. But Billy...'

'What?'

'Don't let on you was with me. My mum is hiding from someone, a copper, I think.' She had quite forgotten the details, so long had it been. 'No one calls us Cotter no more. You're the only one who knows.'

'Well, *I* won't say nothing.'

The band struck up the next dance. Maud reached up to Billy's shoulders as he bent to embrace her in another kiss. This time the two of them lingered and made a better job of it as George and Ronnie and Effie watched from across the dance floor.

That very evening Emmeline Sleet was informed by George and Ronnie, with ribald guffaws, about young Billy's kisses with a pretty little dance partner. 'Know who she is?' asked Em. No, they had never seen the girl before and did not know her name. 'What's she like?' – 'Brunette in a green frock. Just a kid.' – 'Well, if he sees her again find out who she is. We don't want the wrong sort poking around, asking questions.'

Harriet took longer to be told. A week passed before a neighbour mentioned that Maud had been canoodling and spooning with one of those notorious Sleet lads at the Palais. Harriet felt scared. She had never known quite how seriously to take Fisk's warning, and did not want to find out. She wondered now whether to say anything to Maud. After all, it might have been a one-off, a chance encounter.

Instead she raised the subject with Gina, casually repeating her story that the Sleets were just a rough family that Edwin had fallen out with. Nothing more had been heard about the hundred pound reward, and they assumed (if it existed at all) that no one had claimed it. 'All the same, I don't want the Sleets to come knocking,' she said, 'an' now Maud might be having a fling with one of 'em. I don't know if I should interfere.'

Gina said, 'Ask her about it, why shouldn't you? Nip it in the bud.'

'Might be nothing.'

'Well then, if it's nothing, no harm done.'

Before Maud left the house the suspicious Harriet asked breezily, 'Where y'off to then, duck?' – 'Nowhere. Effie's.'

'What you goin'a do there?' – 'Nothing. Listen to records.'

'A'right. I heard you danced wi' one of them Sleet lads.' – 'How d'you hear that?'

'Someone said they seen you at the Palais. What's his name?' – 'I don't remember.'

'You seen him since?' – 'No.'

'Good. The Sleets are a bad lot, Maud. Don't see him no more.' – 'A'right.'

But by that time Maud had already had a second meeting with Billy. Hand in hand they had strolled among shady lakeside trees at the edge of Wanstead Flats, hidden by bushes and shrubs.

And that's where she was going again. Maud hurried from the house to Rabbits Road, over the railway bridge, into shadows where Billy was waiting on his motor bike.

There is no love so consuming as that of two adolescents. Even for the boy the obsession is hardly sexual. It is pristine, unalloyed devotion.

'Here, I made this for you.' he handed her a small square of polished steel, exquisitely smooth, on a flimsy chain. From its centre a heart shape had been cut. 'Made it in the garridge workshop.'

'Oh, blimey, Billy, what a lovely necklace.'

He showed her the steel heart that had been cut out. 'I'm goin'a make this bit into a ring, for myself.'

Maud could not wear the necklace. Her mother would have asked where she got it. She kissed it each night before sleep, kept it with her all day, and clipped it around her neck only when on her way to meet Billy.

*

The snug at the Well Smack inn in Barking had a new sign on the door, *Private*. Under the blind eye and deaf ear of landlord Roland Fisk, here the Sleet family could hold a quiet meeting. Things could be discussed with friends or enemies, negotiations held or a partner entertained.

Men who had had dealings with young Micky averred now that they had always known he would amount to something. They said 'Frostie' was not a lad to get on the wrong side of. Far better to work with him than against him.

Em Sleet truly admired her son. He had sought revenge and got it. Cotter's widow had so far escaped him, but he would find her. He was the type that never gives up. He was a hard man. Yet he could be a charmer when he wanted – his Pa could too. As Em would tell people, say what you like but Micky was always very good to her. He had clever ideas and made things happen. Some might think Micky cold, even heartless, she knew. Em admitted he would not be everyone's cup of tea – who was? All the same, he brought in plenty of the pounds, shillings and pence. Thanks to him, the family home had been extended and done up, with a shed for motor cars and motorcycles, and a stable for a pony and trap. And he treated his mother with respect, as the only woman among men, and head of the family.

The trouble was, Em found, Micky and all the boys hankered for female company. She had no objection except girls could be a risk. Eventually, Em supposed, her boys would marry. It was important they choose wives who could keep their traps shut and stick up for the family. The Sleets had enemies and rivals. She had her sons watching each other to make sure none of them did anything stupid. Apart from Micky, none of the boys was supposed to go anywhere, see anyone or do anything without Em knowing about it. Yet now George and Ronnie were telling her that Billy was always going off by himself for a motorcycle ride.

'Find out where he goes,' she said.

But they could not.

Effie and the girls decided it was far too long since they'd had a Saturday night out at the East Ham Palais. Maud and Billy prepared themselves. They must not let anyone realise that they were – they hardly knew what it was – were they courting? – that they were secretly keeping company, that they were in love. They agreed that when they met on the dance floor, where his brothers and her mother's spies might be watching, they would 'act natural' as if they hardly knew each other. They would make out they did not remember each other's names.

Nothing went to plan. Again the jazz beat and sparkling light were intoxicating, the fast-moving musicians on stage, the smoke and talk, couples in fine clothes turning and moving in each other's arms. George and Ronnie, instructed to 'stick close' to Billy, were at his side as Maud and the girls approached. Effie joked, 'Aha, look who it is, Maud – your beau.' The others smirked and snickered.

It was suddenly obvious that a kiss seen by others becomes public property. The other girls somehow knew, they could see it, that Maud was 'soft' on Billy. It was pointless to pretend.

Billy smiled slightly and touched Maud's hand. Their little subterfuge was abandoned. He said, 'Fancy another dance, then?' as if they had danced a dozen times already that evening.

Effie addressed George and Ronnie, 'Ain't neither one o' you goin'a ask *me* to dance?' George reached out a hand and led her onto the dance floor, leaving Ronnie in sole charge of keeping an eye on things.

'That's a nice frock,' said George, without much feeling.

'You dance nice,' Effie replied, though it was not true.

'You done your hair pretty tonight.'

'Get away with you.'

'Where d'you live then, Ef – round here?'

'Over by the Three Rabbits. What about you?'

'Wall End, by White Gate Bridge. My little brother Billy's totally gone on your friend. Who is she?'

'That's love at first sight, that is! I reckon they're seeing each other, on the quiet. You can just tell, can't you?' George laughed and asked Effie what she knew of her friend.

'What d'you want to know? Her name's Maud Hayes. She lives near me, on the other side o' Romford Road.'

'What street? Just curious, seeing as she's Billy's girl.'

George and Effie talked a great deal more before the end of the evening. The two liked each other. They arranged to meet again.

The last dance came to an end. The crowd streamed out of the Palais into the High Street, walking away in every direction, joined by groups emerging from a dozen nearby pubs at closing time. There was laughing and yelling as usual on a Saturday night. Effie and the girls lit up cigarettes and recounted the evening's successes and failures, the merits or otherwise of their dance partners, as they strolled back up to

Romford Road.

Heading away from the Palais in the opposite direction, George, Ronnie and Billy set off in the cooling night on a half-hour walk to the Sleet family home up the track beyond the new housing. There George tapped on his mother's door and went inside. He reported everything he had learned from Effie. 'This girl of Billy's –they're dead serious about each other. They spent the whole time tonight spooning like a couple of lovebirds!'

'Ha ha! Billy's a bit young for that malarkey. Who is she?'

'Name's Maud Hayes. Lives in Manor Park, near the Rabbits. I got the address. They're no one special. Her mum's some sort of dressmaker. The dad's dead, used to run a pub in Barking.'

'Did he now? Ran a pub in Barking! An' the name is Maud! Using the name of Hayes! Well, well, well. Would you ruddy Adam an' Eve it? Can it really be her? What a stroke of luck if it is. I must get Fisk onto this.'

Harriet heard the front door, Maud's footsteps in the hall and on the stairs. Maud came at once into the shared bedroom, where her mother sat sewing. Harriet stopped her work and pointedly put it aside. 'Had a nice evening, dear? Need to talk to you.'

'What is it, Mum?'

'Did you dance with that Sleet boy at the Palais again?'

'Blimey, why shouldn't I dance with who I want? Who's sneaking on me?'

'I want you to steer clear o' them Sleets. They're crooks, vicious thieving scum, lowlifes.'

'No they ain't!' Maud scoffed. Then, 'Billy ain't like the rest of 'em. He's sweet. He's nice an' got a good job.'

'His mother offered a reward to find out where we live, did you know that?' She still did not know if this was true.

Maud recalled something overheard years ago. 'Never found us though, did she? Billy won't snitch. Anyway, why did they offer it?'

Into Harriet's mind came the unhappy doubt about keeping this secret from her own daughter. But she replied, 'I don't know, pet. Only I'm telling you now, you have to stop seeing that boy.'

'You can't tell me that, you've no right. An' stop saying "that boy". He's Billy. I love him, an' he loves me.' Annoying tears clouded her vision. She grasped his necklace in her pocket.

'I *can* tell you, Maud. I *have* got the right. Oh, darling! Listen!' Harriet pleaded, 'Me an' your father only ever wanted a good life for you. You've got yourself a job in a decent shop. Don't spoil things.'

Maud found the outpouring of maternal concern pointless and embarrassing. 'Only part time.'

'It's a start. Don't throw away our efforts by mixing with that family. They caused your dad's death.'

This was shocking. She had never before heard it said with such certainty. Into Maud's mind came the memory of her father falling to the floor. She struggled to picture the scene more clearly. 'Well, that weren't *Billy's* doing.'

'Look, don't carry on with that boy no more. It's not safe. Promise me you won't. It can't come to nothing anyway. His mother won't allow it.'

'She don't know about it. *He* ain't goin'a tell her. I ain't promising you nothing.' Maud was even more determined now to stand by Billy and be his girl.

*

Billy picked Maud up on his motorcycle and drove beside Wanstead Flats to their lakeside hideaway. Clumps of bluebells had opened in the shady grove. 'Them flowers're pretty,' she said a little shyly.

'There's loads more of 'em up that road. You know the woods in Wanstead Park?'

They lay on Maud's coat and held one another close in long kisses, ran their hands over one another, fumbled under one another's clothes. Maud discovered a few more disconcerting facts to add to her burgeoning knowledge of men and maleness. She told him everything her mother had said. 'She said your family killed my dad.'

'They never! *She* had *my* dad killed, that's what happened, Maud. So my brother Micky said.'

'Oh! Really, you sure?' That would explain the hundred pound reward. And her mother had not told her!

They swore they would never part or stop seeing each other, and would always love each other, and not be driven apart by a family feud that was nothing to do with them.

'Sha' we get married?' breathed Billy into her ear. – 'Yeah, that a show 'em,' she answered.

'How do you, y'know, get married an' that?' – 'You go to a priest an' he fixes it for you.'

'What, a priest in a church?' – She nodded, 'Yeah. Only, *can* you get married at sixteen?'

'Course you can, can't you?' – 'You need permission, don't you?'

'Not bloody likely! We ain't asking no one for no permission.'

While Billy and Maud lay dreaming of marriage, Roland Fisk was in discussion with Micky and Terry Sleet and their mother. He said that with the information given by this lass Effie, he had found Mrs Cotter's home and had it watched. He had not yet been able to get sight of Mrs Cotter herself, but had seen the daughter. He told them who else lived in the house, their names and their movements.

'I don't want no harm done to the kids, Micky,' insisted Em, 'an' keep an eye on Fisk. Don't want the Inspector giving a tip off to his true love.'

'I won't do that,' said Fisk. Beads of sweat lay over his scalp.

'That's right, pal, you won't,' said Terry.

Fisk resumed his account. 'The other woman, Mrs Hayes, she's off to work early. So is the bloke downstairs. Then his missis walks the kids to school and carries on to her own place of work. Then Cotter's girl, Maud, she goes out to her morning job. Mrs Cotter don't go out at all. So by about half eight,' Fisk hung his head, 'everyone's out the house except her,' he admitted with pain. He could think of no way to save her.

Micky nodded to Fisk. 'Oi, you – you're comin'a make sure it's really her. You'll wait with the pony an' trap while I go in an' deal with her.' He turned to Terry. 'You'll watch the back of the house, in case she tries to slip out.'

'Pony an' trap?' queried Terry. 'Why not a motor – faster.'

'No,' replied Micky, 'trap's better. No one takes no notice of a pony an' trap.'

*

It was not especially early when Maud awoke. She washed at the bowl in the bedroom, buttoned her frock and went down to the scullery for a slice of bread. She had the timing to perfection: a brisk walk to the corner of the street and she arrived at the door of the haberdashers' at exactly five minutes to eight, as required.

Micky, Terry and Fisk had the timing right too. As Maud slammed the door behind her and began her walk to the shop, Roland Fisk drew up in the Sleets' pony and trap. He stopped not at the house but at the entrance to a narrow pathway behind the back gardens, one of the little paths that gave coalmen and dustmen access to the rear of terraced houses. There Terry alighted and moved along the path. Fisk now drove the pony further along the street, stopping with a clear view of Harriet's front door.

Micky descended from the trap holding a length of cord and a can of petrol. With these in his hand he went to the front door, raised the knocker and heard its echoing sound inside.

Fisk's mind raced round and round in its small cage, looking for an escape. He could find no way out. The instructions were simple. If the woman who answered the door was Harriet Cotter, he was to nod and touch his cap. If she was not, he would keep his head still and leave his cap alone.

He loathed himself. He loved Harriet. He desired her, daydreamed about her, so shapely, with natural elegance and lovely hair. His greatest pleasure for years had been the day he kissed her and put his arms around her in the snug bar. He longed to possess Harriet Cotter utterly, mind and body, cherish her and care for her. He had chosen instead to save his own skin from the Sleets.

Micky stood on the doorstep waiting.

Harriet heard the knocking. No one ever came to the house during the working day. She approached the window and peeked out, but could see no one. That was the trouble with a porch. A pony and trap waited in the street. The driver looked like Fisk. She could not be sure, with his hat and muffler. Likely it was not him. She preferred not to take a risk.

A second knock came, insistent, and a man's voice yelled through the door: 'Urgent telegram for Mrs Hayes.'

No one would send her an urgent telegram. He must mean Aunt

Gina rather than herself. She called out, 'Put it through the letter box, would you?'

The voice called back, 'Sorry not allowed, Madam.'

She did not know if that was true. She had never received a telegram in her life.

Should she answer the door? Suppose there really was an urgent telegram for Gina. Perhaps a death on her side of the family. Or someone gravely ill.

Taking her large fabric scissors to defend herself if need be, she left the front room and stepped into the hall. She feared she was being foolish, that she was in fact incurably foolish.

'Just a minute,' she called. She fixed the security chain in place and opened the door slightly. Through the gap she could see a man standing. He did not appear to be a telegram boy, and was not in uniform. Nor was he holding a telegram.

The slender security chain gave way in a single shove, wrenching the screws from the door frame and splintering the wood. Seeing the scissors in her hand, Micky at once grabbed her arm and took them from her. He held her up bodily in his grip at the front door and gestured to Fisk to confirm whether or not this was Harriet Cotter.

Fisk nodded and touched his hat.

To Harriet it seemed almost as though Fisk were greeting her. So it *was* him sitting on the trap. She tried to understand. This other man, she supposed, must be here to drag her out of the house so that Fisk could drive her away.

Her fear turned to terror: Micky did not drag her out of the house. Instead he pushed her inside and closed the door behind him. Then she saw the rope and the jerry can.

2

Micky forced Harriet into the downstairs back room, Phyl and Sam's family bedroom. 'What d'you want – you ain't brought a telegram?' she said stupidly.

'Nah,' Micky was amused by her incomprehension, 'no telegram, Missis, though I have brought a message – from Charlie.' He had already begun tying her hands behind her back. He moved so quickly that in the first shock and confusion she remained passive.

'Charlie –?'

Suddenly, vigorously, she found the strength to struggle. It was hopeless; he did not even notice. He seemed like iron machinery, herself a threadbare glove-puppet.

'Yeah, you remember old Charlie Sleet? My Pa. Funny how what goes around comes around.'

'You're his son?' She knew not what to fear. In what ways would he hurt her, how painful would it be? How much worse than ordinary pain? Would he rape her, use her like that in some way? Perhaps very viciously? She thanked God she was no longer so attractive to men. Or hang her, as she heard Charlie Sleet had been hanged? She felt physically sick in her growing terror, unable to stop trembling, as though she might at any moment lose control of her bladder and bowels. Without the sharp scissors to defend herself, small as she was and he so big, she powerless and he apparently omnipotent, she had no more plan of action than a mouse beneath the paw of a cat. Yet somehow she retorted defiantly, 'What about Mr Fisk – why you letting him off the hook?'

'Fisk ain't off the hook. He's right on it.'

Strangely it had not occurred to her until now to shout for help. It was something she had never done before. She raised her voice to a piercing scream and yelled, 'Help me, help me!' Micky smiled and instantly wound the rope across her open mouth like a horse's bit, stopping her cries. She was impressed by how deft he was, how unflustered. He ran the rope around her face a couple of times, then down to her ankles which he tied together.

Trussed and lying on the floor, she watched as Micky unscrewed the cap of the jerry can. He poured liberally in a circle around the room, sprinkling a little over her legs. With the rope in her mouth she could not ask him what the liquid was. It smelled like paraffin.

Outside, Fisk looked at his pocket watch. Micky had told him to wait a few minutes. He could hardly bear the thought of what might be happening to Harriet. The pitiful sight of her emaciated form at the door had been agony for him. She was showing her age so pathetically, he thought, the face so weary and lined, her hair lank and fading! How did she come to be in such a state? He lifted the reins and whipped the pony forward.

Maud, he knew, worked at the haberdashers' round the corner in Romford Road. On an impulse he drove to the end of the street and descended quickly from his seat, leaving the pony unattended as he darted on foot along the pavement. He pushed open the shop door and without preamble, ignoring a queue of women, called out, 'Miss Hayes! Miss Maud Hayes, Maud Hayes!' Every face turned, astonished. Maud looked up from the counter.

'Get home straight away,' he bellowed, 'your mother needs help urgent. There's been a serious accident.'

Maud stared for a moment and meant to ask him a question, but Fisk was gone. She had a recollection of having seen the man before, but for the moment could not place him. Fisk ran back to the pony and returned to his post at the house, for if he were not in place when Micky came out there would be a terrible price. Fisk looked again at his pocket watch. It was still not ten minutes since Micky went inside.

Everyone in the shop heard Fisk's message. Even so, Maud felt she must at least ask the haberdasher if she might be excused for the rest of the morning. It delayed her only a moment. She was told to go home at once. Back in his position, Fisk watched her approach. She ran fast. Fisk looked nervously at his watch once more. Now it was a full ten minutes. He cursed himself for a fool: if Maud were to arrive while Micky was still in there, she too would be in danger.

What was Micky doing to the poor woman? In the sixty seconds before Maud reached the house, Micky emerged. He had lingered to watch as Harriet writhed to escape the flame racing towards her and to hear the first howl of pain as the fire touched her legs and took hold of her dress. Gratified, he strolled calmly across the road and climbed into the trap. Fisk urged the pony to trot away. Micky said, 'Well, it's all over for your sweetheart, Inspector.' They went as far as the corner, stopping beside the little path. 'Wait here,' said Micky. 'I'll run an' get Terry.'

She saw the broken door frame, her mother's fabric scissors on the floor, dark smoke creeping from the back room. Foolish though Maud could sometimes be, a forceful common sense seized her now. She dashed inside and at once emptied the washstand jug over her mother's clothes. She struck at the flames with her own bare hands and with blankets dragged from the beds. She dragged the tied body into the hall. She seized the fabric scissors. The rope, already scorching through, gave way under the sharp blades as Maud worked with maddened strength. With both arms she hauled her mother up and pushed her to the front door, half-screaming to the world at large, 'Fire! Help, fire!'

Released and able to speak, with skin scorched and peeling on her legs, yet Harriet would not go out. She shook off her daughter. 'My fabrics! Upstairs!'

'No time, Mum, no time.'

'Too expensive, clients' money, can't afford to lose it.' A lick of heat and flame burst from the back room. Ignoring her pain or hardly aware of it, Harriet scrambled in frantic haste up the stairs. In smoke Maud stood shouting by the door. 'Too late, Mum, the fabric's done for! Come down, come down!'

Harriet continued into the bedroom, where her clients' dress fabrics were kept. Nothing mattered but her terror of the ruin and debt that would follow if her poplin, satin and lace were lost. The floor felt terribly hot underfoot, as if about to erupt. Still, there was no smoke in this room yet. All the while came Maud's desperate cry, 'Come down! Come down, Mum!'

Harriet grabbed her carpetbag from under the bed and pushed in the precious lengths of cloth – and saw at the bottom of the bag, where it had lain these last years, Edwin's loaded revolver.

The picture of Edwin she took down from the wall and rested it on top of the fabrics. Her eyes moved around the room frantically; what must she take, what must she leave behind forever? From a drawer she grabbed clean underwear and sanitary cloths and the valuable little stolen enamelled bag with a few shillings inside. She wondered whether to throw the filled carpet bag from the window down into the garden, or take her chances with it on the stairs and in the hall. Could she herself somehow escape by the window? She raised the window and looked into the garden for a way out. There she saw Terry standing guard. She heard Micky's voice calling to him, 'It's done, Terry, let's go.'

She pulled Edwin's handgun from the bag, cocked it and peered through the sights. The weapon was too heavy to hold steadily. She rested its weight on the windowsill and pulled the trigger. To her surprise the effect was instantaneous. Terry shouted and fell in the same moment that the gun made its immense jerking bang.

Micky came into view, staring up, uncertain where the shot had come from. She pointed the gun in his direction, peered along the barrel and pulled the trigger. She heard the loud bang, felt the wrench in her wrist, but when she looked, Micky was still upright, staring about. Micky ran to his fallen brother and called back – 'Oi, Fisk, get over here an' help.' Fisk came into view, running along the pathway until he reached the two brothers.

It was something she had long wanted to do: she turned the gun towards Roland Fisk and again pulled the trigger. Another cry as Fisk grasped his left shoulder and reeled back against the garden fences. His rapid, searching gaze found her at the window. Despite the injury, with his other hand he helped Micky carry Terry away, beyond the point where she could see them clearly.

The heat from the floor was becoming unbearable. Black smoke seeped between the boards. She knew that at any second it would collapse into the conflagration below. Out of the room, onto the landing, Harriet clutched the bag tight; smoke billowed up the staircase, blinding and suffocating. She almost threw herself down the steps into flames blazing in the hall and ran screaming out of the front door with her hair and dress on fire.

Maud threw a coat over her, striking at the flames with her hands, herself screaming with the pain. Neighbours ran forward with jugs and pails of water. 'My God, look at you!' cried Maud, tears streaming down. 'Let's get you to the hospital, Mum.' Somehow her mother, skin horribly raw and blackened, her hair singed away, would have to be taken to East Ham Hospital. She did not know how. She shouted out, 'Please God, fetch a doctor!' and a young man did race away.

Someone was attending to her burns in the street. A fire engine had arrived – she did not remember it coming – the firemen pumping water deep into the house. Harriet sat on the road amid a crowd watching flames consume her hiding place, her home and her place of work. A greater, unbearable anguish was that she was responsible for the destruction of Sam and Phyllis's home too, and their children's, and Aunt Gina's, and their dearest possessions. If it had not been for her, this catastrophe would not have fallen upon them. They had been generous and this was how she repaid their kindness. And of course, now Maud also had no home. 'Maud, dear,' she murmured, 'take my bag round to Cousin Will and tell him what's happened.'

*

Em watched in horror as the groaning, half-conscious Terry was laid out on the kitchen table. Dark blood dripped from his clothes and trickled across the quarry tiles.

'She flipping shot at us,' said Micky, 'in broad bloody daylight.'

'What, not the publican's widder – she *shot* at you? The cow! What with?'

It was Fisk who answered. 'Couldn't see clearly. Sounded like an old pistol. She got a lucky strike with Terry, who's never done her no harm.' Fisk's jacket was ripped apart at the left shoulder where it ran red and wet. In pain; he held the arm against his belly. 'I need a doctor. What Terry needs I don't know. He looks mortal bad.'

'Get cloths to soak up this mess. You should've took Terry straight to East Ham Hospital.'

'It would o' meant explaining,' said Micky. 'Too many questions.'

'No, no, you're right, son. Where's he hit?'

'In the guts.'

They stripped away the blood-soaked clothes. Unflinchingly, Micky looked into the wound. 'There's bits of him bursting out.'

Em grimaced at the ghastly sight. 'Oh, poor lad! We need to staunch it. Strap it up tight.' She began artlessly wiping blood away and pressing down towels. A gruesome substance oozed onto the table, but the flow was gradually reduced. Ordinary leather belts held everything in place, which seemed to work.

Terry fell into unconsciousness, which Em believed was a health-giving sleep. She sat beside him for some hours as he made no sound other than shallow, scraping breaths. She was hopeful.

In the afternoon, Billy and the other brothers came in, crying out at the sight. They were quickly informed – for once, a plan of Micky's had gone wrong. They learned what he had done. Somehow the woman had freed herself and escaped her punishment. Micky said, 'Someone must'a cut her loose.' It might have been a neighbour. Or had another person been inside the house all along? Or, his calculating, suspicious intuition at work, he guessed most likely the daughter had returned home. His mind was working on what the reason for that might be.

Em's certainty that all would be well deserted her. 'Oh, my good, lovely boy! My Terry, my Tel, my darling! I don't want to lose you! Bloody bitch should be done for this – shooting at people!'

'If he dies,' pronounced Micky, 'it'll be out an' out murder. Then we'll go for the girl an' all, the daughter. Slice the girl an' make the mother watch.'

Billy protested, 'What, go for Maud? *That* ain't fair! It ain't nothin'a do with her.'

'You ain't seeing that girl no more,' said Em, 'not after this. I *forbid* you to see her, Billy, that's final.'

'No, Ma, he's to see her,' Micky countered, 'an' find out where they're putting up. I'll do the job right this time. The pair of 'em are dead meat. So'll you be if you try anything, Billy. No funny business.'

Terry's breaths became more rasping. Fisk leaned over him, 'Feel the heat coming off. That's a fever, that is!'

'Can we stitch him up ourselves?' said Em.

'I reckon,' said Micky, 'if there's a bullet in there, we must take it out.'

'How *do* you get it out?' Em wondered.

Fisk said, 'We want to be careful. That's a job for a proper surgeon.'

'Where can we get a surgeon?'

Fisk shook his head in doubt. 'The only place has got to be East

Ham Hospital, but I...' He wanted to prepare them for the worst.

'Well, bloody well go there an' get one then, what you fucking standing about here for?' interrupted Em sharply, 'An' never mind the cost. Take what you need from the cash tin. Bring a surgeon we can trust.'

*

The doctor waived his one shilling fee. Harriet was taken to hospital as a charity patient, accompanied by a police constable. She told him that a strange man had broken into her house and set fire to it, apparently under the impression she was someone else. She had never seen the man before. She described Micky Sleet to the last detail. The constable jotted it all slowly in his notebook, *Arson attack on home of Mrs Harriet Hayes, case of mistaken identity. Victim describes perpetrator. Tall young man, very blond, local accent. Could identify.*

'Now then,' said the policeman, 'some of your neighbours report hearing gunshots. You know anything about that?' Harriet said she had heard three or four gunshots; they seemed to be behind the house, in the gardens; it sounded like two different guns, she said; she believed her attacker was exchanging fire with someone.

After the officer had wished her well and gone away, Harriet was injected with morphine and fell into the best sleep she had known in years. When she next opened her eyes, it was evening. Maud was sitting at her bedside. She too had been washed and treated for burns. There were flannel wrappings around her forearms and the palms of her hands.

'You a'right, dear?' Harriet murmured.

'The nurse reckons I'll be a'right in a fortnight. You're pretty bad. Doc says yours'll take a long time.'

'Thank you for' – Harriet wanted to say, for saving her life, which was no more than the truth but would sound melodramatic; besides, she was trying to understand Maud's part in the incident; how the Sleets found her address, and why Maud had come back early from work – 'everything you did for me.'

'Will's here,' said Maud. They were provided with ointment, mixtures, pills and bandages and Will took Harriet away on his handcart, Maud walking along beside.

At his squalid house, Will offered Harriet and Maud his bed for the night. As for himself – 'I'll be a'right on the floor. We'll sort something out.'

'Bless you, Will, bless you! I keep thinking, how'll I do my work? My sewing machine is in the house! It'll be ruined!'

'Don't worry, Hat, we'll find a way. Who done this to you? Can't be Fisk – he wants to bed you, not kill you.'

'The bloke what done this said he was the son of Charlie Sleet. What that's supposed to mean, I don't know. But Fisk *is* something to do with it. Cause he was sat outside in a pony an' trap.'

'Was he? One of these days, Hattie, tell me what's the hell's going on between you an' the Sleets. Why would they do this, when you say you don't even know 'em?'

She simply could not admit the reason. She said, 'Ted crossed them somehow. They're a family o' villains, wicked an' vengeful, that's all. I don't know what Fisk has to do with 'em, except he was a copper. This is Maud's doing – she's mixed up with the Sleets. That's how they found us.'

Maud burst out, 'How is it *my* doing? I don't know the Sleets any more'n you do.'

'Didn't I say to stop seeing that Sleet boy? From now on, you're *not* to see him. Not ever again.'

'This ain't nothin'a do with Billy. It weren't *me* told 'em where we live. It was Effie.'

'Effie! Wouldn't you flipping know it!' Harriet exclaimed. 'Another one o' your pals. So that's it! I told you that friend o' yours was no good. Stay clear of Effie, l always said. Now look where she's landed us.'

Angrily and guiltily Maud rushed out of the room. She could not recall ever telling Effie to keep quiet about their address. If she had, it was years ago. She dashed about trying to tidy and clean Will's house as well as she could despite her pain and bandages, sweeping, brushing and dusting in a fury. She did not fancy sharing a bed with her injured, unjust mother, and even less did she fancy sleeping between the filthy bedsheets of Mum's hairy, unwashed cousin, but eventually she did lie down exhausted and depressed on his bed and fell fast asleep.

In the kitchen Harriet talked to Will about her next steps. 'What's to become of Aunt Gina?' she fretted. 'An' Sam an' Phyl an' the little ones? Where they to go?'

'We know what becomes of people, don't we, Hat, when they ain't got no home to live in? I'll walk over to meet 'em from work an' see if there's anything I can do.'

*

It might have been best for Fisk to go straight to East Ham Hospital in search of a surgeon. He did want to do that, if only to have his own injury stitched up. He was afraid, though, that the hospital would inform the police of anyone with a gunshot wound. Leaving that aside, he dreaded the mission to find a surgeon to treat Terry 'no questions asked'.

Instead, tortured by remorse, he drove the pony and trap to Harriet's burned-out home. Smoke and soot lingered in the air a mile distant, the distinctive, acrid stink of a housefire. The firemen had done their work: the brickwork was soaked, the window glass gone. Through blackened window frames he saw plaster falling free from the walls and ceiling. The roof was still intact, no doubt held up by a scorched remnant of the timbers.

A rough-looking workman was pacing about outside, apparently waiting for someone. It was Harriet's cousin Will, but the two men were strangers to each other.

Fisk spoke to him. 'I wonder who the poor devils are that've lost their home.'

'Six kids and their mother taking shelter in the church. The husband not back from work, nor one of the ladies what lived here. They've a nasty shock coming when they get home. The other lady that was in the house, and her daughter, the two of 'em burned an' been took to the hospital.'

'So that's where they are. D'you know them?'

'Oh, I know 'em all right! It's my own family, them that went to the hospital.'

'Your own family! Why, what name is it?'

At this Cousin Will gazed more closely. The question, and the tone of the questioner, struck him as odd. It occurred to him, suddenly wary, that this might be one of the Sleet family. He asked, 'Why, what name are you after?'

'She might be someone I know, a dressmaker in this street by the name of Mrs Cotter, or Mrs Hayes.'

Will was considering – on reflection, this flabby Bunter of a creature was much too old to be one of the Sleet boys. He recalled Harriet saying Fisk had driven the Sleet's pony and trap.

'That's her. You look as if you should be in hospital yourself.' Blood coloured the whole left side of Fisk's jacket.

'As it happens I am on my way to the hospital.'

'You won't find her there, if that's what you think. They've let her go.'

'If she's left the hospital already, it can't be too bad. Thank God!'

'I believe I know you,' Will ventured brazenly, 'Mr Fisk, is it, the new landlord of the Smack in Barking?'

'That's it. Do you frequent the Smack? I don't usually forget a customer's face.'

'Well then, Mrs Hayes told me all about you. I happen to know she'd prefer you to keep away.'

'Listen, friend, I know what Micky Sleet done to her today. She's shot at me and done this, but what's worse is she's shot one of the Sleet boys. He's like to die, and if he does it will change everything for her.'

The shooting was astonishing news to Will.

It was clear Harriet had never been straight with him. There would be a good reason, he was sure. He wanted to get to the bottom of it. Why would anyone try to kill a harmless widow? Indeed, *was* she harmless, if she really had shot a man? He replied evenly, 'I daresay she's a few bullets left an' willing to use 'em.'

'Maybe so, but I've come to help her if I can. It troubles me what's happened.'

'How d'you mean, help?'

'Can I trust you?'

'More'n I trust you.'

'I think you know where she is. Well then, if you do, will you take something to her?'

Fisk pulled from under his coat a great quantity of banknotes tied into a small bundle with a piece of ribbon. Will was shocked by the sight. Fisk had brought three such bundles, three hundred pounds, to bribe a surgeon, but now suddenly he thought that task – if it could be done at all – could be done with two hundred. The other hundred he handed over to Will.

'If the Sleets find out, that is literally the death of me. Give this to Mrs Cotter with sincere apologies from the bottom of my heart. It'll get her on her feet again.'

Cousin Will waited outside the burned-out house until first Sam and then Aunt Gina came from work. Sam stood and stared at the wreckage of his home with no reaction. It seemed almost that he had been expecting such a blow to fall sooner or later. The two men did not converse. Sam asked bleakly only if his wife and children were hurt and, hearing that they were safe at the church, went to join them. Gina was more distraught, yet quiet. There were no tears, no cries. She murmured that she was damned if she would go to the workhouse, nor be cared for by the church, nor by some do-gooding charity. She told Will she would rather throw herself in the River. 'It weren't much, not even our own place, but that's where me an' my husband had our time together, him an' me, man an' wife an' our boys,' she said. 'Everything good that I had was took off me, first him, then the boys, now this. Not even their photos left.' She turned away, refusing to look at the smouldering ruin.

He walked her back to his own cluttered kitchen. Seeing Harriet's bandaged legs, without a word Gina clasped her niece in an unaccustomed embrace. She said, 'Oh, your lovely hair, all burnt! Let me tidy it for you, pet.' Will placed cups of tea on the table. He turned to Harriet: 'You ain't goin'a believe this, but Fisk come to the house. He asked me to give you something.'

'He can bugger right off. I don't want nothing.'

Without drama Will brought out the tied-up banknotes.

'Bloody hell,' cried Gina, 'what's that?'

Harriet merely stared in horror, fearful of some trap or bribe.

'With apologies for all what you been through, from the bottom of his heart. He asked me to tell you that.'

'So he *did* have something to do with it. I knew it!'

Will did not mention that Fisk had been bleeding from a wound. He would have liked to ask Harriet about the shooting, and as soon as possible he must pass on that a man she shot was likely to die – murdered, in effect.

He did not want to talk about these things in front of Aunt Gina. Probably Harriet had never discussed the Sleets with her aunt, who in any case had enough to worry about. He would have to wait until he and Harriet were alone.

She untied the bundle. The banknotes were of different sizes, colours and amounts. She pulled one out and felt it between finger and thumb as if to check she was not dreaming. It was a pound note. She contemplated its picture of the King, and the Houses of Parliament on the other side, hardly believing she was in the very same city as those institutions. She handed the note to her cousin. 'Here, you have this one, Will.'

'No, Hat, it's yours.'

Together they counted out the rest on the kitchen table. Fisk had given her a fortune.

'*Your* ship's come in, hasn' it?' Gina said bitterly. 'What's to happen to the bloody rest of us?'

Harriet promptly divided the pile into four. 'Here,' she pushed one quarter to Gina, 'that's for you, Auntie. Find a decent room. That's rent for a whole year, that is.' A second stack she pushed towards her cousin. 'This is yours, Will, no arguments.' She picked up the third heap of notes, 'Can you get this to Sam an' Phyl somehow?'

She rested her hand on the final quarter. 'I'll take this, wherever it is I'm going.'

'Now wait a minute,' argued Gina, 'you ain't going nowhere, not without me.'

'No, I've give everyone enough trouble. I'll get out o' your way.'

And she knew now where she must go. So obvious, really.

*

Past the snarling dogs Fisk hastened with the surgeon, a big, bluff well-bred man bearing two bulging leather bags, into the Sleet family home. Other than Fisk himself, few outsiders had been inside the house. Even in Charlie's day visitors had not been welcome. Since then the dirt-track wasteland cottage between Wall End and the River Roding had been transformed into a good, sizeable house enclosed by high fences. The doctor was greeted by the suspicious faces of Emmeline and all but one of her sons. The other lay unconscious on the table. The doctor understood at once what the family were.

Having said he could do the job for one hundred pounds and no questions asked, on a single glance at the patient the doctor shook his head. 'You didn't tell me he was this bad,' he accused Fisk.

'Can you save my boy or not?' demanded Em.

'I don't know.' The doctor spent some minutes in close study of the wound. 'I won't say it's impossible. There's an outside chance. It depends whether suitable blood can be obtained for a transfusion. It's not a simple case of removing a bullet. That's the least of his problems. I see fragments of bone and fragments of bullet. The damage to his vital organs is extensive, probably terminal. Particles may have struck the spinal cord. He must be taken to hospital at once for an emergency operation.'

'No, do it here, not at the hospital.'

'It can't be done here.' The surgeon grimaced and shook his head. 'The damage is too serious. Antibacterial drugs might control his infection, if we can get them, but he's lost too much blood.'

'Save him,' snapped Em, 'at any cost.'

'Or you'll be sorry,' added Micky.

'Threats make no difference to the outcome of an operation like this, nor does money. Life, unlike death, is not always something money can buy. I'll do my best for him, no more, no less.'

'Stop jabbering an' get on with it,' said Micky. 'Save him or you're a dead man.'

'He's going to hospital or *he's* the dead man. Frankly I'm surprised he's not already dead. Is there a telephone booth near here, or a police box, to call an ambulance?'

'No, no, no! We don't want no one coming out,' Em replied sharply. 'Anyway there's no boxes round this way.'

Under the surgeon's direction Micky's car was prepared with towels, cushions, rugs and blankets. Terry was carried out on a makeshift stretcher. Micky was to drive, Em in the passenger seat beside him, and the doctor in the back with the patient. Before they set off, Fisk asked the doctor, 'Tell me the truth, doc, what're his chances?'

'Fifty-fifty, if we can get the right blood for him.'

Em insisted desperately, 'Terry'll make it. He'll pull through. He will, won't he, doctor?'

3

During the night Harriet woke in pain. Maud sat up to measure out the prescribed drops of tincture. When morning came, Harriet lay with eyes half open, lost in thought, drowsy from the drug. She was awake enough, though, to ask Maud to visit a client. 'Tell her I need a few days more to finish the dress.'

'How you goin'a finish it? You ain't fit, an' got nowhere to work.'

'Never mind that, after you're done in the shop go an' tell her.'

'I ain't going to the shop today. My frock's filthy-dirty, an' I can't work with bandages on my hands.'

'Give the frock a brush-down. Your fingers are good enough for work. Go to the shop or you'll lose a day's pay.'

'It won't look right, being behind the counter with bandages.'

'Yes it will,' Harriet insisted. 'Say we had an house fire an' she'll think it's good o' you to show up at all.'

Maud promised she would go to work. Other than what she was wearing, all her clothes had been destroyed. She brushed and smoothed the soiled, sooty frock as well as she could. She was only thankful that Billy's necklace was safe in her pocket as always. Will had a washboard and a tub in the outhouse, and a wringer, too, so if it had not been for the bandages and burns and the presence of a man, Maud might have taken off the dress off and washed it. With bandaged hands and no privacy she could not wash even herself, let alone her clothes. It would be embarrassing to turn up at the shop like that.

Maud ate a slice of bread at Will's unsavoury kitchen table and left the house. However, she did not fulfil her promise. Instead she hurried to the home of one of Effie's gang. She would have liked to call on Effie herself, but Effie would also be at work. Maud borrowed a cheap cotton frock in the loose, low-waist style Billy especially fancied. Yesterday's dirty dress she took off at last and washed in a copper on the stove, simply poking it around and lifting it out with the dolly stick in an attempt to keep her bandages dry. She ran the wet cloth through the mangle and ironed out the creases. 'I'll pick it up later,' she said.

Now she clipped Billy's necklace around her neck.

Effie's friend agreed to take a note to Sleet Motors in Forest Gate. Maud gave her a penny for the tram and laboured to write her message. *Usual place waiting for you darling M.*

'Hand it to Billy, no one else.'

Billy turned up on his motorbike. He was wearing his oily garage overalls beneath a leather blouson. 'My God, look at you, your arms,' he cried at once.

'You know what happened, Billy? Did your brother tell you he set light to my mum? He burned down the house! I got this tryin'a save her, that's what!'

'Yeah, I know what he did. So it *was* you who untied her – that's what he thought. We can't stay here. They'll come looking. Get on.' Maud settled herself onto the pillion. With her bandaged arms wrapped around him, her head resting on his back, he drove furiously beside the bleak heathland of Wanstead Flats until he reached the lake, their lake, their private place. There they dismounted miserably. He let the bike fall against some bushes.

Maud said simply, 'Billy...' and began to weep. He held her close, standing among waterside trees and shrubs. She looked into his own unhappy eyes. 'Say something, Billy.'

'D'you still want to marry me, pet, even after this?'

'You know I do! Only you have to *not* be the son of Charlie Sleet, an' I have to *not* be the daughter of Ted Cotter.'

'Why've we got to be kept apart by old history? Them people ain't alive no more! If only I *could* give up being a Sleet! My brains an' hands an' face an' everything ain't "Sleet" – it's *me*, it's Billy. Even *that* don't mean a ruddy thing! Two lovey-dovey pigeons cooing on a bleeding rooftop, or a couple of little sparrers playing hopscotch on the pavement, or a pair of swallers like darts in the sky, all having the life of flipping Riley, *none of 'em ain't got no names* – think of it, Maud! See what I mean? They don't even know what country they're in nor nothing! They're just *alive!*'

'Even if we didn't have no names, we'd still be *us!* You an' me.'

'Whatever your name is, Miss, I love you. I'll love you all my life, that's a promise. An' you'll love me an' we'll *always* be just us.' He held her tenderly and touched her lips with his. 'Whatever happens.'

'A'right then, I'll give up the name Maud Cotter. You change your name. We'll belong to each other, not to our families. We'll be whoever we want to be.'

Billy gave a slight, bitter laugh. 'That'd be nice, only...' He said that *his* family were watching him like a ruddy hawk. He got away this morning by pretending he was giving a friend a lift. Any minute now they would send someone out to find him. 'First Ma has *forbade* me to see you. Then my brother Micky *ordered* me to see you an' find out where you're staying. He even *threatened* me if I don't find out.'

'Same. Mum said I must never ever see you again, not ever. But what I think is,' she said, and he watched her lips utter the impossible words he knew were coming, 'let's go away together.'

Again they kissed. 'The trouble is, pet, it ain't so easy. Your mum shot my brother Terry an' he might die. Micky says if he does we're to go after *you*. Go after the daughter, he said.' He did not utter the full horror of what Micky had suggested.

'Christ, that's wicked! It ain't even true. I never saw her shoot no gun!' retorted Maud. 'But if you truly love me, Billy, none of it won't matter – not even that – so long as you an' me's together.'

'I do truly love you, Maud, heart an' soul! I do! But we won't have no peace. Never. They'll always be after us.'

'No one'll find us.'

'Oh, Maud, they would. This is our last little minute together.'

'What you saying, Billy?' Incredulous tears ran from her eyes. 'No! I want to keep seeing you. We'll meet here every day.'

'No, pet,' he replied tenderly, 'even this place won't be safe.' He raised his motorcycle from the bushes. 'Anyway, I got to go now.'

'You ain't going back to the garridge, after what we've said?'

'I must.' He threw a leg over the seat and started the engine. 'They'll be out looking for me. I don't want to lead 'em to you. I'll take you to Manor Park an' we'll kiss goodbye.'

*

Alone, Harriet raised herself to a sitting position. She dimly recalled being undressed and put to bed by Aunt Gina. Carefully she unwound the dressings from her calves. Revealed was a repulsive archipelago of peach-coloured patches in a lurid sea of red slime. Each of the patches had a shining, moist surface rising and falling in blisters. She would have expected flesh so damaged to hurt a great deal more than it did. Following the hospital's instructions, she did not touch the place but simply tied bandages over until all was again concealed.

She had to throw away the used dressing, vile with stains. She tried shuffling across the room to a bin. It was not difficult. Walking, she found, did not hurt terribly. Turning the leg was painful, or anything brushing against it.

She lay back in bed, idle for the first time since she gave birth to Maud, or perhaps since she was a babe herself. She could hear Will hammering in the back yard. She supposed Gina was at work. Maud would come in later from the shop. She raised herself again to pull at the carpetbag on the floor beside her.

Inside the bag, her pieces of dress fabric were unharmed. Ted's pistol and cosh were again lying beneath. The tinted photograph of him had survived the tumult. She took it in her hand and in painful longing gazed at the image, seeming to feel her husband's broad shoulders in her arms, the kind, dashing, handsome man.

It's all because, she chided him, *you're so bloody kind. No good's come of it. If you hadn'a saved them Jews from Sleet's mob, everything'd still be all right.*

Harriet did not ask Maud how she managed at the shop this morning. There was no time to ask and no time to answer. They had to leave at once, quietly and quickly, while Will worked in the yard.

Electric trams clattered and clanged up and down Romford Road, together with motorbuses and jostling motorcars and swarms of noisy motorcycles. Tram number 63 ran along Romford Road all the way from the East End to the outer reaches of East London and back again, and back again, and back again every hour, ferrying labourers and factory workers, tradesmen, clerks and cooks, maidservants, warehousemen and shop assistants. Harriet and Maud boarded the tram and stayed on it all the way to the Aldgate terminus.

From Edwin's description of his journey on that night of the mobs, Harriet had a notion of what to do next. They turned through crowded, rubbish-stacked streets and lanes off Middlesex Street towards Spitalfields market. Maud remained silent. Her mother had gone mad. Because of her mother, she was being taken away without a word of apology. Old enough to leave home and find a place of her own, yet she had been brought against her will into this horribly strange world. She should have refused; would have refused if she had only known where else to go. Harriet waylaid foreign-looking women clad in blanket-like shawls to ask if they knew Zuckerman, the sweet-maker. Unknown and untrusted, she was rudely brushed off.

Edwin had mentioned the nauseating alleys, barefoot children in the dark, ragged girls offering satisfaction for fourpence, foul tenements brimming over with filth, squalor and degradation. He seemed never to recover from leaving Mr and Mrs Zuckerman and their boy in such a place, and recounted their absurd offer to repay the favour one day. Harriet recalled the same unlikely offer from the wife as they set off from the Well Smack inn that night.

Maud too knew the savage reputation of the area, the drunkenness, fighting and thievery. Yet as they progressed around Spitalfields Market and either side of Brick Lane, it was not as they expected. There were different streets, different peoples, one corner seething with idleness, the next teeming with industry; some figures crushed beyond any hope, men and women dead drunk on the pavement or propped in doorways, some not decently dressed, stinking enough to make a passer-by retch, others dandified, swaggering and sneering defiantly, some out of their minds, ranting and yelling, others sober and serious, correctly turned out in shirt and collar, hat and coat, walking intent upon inscrutable business.

There was not a single nook of tranquillity in the narrow thoroughfares, everywhere a din of crying hawkers and touts, squealing children, shouted foreign talk. The very air was alien with its odors. Clattering handcarts moved about like shoals of fish, boxes and crates and bundles and chests ceaselessly delivered or taken away. Harriet moved forward slowly and cautiously, Maud carrying her bag. Every face turned towards them, staring unabashed.

Everywhere they asked for Zuckerman, sweet-maker. Perhaps they were asking the wrong kind of people. Countless Jews lived here, but there were other nations, plenty of English and Irish, and pub corners and dark blocks and tenements where they doubted any Jew would dare venture. Edwin had told her he left them in a street where every single shop and factory bore a Jewish name. Perhaps the Zuckermans had moved on since then, and would not be found. Harriet was afraid:

what would she do then? It occurred to her to ask fellow Englishwomen when she saw them, and soon they were directed into a neighbourhood where indeed every man, woman and child must surely be a Jew; where signs, posters and bills on walls and windows were printed in the unreadable letters, and above every shopfront and workshop in their own familiar alphabet were painted many names of that restless, harried tribe, Rosen and Bloom, Abrahams, Isaacs and Jacobs, Silver and Goldstein, Cohen, Levy and Israel. Here they stopped again to ask and, eyed warily, were led by a woman to the very door of Aaron and Lieba Zuckerman.

*

The *Barking, East Ham & Ilford Advertiser* covered the story with a front-page splash and a photograph of the smouldering house. Its usual litany of brief court cases of men sentenced to a ten shilling fine or a month in prison for affray, gambling or failing to maintain a wife, for hooliganism, drunkenness, and driving a cart recklessly, was pushed aside by the truly sensational and puzzling account of a house fire, attempted murder and shoot-out in a respectable Manor Park street which had left a poor widowed dressmaker almost burned to death.

The *East London Observer* and *Stratford Express* took up the pitiful story, and then the *Evening News*, hawked at newsstands all over London. Whatever else had occurred in the shocking incident, lamented the editorials, the pity of it was that the police had done nothing. Finally it merited a comment in *The Times* to the effect that the vice and criminality of Whitechapel and Stepney was a contagion gradually spreading along Romford Road into Metropolitan Essex. Working-class districts of East London, the paper warned, were being permitted to fall victim to a lawlessness not accepted in other parts of the city. According to their writer, London's police were believed locally to be in the pocket of criminals.

The constituency MP was asked, and thundered the same question in his turn, why so little was done to bring London's criminal fraternities to justice. Police corruption, declared the MP to the House, was an evil that must be rooted out forthwith, and honest, upright law-enforcement restored. The police protested that the incident was being scrupulously investigated and that there was no evidence at all of the involvement of any criminal fraternity. Furthermore, no witness to the supposed shooting had come forward; nor to the arson. Nor could they find any trace of the so-called poor dressmaker.

*

Maud was furious with her mother and with the world, and with Billy, and his vile family, and furious with herself for not rebelling. She and Harriet were welcomed into the Zuckerman home with amazed cries, drawn inside with offers of food, shelter and help of any kind. Maud could hardly hide her disgust at such excessive emotion, welling tears, horrid embraces. The building seemed crammed with bizarre characters, the rooms decrepit yet strangely elaborate, dark with ruined panelling and high, ornate ceilings. She imagined herself in some monstrous Victorian fairytale.

To stay with the sweetshop family from all those years ago, whom she hardly remembered, struck her as senseless and unreal. Mr Zuckerman seemed to have forgotten his broken English and now spoke only in the Jews' own language. Yitzy, their dark-haired little boy, was now sixteen years old and barely recognisable and had two brothers and two sisters. *Their* English was as good as anybody's, but in strange accents and all talking at once.

Maud was led up a rickety, richly carved spiral stair by an old servant who spoke no English, to sleep on the floor of a bedroom with the two girls and – even more aggravating – with the servant herself. The servant, she realised, was simply a destitute local woman who worked in exchange for bed and board.

There was no privacy, no wash-stand, nothing made sense. The street, the house, and all the people, looked, sounded and smelt peculiar to her. Pungent, sickly air from Mr Zuckerman's workshop fused with malty vapours from a neighbouring brewery to create a nauseating stench.

Her mother had not even come upstairs, leaving her to face things on her own. Lieba and Harriet stayed in the room over the shop, working together into the night on Harriet's urgent dress orders at a table and sewing machine.

'*Azoy sheyn*, so beautiful,' Lieba murmured. '*Di unter rekl*, the… underneath.' She ran an appreciative finger over the fabric, held it up in incredulous admiration. '*You* made this?'

Harriet assured her that it was her own handiwork.

'Like this, you can work in the high-class. This you can sell in fashion house! Bond Street, Mayfair.'

Harriet gave a mocking laugh. 'They wouldn't let someone like me through the door. Anyway, you need different fabrics for the high-class work. You have to know how to cut an' sew rare silks, tussore, taffeta, how to use embroidered lace, guipure, faille. I've not had enough practice. It's a different job.'

'You *do* know how. You *can* do this. We will ask for you, friends in the shmutter business. Friends open doors.'

'The what?'

'Rag trade, fine suitings, dress-making, garments, couture!'

Lieba sat with Harriet until four in the morning. She asked, 'What happened to you? What about your husband?' As they worked, Harriet gave her an account of the years that had passed, starting with the death of Edwin and ending with the fire. The tale was abridged. There was no need to mention Fisk. That would be too hard to explain. Nor the pistol, she did not mention that. Micky Sleet was, after all, the point of the story, son of the man who had led the attack on the Zuckermans' shop in Barking. .

On the other side of the room stood a cheap upright piano. Harriet asked if she could play it from time to time. 'Harriet,' – Lieba pronounced the name with a guttural H, rolling R and sibilant T –'use the sewing machine and play the piano. And Maud, she should play, and Yitzhak on his clarinet, Aaron will take the fiddle, and we will all sing, sing like birds, like birds,' she laughed.

'Ha ha! What kind o' birds – crows?'

An alarm woke her in the dark. She heard the elderly servant moving in another room. Harriet lay pondering what to do next, remembering that she had absolutely no reason to get up. She had been under her covers for less than an hour, the burns madly itching and sore. Yet from long habit she was wide awake. She sat up and took her medication. She carefully changed the dressings on her wounds, which looked as lurid as before. The falling and rising cadence of Aaron and Lieba's voices could be heard through the floor, speaking their own language. Harriet put on yesterday's clothes and went down. If Lieba could get up after less than an hour's sleep, then she would too.

They were horrified. 'Go back to bed, rest!' But she sat with them at the small kitchen table. The air in the room seemed curiously scented, sour with fats, savoury with oils. Something white hanging in loosely woven muslin dripped whey into a bowl. Breakfast was unfamiliar, black bread and black tea with a spoonful of jam. Struggling with his English, Aaron expressed great sorrow and condolences about Edwin's death and dismay at the way things had turned out. 'Such a fine man,' he said, 'such a golden heart,' in a voice so tender that suddenly Harriet felt the choke of misery. Tears rimmed her eyes. She had forgotten to think about her husband in that way.

Lieba patted her hand. 'We must think now, dear,' she said, 'where to find for you one or two rooms.'

The willing generosity of the remark almost frightened Harriet. She had truly left her own world behind with little hope of return. She depended utterly upon these foreigners, people she barely knew. Desolate and apprehensive, she murmured, 'How can I repay you?'

Aaron shook his head to banish the remark. Lieba said, 'No, darling, we are repaying you!'

They discussed what work Maud could do. Returning to her job in Manor Park was ruled out, for surely that was where the Sleets would search first. Besides, she would have been replaced by now. Serve in the Zuckermans' sweetshop, perhaps, or on the market stall? But no, for she could not serve their customers without knowing Yiddish.

'And such work,' argued Lieba, 'is not for Maud. She must better herself.'

Aaron had another idea: he was thinking of selling a new product, gift boxes of luxury candies. 'Praline, nougat, fudge, truffle, sugar almond,' he explained. He needed someone for two weeks or so to pack attractive sample boxes. It was delicate, light work, something Maud could do. She would wear spotless gloves of thin cotton.

By the time Maud came downstairs for her own slice of bread, Aaron and Yitzhak had departed to the workshop, the younger children were at school and Lieba was selling sweets at her market stall.

Harriet helped change Maud's dressings. She broke the news that Aaron had some short-term work for her packing boxes of sweets. She said it had also been decided Maud should try for a job as a shop girl at a West End department store.

'What, you already decided without asking me?'

'Well, you must do something, dear, mustn't you? Yitzy says one o' the big stores in Oxford Street will be advertising for more girls in a couple of weeks. He found out somehow.' She added that the shop was Bourne & Hollingsworth, a grand name familiar to both of them although of the shop itself neither knew anything except that it was not the kind of place that they themselves would dare set foot.

Maud dismissed the suggestion with sarcasm. 'Can't do work like that with bandages, now can I, Mum?'

'It don't start for a couple of weeks. You might be all right.' Yitzy was to take her there before the "staff wanted" notices were published to make sure she spoke to the right person. At the same time he would give samples of Aaron's gift boxes to the confectionery buyers there and at other West End stores. No one was troubled by the thought of a sixteen-year-old girl and a sixteen-year-old boy spending the day together. On the contrary, Harriet thought it might help to get Billy Sleet out of Maud's mind.

Maud admitted to herself that Yitzy had become rather handsome. He was lithe and slim, had a quiet manner and gentle eyes, and looked painfully thoughtful. 'To work in these places,' Yitzy advised her, 'you need to speak right and do things nicely.' – 'Yeah, I know about being polite to every-bloody-one,' returned Maud sharply.

'Polite? Of course! That's obvious. No, I mean you got to learn to talk nice, dress nice, look nice. And even – if you can force yourself – actually *be* nice. Be ladylike.' He spoke lightly and easily, looked at her with his beautiful eyes and lovely smile. She warmed to him. With playful seriousness he urged her to talk 'properly'.

She tittered at the thought. 'I'll talk how I ruddy want.'

'Oh, you do as you like. But if you want to get on, talk the King's English. At home, too. How you talk is everything in this country.'

'Nah, you can't hide what you are. *That's* the thing in this country.'

'If you say so.'

She abruptly changed the subject. 'You walking out with anyone?'

Yitzy snorted. 'No, I'm not, what with working late and night school.'

'Night school?'

'Yeah, at the Evening Institute. Courses and classes to improve your prospects. It's cheap. Free, some of the classes. What about you? Seeing anyone special?'

'Mm.' She tightened her lips. 'How can I see him, now we've come here? Anyway our families don't approve.'

'Oh! Who is it? D'you love him?'

'I do, that's a fact. An' he loves me. He lives in Wall End, if you know where that is.' She did not mention why her mother disapproved.

'Just catch a bus. It's not that far.'

'It's not easy, with his family. Why ain't you at work today?'

'I *am* working. I'm to show these samples at the stores.'

'Don't you never have no time off?'

'Course I do. I go to the comedy theatre and the pictures or dancing sometimes. On a Thursday night or Saturday night.'

'Where d'you go dancing?'

'Stepney Assembly Rooms, mostly. Or the Tivoli.'

'What, not the Tivoli in the Strand?' She was impressed. To her mind it was a fantastically glamorous nightspot.

He smiled at her naivety, not unkindly. 'That's the one. You want go this Saturday night?'

'What, dancing at the Tivoli? A'right then.'

*

Emmeline and Micky took their places by the hearth, Ronnie and George lounging beside them. Billy and Arthur had not come; they were "minding the shop" at Sleet Motors. Into the snug Roland Fisk carried a tray loaded with cheese and cold meats, a glass of port and lemon for Em and pints of pale for the brothers.

These days Fisk had an under-manager and senior barman, a cellarman, two junior men and two barmaids, but he maintained that to serve the Sleets with his own hands was a pleasure. He was panting noisily with the effort. No one rose to help him. They watched as Fisk placed their food and drink carefully upon the table, every item in its right place. He then dropped wearily into a chair, wiped his moist scalp with a folded handkerchief and lit up his pipe.

'Look at the bleeding state of you,' said Micky.

'You got heart trouble?' Em asked.

George said, 'Fisk, if you ain't well, transfer the pub licence to me.'

'George!' said Em, 'We ain't never spoke about that!'

'Yeah, well, I want to take this place over.'

'*Do* you?' Micky and Em stared thoughtfully at one another. 'Not a bad idea,' said Em.

'I'm fine, I'm perfectly well,' responded Fisk nervously. He knew that the day he was not useful to the Sleets, they would dispose of him. 'I'm happy to teach George the business, course I am.'

Glasses were raised to Terry, very ill in hospital. It was not yet clear if the operation had been a success.

'You need to know,' said Fisk, 'the police'll look into this an' I can't stop 'em. Setting people alight, shots fired an' that. Even the ruddy MP poking his nose in. You're like to be called as witnesses if you ain't charged with something.'

'All this fuss,' mused Em, 'over a flipping dressmaker!'

'*We* never fired no shots!' protested Micky. 'It's wild accusations, that's what it is. They better fucking not try an' pin nothing on *us*.'

Fisk shrugged, 'It won't be ignored, that's all.'

'Shut up, Inspector. Neighbours seen nothing. Ordinary house fire. Chip-pan blaze or a dropped cigarette'

'S'pose they ask about Terry being shot?' queried George. 'Why not come right out with it that she fired at us?'

'No, no – the court will ask what we was doing there,' counselled Fisk, 'an' *why* she took a shot at us. Stuff gets dragged out in court, people cross-examined. Least said, soonest mended. No case to answer.'

'I agree wi' that,' declared Em. 'None of you was anywhere near the place, right? We don't know what happened an' poor Terry ain't well enough to tell us. Someone took a potshot at him for no reason as he went about his lawful business, *that's* what happened. Nothin'a do wi' this fire. We need to forget this Cotter woman for a bit. She's caused us enough trouble.'

Micky said sharply. 'No, Ma, we can't leave things like this. We ain't letting her get away with it.'

'Thing is, Micky, we don't know where she is. Could be anywhere. She'll turn up, you mark my words. People always do.' She sipped her port. '*Then* we'll have her. All in good time.'

4

With her personal introduction from Yitzy, Maud landed a position as a sales girl. The entire palatial interior of the shop, done out in the latest Art Deco style, was breathtakingly grand and opulent. Below stairs as well, she had never been inside a space so clean and spacious, with facilities that were barely credible, a staff canteen, even a doctor and nurse on hand without charge. Staff were given their instructions calmly and politely and treated better than Maud had dreamed possible. The store even ran a hall of residence for its unmarried shop girls, but Maud stayed with her mother, who, she explained, was a widow who needed her at home. On the other hand, anyone who failed to carry out her tasks correctly was dismissed at once. All the girls must arrive on time, eat breakfast quietly in the canteen and change into a spotless black dress. Everyone wore an elegant metal name badge. They were taught to speak correctly and how to address their wealthy, refined customers.

Such a servile job felt to Maud like falling into riches. She adored Yitzy for the part he had played. Thereafter she followed his advice to the letter and was meticulous in keeping herself neat, tidy and ladylike. Admittedly she felt a little embarrassed by Yitzy's elocution lessons. Yet she submitted to his coaching and step by faltering step *yer* became you, Hs and Gs and Ts found their proper place, tenses were given a polish and double negatives excised. Far away from her old friends, there was no one to call her stuck-up.

Maud liked especially that she had been put on the millinery. With such good wages and the staff discount, she treated her mother and herself to a new coat, veiled hat, woollen headscarf and pair of shoes in the new style. She did not feel so bad anymore about the way things had turned out, especially when she and her mother moved into their own rooms. After all, Billy himself had warned her to stay away. Maud was beginning to feel that her mother had made the right choice, bringing them to this bizarre hiding place.

Harriet's new rooms went with a job. Aaron's rag trade acquaintances found her a position as a 'whole-time homeworker' for a West End fashion wholesaler. She moved into their live-in workshop, in fact two adjoining small rooms in an alley parallel to Brick Lane, close to the railway line and overshadowed by the brewery. One room was entirely filled with a three-quarter bed for Harriet and Maud to share, the other was a day room with a large window and good light, fitted out for professional dressmaking with a top-quality machine.

They were on the first floor of a densely crowded four-storey dwelling with a weaver's loft on top and a shop down below. The plasterwork and joinery had been patched and re-patched over the centuries, keeping the house more or less dry, sound and habitable. There was a shared privy at the back and a scullery on the landing. Scores of seamstresses, tailors and dressmakers were living and working in the building. A local man from the firm collected and delivered, with hanging racks instead of seats in the back of a motor car.

Harriet felt she could do no better. She said nothing to anyone about her experiences. There was too much shame in it, being set on fire as if one were not human at all, of no more value than rags and kindling.

Flames flickering in the tiny grate set off memories. Her nerves were on edge. She slept badly, had nightmares, and when awake was seized with moments of terror. She was scared too of the incomprehensible desert island onto which she had cast herself, its weird babbling jargon, chaotic goings-on, oddly pungent shops.

Harriet sent a letter to Cousin Will with no return address (Maud posted it in Oxford Street) to let everyone know she was safe. Other than that she could not think what to say. Besides, she believed that she was a bringer of bad luck. It came into her mind that even opening a letter from her might do them harm.

'I want to give you a treat, Mum.' – 'A *treat*? Like what?'

'I'll take you out somewhere.' – 'Oh no, I don't fancy that!'

'I only mean tea at one of them teashop places.' – 'No, well, we can have a cup of tea at home, can't we?'

'Wouldn't be a treat, then, would it?'

Harriet saw that it might be a mistake to rebuff her daughter's thoughtfulness. She must be careful not to fall out with her. She said,

'Oh, well then, if you like. If we're careful.'

On the day, Maud went out to hail a taxi. Harriet's face was hidden by a thick silk scarf and a veil hat. The taxi journey itself was marvellous to her. The city had always remained a mysterious, unvisited entity. They descended from the cab at Lyons' Corner House, a few paces from Piccadilly Circus. The bright cafeteria, with clattering and chatter and customers crammed at little tables, was the smartest place Harriet had ever entered. It was the first time she had been inside a restaurant other than a pub or a music hall.

Maud gave her name to a man in a tailcoat. He led them upstairs to a more formal room glorious with Art Deco lamps, marble walls, stucco ceiling and tables cloaked in white linen laid with silverware and china. Harriet struggled to focus. She saw gleaming urns, waitresses uniformed in black and white, trays of sandwiches, platters of cakes. A quintet played jaunty dance music from a small stage. Couples were actually dancing a quickstep, swirling around in each other's arms in front of everyone on a little dancefloor! In a tea shop! Goodness, so *this* was a "tea dance"! She had heard of them. Harriet had spent so long indoors, she was nearly overflowing with emotion, afraid she might faint.

'We only want a cup of tea, don't we duck?' she said nervously.

'No, well,' asserted Maud, 'you got to have a sandwich and cake.'

'Expecting two more, Miss?' asked the man politely. At that moment, adding to Harriet's utter astonishment, they arrived: Aunt Gina in her best dress and Cousin Will spruce in a three-piece suit and trilby hat. They were as overawed as Harriet, staring about open-mouthed. There were hugs and kisses, apologies and heartfelt explanations, and Harriet screwed up her face to forestall tears.

'Come on, Hattie,' said Cousin Will, 'dance wi' me.'

*

Maud watched disappointed as groups of singing suffragists with banners raised marched to the polling station. It was the first general election in which all women over twenty-one years old could cast a vote. Maud was two weeks short of her twenty-first birthday. To her surprise the officials were very strict. They insisted that if you were under twenty-one, you could not vote.

On the bus, in the street, she found herself looking at women differently. These ordinary people in cheap coats and dresses, headscarves and block-heel boots, carrying shopping baskets and handbags, now had a part in running the country.

Harriet could not vote either, because she would not give her name and address. In the event, the constituency of Whitechapel and St Georges returned a Labour MP with a large majority. As it happened, one year later the MP died and a by-election was called. Maud had now passed her twenty-first birthday and insisted that this time she would vote. This weakened Harriet's resolve and both of them went to the Town Hall to register.

The main issues of the day were the Great Crash, unemployment, the trades unions, Ireland and restrictions on the number of Jews allowed into Palestine, about which topics neither Harriet nor Maud knew anything at all. After a discussion with Yitzy, who was a passionate Socialist, and with Lieba, who strongly supported the Liberals, Maud and Harriet decided to vote Conservative. They walked quietly together to the polling station in the local primary school. The solitary experience of standing within a polling booth and placing her X upon the paper was more awesome than either had expected. Maud emerged with tears running down her cheeks. Harriet had no tears but raised eyebrows and tight lips showed that her emotion was the same.

Maud wiped her eyes. 'Ladies went to prison so we could do that. Force-fed.'

'I know. Well, it's done at last,' said Harriet. 'I reckon that deserves a drink.'

The next day it was announced that Labour had again been elected in Whitechapel and St Georges.

*

Emmeline Sleet never had any time for suffragists. She believed votes did not matter. She believed that powerful men would always rule, votes or no votes. She believed what mattered to people was not their Government but their family.

Things had been going extremely well for her own family. The General Strike and its aftermath, and now the Wall Street Crash, had been all to the good. Shortages had pushed prices sky high. Shops were closing down. Workless families were desperate for the bare essentials. Back-of-a-lorry, under-the-counter, on-the-sly business boomed. Micky, Ronnie and Arthur were busy with one job after another, jump-ups, hijacks, smash-and-grabs, robberies. They would target places out of town, an easy drive into Essex, where warehouses, banks, shops and offices had no preparations for a hold-up. George and Emmeline disposed of the goods.

Billy had a different job to do. He was left at the garage, minding the shop and playing the straight man. And in fact the others were also officially working with him at Sleet Motors.

Naturally Terry did not take part. He had survived the shooting but would never be a fit man. He would need help for the rest of his life. Terry's idea was to open a string of shops – he meant knocking shops. Micky and the boys approved. It was something Terry could handle, and it would expand the business.

Em advised caution. 'We'll be treading on the toes of fellers who think this is their patch.'

'Let's take 'em on,' said Micky. 'Deal with it once an' for all.'

'No.' Em did not want to take on their rivals. She spelled out a more prudent scheme. 'That Winslow lass is a looker. D'you like her? S'pose you fancy her and she fancies you. Well then, that could be a friendly alliance right there. If the Winslows and the Sleets got together, just think what that would do.'

'Ada Winslow, you mean? Matt Winslow's got three other girls besides her.'

'You ever asked any of 'em for a dance?'

'No. They go dancing in Stepney, at the Assembly Rooms.'

'Why go all the way to Stepney for a dance?'

'Because Ada Winslow is walking out with Johnny Renvoize, that's why. You know the Renvoize mob, Ma? Renvoize run everything down that way, spielers, tarts, protection, you name it. They've got muscle. The Assembly Rooms is theirs. The Renvoize mob got the same idea as you, see – link up with the Winslows.'

'*Oh* no, I don't like that! What, Winslow an' Renvoize team up? We must chuck a spanner into that quick as you like. I want you to go dancing at the Assembly Rooms this Saturday, the whole lot of you. One of you find a Winslow girl.'

'What if they don't fancy us? I'm too old for them.'

'Get friendly with Ada an' I'll talk to her mother. A wedding band can work wonders.'

'Not by itself, Ma, no. Matt Winslow won't give something for nothing, not even if his daughter's wearing my ring. We'd still have to take 'em on to settle things.'

'No, we want friends, not enemies. Choose the right girl an' we'll see how it plays out.'

Em settled back comfortably in her favourite armchair with a cup of tea and a biscuit, musing about weddings. She visualised herself at a big reception, no expense spared. There would be gilt and lights, French champagne and massive, fragrant bouquets. She would have a fitted gown with great quantities of ruffles over the bust, tasteful and flattering. Since she had no daughter, it would be nice to have a daughter-in-law to chat to. And she would like especially to have a dear little granddaughter one day. She would spoil her rotten, cover her with kisses and cuddles, give her presents.

*

Aaron Zuckerman's luxury gift boxes were a success. He leased a warehouse on the other side of Whitechapel High Street to handle that side of the business and installed Yitzy as manager. There was a roomy apartment above where he could now live away from his parents, read, study and practice his clarinet.

Maud did not join Yitzy at evening classes. Going to a dance with him, though, became a regular thing. They talked easily. He made her laugh. They were not "walking out", just hanging around. When Yitzy and some of his musical friends put together a combo, they roped in Maud too. They began to play traditional jazz mixed with Yiddish music at Jewish clubs and events. Most in the audience assumed – small, vivacious and dark as she was – that the young pianist was also Jewish. Then there was a breakthrough; a regular paid gig at the Aldgate Tavern, a big old inn close to Yitzy's new home. It was the first of their non-Jewish venues.

In an odd way, Yitzy and Maud fell into something like love. They did not kiss, never. They would smile and shake hands at the end of a good session or a happy evening. Their clasped hands might linger for an extra moment of fondness. Yitzy did not like any other girl as much as he liked Maud. However, he was under strict orders not to fall for a shiksa and certainly he did not wish to. In any case Maud had told him, and believed it herself, that she was promised to another. She still held Billy's necklace in her pocket.

Naturally Maud picked up some Yiddish. She could greet a neighbour, understand a joke, read a poster, and developed a taste for pickled herring, boiled bygels and lokshen pudding. On Shabbat she performed tasks for the Zuckermans that were forbidden them on the holy day, and they did favours for her in return.

In Maud's opinion a mania afflicted Jewish people, a mental frenzy, a restless zeal, an impatience, an excess of imagination. Behind the shabby doors of Spitalfields was ceaseless peevishness and debate, candour and insult, wild-eyed fervour, pleading to God, denouncing God, and regaling one another with anecdotes, sad or angry or comic, pouring out the whole gamut of emotion.

Yet Jews remained an enigma to her. Were they foreign? They were from Russia and Poland but insisted they were not Russian or Polish. Their world and their story were like richly decorated pages in a manuscript she could not decipher. They were explained to her as people 'of a different faith'. Yitzy said he had no faith at all; he went so far as to denounce faith. The Zuckermans seemingly did not regard their observance as religion, merely as a routine. The all-important "Friday night" with its rituals and benedictions, twin loaves and twin candles, amounted to a comfortable, dependable family dinner.

On Saturday every shop and factory was shuttered. Men and boys from the oldest to the youngest streamed to and from synagogues and prayer halls. Some were strangely costumed. She had never seen such numbers streaming to any place of worship in Manor Park. Few women went to places of prayer. Lieba was occasionally among them on festivals. Having hardly looked inside a church, Maud did not ask to visit a synagogue.

According to Yitzy, the injunction not to work on the holy day depended what line of business you were in. If you could afford it, you rested on the Sabbath. Those employed six days a week by non-Jews went to work. Some men, he told her, turned up at synagogue in shop coats or overalls, hurriedly returning to their jobs afterwards. We assume, explained the atheist, that God does not want his people to get the sack.

At the Aldgate Tavern the clarinet sang and Maud's fingers moved fast over the keys. Now *she* was the young lady at the piano, beaming at the audience! One young man among the others, standing tall, upright, broad-shouldered, with a neatly clipped moustache and a pint in his hand, smiled back.

She recognised him from somewhere. Then she remembered: she did not know him at all. London is full of strangers, yet there are men and women one sees again and again in the daily round, familiar faces at the shops, in the street, on the journey to work. An occasional individual catches our eye.

Each workday morning the pavements around Liverpool Street station were crowded with thousands in their hats and coats, carrying bags, toolkits, briefcases, changing stations, hurrying to bus stops. *That's* who he was, the good-looking man with a pint.

The next time they passed on the Liverpool Street forecourt she grinned and said, 'Morning.' He smiled, 'That was a damn good session.' She liked his quiet manner, his voice and his smile. There was something else she liked, something in the eyes and lips, something tough-minded. And he really was handsome, like a film star, with a square chin, lovely teeth, a large, lean physique and beautiful brown hair slicked back.

He said, 'I noticed you loads of times, walking by. On your way to work?'

'Yeah.'

'Me too. The band introduced you as "Miss Maud at the keyboard". Hello, Maud.' He held out a hand. 'Leonard Blake.'

*

Over tea Maud said, 'I'm out Saturday night, Mum, going to a dance.'

'With Yitzy?' – 'No, not this time. With a feller I met. He's from Manor Park. He lives with his mum. She's got a house there.' – 'Really? You met a nice man from Manor Park whose mother owns her own home an' he's taking you dancing? What's his name?' – 'Len.' – 'Is he a Jew?' – 'No, he's as English as they come.'

'An' he's nothin'a do with the Sleets, nor with Fisk?'

'God no, course not. He goes to our jazz sessions at the Tavern. We meet sometimes for a cuppa in Liverpool Street station. His job is in Covent Garden.'

'Covent Garden? What is he, a market trader, a porter?'

Maud smiled. 'He's a printer.'

'Apprenticed, did you say?'

'No, a printer. He said it's called a process engraver. That's a skilled trade. He's at a print works there.'

'Blimey. A printer! Is he in the union?'

'Well, I didn't ask, but he must be, I suppose.'

'What does his father do?'

'He was in the print, too, but he got killed in the Great War. His mum's side were army people, sergeants and that. He's good-looking. I really like him.'

'What d'you say his name was?'

'Len. Leonard Blake.'

'Well, well.' Harriet advised Maud to stick with Len Blake. 'Sounds like a good family, very respectable.' – 'Well, yes, respectable, of course.' – 'Printers earn good money, *very* good. What are his wages, I wonder?'

'I don't know.' Maud realised that she would be embarrassed by her mother. 'Don't talk about that when you meet him. He reads a lot, and likes films and jazz. Talk about that.'

Harriet took note that she was to actually meet this friend of Maud's. 'Where's he taking you – up West?'

'No, he doesn't like fancy places. We're going to the Assembly Rooms in Stepney. Don't worry, Mum, that's not far away. He says there's a good band playing there this Saturday.'

'Don't let him take advantage. Be careful. Stay away from trouble.'

'Don't be silly, Mum. There won't be trouble.'

The vast ballroom was sheer delight, crowded, pretty with chandeliers sparkling above the smoke, loud with music from a spotlit stage. Everything was in full swing, couples moving fast, some merely embracing, others dancing with elegance and skill, everyone in modern suits and ties, fitted dresses, hair brushed and slicked. Len took Maud's hand and led her straight onto the dance floor. With his arm around her, his kiss on her cheek, she smiled overflowing with joy, reached up a hand to his broad shoulder and they began – step, step, side, together – step, step, side, together. He drew her very close. She pressed herself to him, conscious that he could feel her breasts against his body. The place was filling even more. A tang of sweat, cologne, cigarettes and beer was to Maud and Len the good smell of a Saturday night.

A little knot of toughs, clad in leather jackets over shirt and tie, were stationed at the back as always, supposedly to keep order. More surprising was the arrival of half-a-dozen men in black shirts, black trousers, black shoes and black leather belts with shining buckles, which sent a frisson through the crowd. Len knew what they were: they called themselves Fascists, followers of Oswald Mosley. He had never before seen them in a dance hall.

'Blimey, what they doing here?' He pointed them out to Maud.

'Jew-baiting, I shouldn't wonder. They've come from Bethnal Green, I reckon. Mosley's got a new place there. I hope there won't be no trouble.' The Fascists took a position to one side, glancing about oddly, as if waiting. Dances at the Assembly Rooms always drew in great numbers of local people. The place was packed tonight. Maud reckoned half the crowd were Jewish.

Maud was perfectly aware of the British Union of Fascists. Everyone around Spitalfields talked about them and feared them. Buoyed by Hitler's robust takeover of Germany, the Fascists believed the hour of the blackshirt and jackboot had come. Mosley was gaining support from all corners, Left and Right, men and women (including suffragettes), rich and poor, old and young, all who admired strength, force and action. Lately Maud had watched gangs of Mosley's black-clad louts shouldering their way along Whitechapel pavements, jeering at Jews, threatening them. Every Sunday crowds of blackshirts emerged proudly from wretched East End tenements and terraces to parade as a shouting rabble through Jewish streets and markets with the chant of *Yids, Yids, Yids, got to get rid of the Yids.*

'Let's hope they only came to dance,' she said wryly. They clearly had not. As Maud gazed at the uniformed men, she caught sight of a familiar face coming through the door. 'Oh no!'

'Why, what's up?'

'See them tall blokes coming in now? The fair-haired ones? That's the Sleet brothers. Family of villains. You know Sleet Motors, in Forest Gate? That's theirs. Big troublemakers.'

Billy was among them. It was the first time Maud had seen him since that farewell kiss of agonising memory. Since then he had become so different, so much like the rest of his brothers, so much more of a man. He was bulkier, more thickset and even looked – just a little bit – it grieved her – more sly and sneering and dishonest, like the rest of them. She reflected, amazed as she made the calculation, how long had passed. Yes, she had lived in Spitalfields ten years! Truly they had been just kids. Yet the pang was there, the pain of love, stinging sharp.

'They look a bad lot,' said Len.

Maud adored the sight of Billy even now. She watched as he moved. She saw his shock when, finally, his eyes found hers. Their gaze held like an embrace, as if a magnetic force locked together. The space between them seemed suddenly void, empty, silent, even as Len's arms still guided her, step, step, step, step. No time or space could separate them. But Billy shook his head urgently, moving his hands in a frantic message to her, the meaning clear: to keep far away from him and his brothers.

5

O n walking into the dancehall with his brothers, Micky Sleet had spotted Johnny Renvoize immediately. It was clear the Winslow girls had not yet arrived. Micky decided to assess his rival without delay. He introduced himself: 'Wotcher mate – Johnny Renvoize? Frostie Sleet. Good to meet you.'

'Likewise, I'm sure,' Renvoize replied with a curled lip. 'Long way from home.'

Micky laughed. 'Heard there's a good band tonight. Just here to dance.'

'Well then, welcome mate.' The welcome was not, however, very warm. Johnny Renvoize suspected that Micky Sleet would not go anywhere simply to dance.

Micky gestured towards the blackshirts. 'Why d'you let them in?'

'If I'm honest with you, they're hard to get rid of. Take no notice of 'em.'

Micky moved aside, watching for the arrival of the Winslow girls. Johnny Renvoize too was waiting, looking forward to seeing Ada Winslow.

Four young women, one of them unusually alluring, entered the ballroom. They were show-offish and loud, heavily made-up, tasteless and provocative. All four were delighted, as Maud had been, by the pleasantness of the scene. Two great muscular brutes came in with them, minders whose job it was to prevent any nuisance to the girls. Johnny Renvoize stepped forward with hands outstretched. 'Hello doll. Been waiting for you.'

Micky also stepped forward and he too addressed Ada Winslow with an endearing grin. As his mother always said, Micky could be a charmer. 'Hello, Ada! I remember you. I'm Frostie Sleet. Nice to see you again. That's a pretty frock. May I have a dance?'

Her minder looked at him quizzically, Johnny angrily. Ada was puzzled. This striking man with hair like silver said he remembered her. Yet she did not recall meeting him before. She was amused and flattered by his audacity. 'Why not?' said she. 'A'right, Johnny?'

'No, not bloody all right.' Johnny Renvoize stared in outrage. 'See that 'gagement ring on her finger? ' he said to Micky. 'What d'you think that is?'

'I never meant no harm, Johnny, my apologies.' His tone was ironic. There was a hint of mockery.

What he expected to happen – that Ada would dance with him anyway – did not happen. Instead Johnny said, 'Well, pal, I don't accept your fucking apology. You come here special to pick up Ada. I saw you waiting by the door like a bleeding ambush. Fuck right off. Get out.'

Micky saw an opportunity. 'Or what, friend?'

'I ain't your friend. This is the "or what".' Johnny Renvoize pulled a razor from his pocket and flicked it open. 'Now clear off out of it.'

Ada placed a restraining hand on his arm. 'No, Johnny, don't.'

Micky considered Johnny had made a bad move. A razor justifies a response. Micky was considering his larger objective and how to achieve it.

It occurred to him that his mother's plan was flawed. Whether Ada Winslow chose him or not, Johnny would not forget this affront. If it should happen – as seemed likely – that *none* of the Sleet boys found a suitable Winslow partner, and especially if Ada Winslow eventually hitched up with Johnny Renvoize, then the united Winslow and Renvoize clans would be unforgiving. They would try to wipe out the Sleets. But with Johnny's blade drawn, there was now a different opportunity.

He smiled and called out to his young brother. 'Oi, Billy, pop over an' tell the band if they hear a kerfuffle they're to keep playing no matter what. Give 'em something for their trouble.'

Instantly a broad knife appeared in Micky's hand as if from nowhere. Aiming not at Johnny but at the minders beside him, with a swift, startling move he slashed both of them across the forehead in a single sweep of the hand. Blood gushed across the whole width of their faces. The two retreated in shock among horrified gasps and squeals.

Johnny always had the advantage when things were done the usual way. The usual way was to step back, raise a conciliatory hand, avoid damage and bloodshed. Micky had done something different. He approached bloodshed with relish and sincerity. It was Johnny who stepped back.

Len pointed it out to Maud as they danced. 'Look, couple of blokes having a to-do over a girl or something,'

'There's fellers been cut,' she said. 'That's the Sleets causing trouble.'

They watched as Johnny moved warily, head back, arm forward, razor handle gripped tightly, the sharp edge hovering like a steel horsefly waiting to taste blood.

Only Micky remained at ease. 'Come on, mate, if you want to go home looking like minced meat.'

Micky's brothers drew out their razors. Only Billy was unaware, innocently returning from his journey to the stage. At the other end of the room he had heard only music. One of Johnny's men moved forward to meet him, blade open.

Maud let out a shriek. Eyes turned towards her. 'No! No, not Billy!'

Billy raised his hands to protect his face. The blade caught his jaw in a slash from which sprang a line of vivid colour. He flinched and cried out. Len could not imagine why Maud would be so concerned for this hoodlum. Yet he understood what he must do.

In four paces Len reached Billy's attacker. He continued without pause, swinging a powerful punch that sent Johnny's man reeling back, dropping his razor, stumbling and falling senseless onto the dance floor.

'He's dead!' cried Ada, 'Bloody hell, he's dead!'

Yet still the band played, as Billy had asked them to do. Even now most in the vast hall danced unawares. Len walked away from the unconscious man. Hardly sixty seconds had passed.

Maud kissed his cheek. 'That was a marvellous punch!' She stared anxiously over his shoulder but could not see Billy anywhere.

'I learned to box as a kid. I belong to a boxing club in Bethnal Green.'

'Do you? Let's leave now, shall we, Len? Live to dance another day.'

'No, course not!' He shrugged unconcerned. 'You don't want to go yet, do you? Don't worry, pet, nothing else will happen tonight. Let's dance.'

Micky considered Len's intervention extraordinarily timely. It interrupted the fight at a moment when he was seen to have the upper hand, and gave Johnny an opportunity to back down without losing face. But he who asks first for a ceasefire has already lost the battle. Johnny lowered his razor. He said, 'A'right, Frostie, stay if you like.' He gestured towards his fallen comrade, 'I better check he *ain't* dead. An' this claret needs mopping up.'

Whether their fight was now settled or merely paused, Micky did not know for sure.

Perhaps aroused by the sight of blades and blood, the blackshirts began to taunt a group of Jewish boys. Johnny said, 'Fuck these Mosley scum.'

'I'll get rid of 'em for you.' Micky turned to the row of Fascists. Without warning his knife sliced cleanly through the polished leather of a young man's belt. With the man's own belt he whipped him, each strike landing the broad metal buckle on his head. 'Bully boys! Gertcha,' he laughed, landing savage blows as the blackshirts backed out of the hall. They had seen Micky's fight with Johnny and were not inclined to confront him.

Johnny said, 'Blimey, that was well done, Frostie. That's a damn good trick with the belt.'

'We quits then?'

'So long as you don't ask my girl for a dance.'

One of the other Winslow sisters spoke up, 'Here, I'll dance with you, mate.'

Micky looked her over. She certainly did not have Ada's advantages. She was the oldest of the four and the plainest. 'That a be nice. What's y'name?'

'Dora.'

'That's a pretty name.'

'Don't talk rubbish.'

'Nah, really it is. Nice frock an' all.'

'Give it a rest, will you? Get on an' dance.'

Micky put his arm around Dora's sturdy waist and she took his hand. He decided Dora was the type he called a hard-as-nails bitch. He liked them like that. They reminded him of his mother.

The band played. Blood was wiped up as if it were spilled beer. The fighting began to seem like a brief interlude, now passed.

As the band paused between numbers Micky pulled George aside, 'That geezer wi' the knockout punch – why did he help Billy?'

'Don't know who the bloke is, but I reckon the girl is Cotter's daughter,' said George. 'I recognise her.'

'Is that really her?' Micky paused to examine Maud and Len. 'Ain't this the chance we been waiting for?'

'No,' George shook his head, 'I wouldn't take that geezer on, not right now anyway, not here, not even with a blade. Look at him, cool as you like!' The band began a new number. 'Leave it for now. Ma told us to focus on business. We come here to meet the Winslow girls. Nothing else.'

Micky nodded. 'No, you're right.' He asked Dora for another dance. Again he slipped his arm around her and she gazed up at him with a thoughtful grin. He had glimpsed the future this evening and so had she.

Maud and Len strolled back along Mile End Road. 'You was good in there, Len,' she said admiringly. 'Thank you for what you done. Don't tell Mum.'

'Oh, she won't care, will she? She used to run a pub in Barking, you said. A bit of argy-bargy and some blokes chucked out – that's a normal evening, isn't it?'

'Please don't tell her it was the Sleets,' she said. 'That *would* worry her. There's a history. There's bad blood. Very. No one coming after us, is there?' They turned around, studying the darkness. They saw no one behind.

'So why didn't you want Billy Sleet to get hurt?'

'It's a long story.'

'Let's hear it, then.'

'Him and me had a bit of a romance years ago. Our families didn't approve.'

'Why's there bad blood?'

She supposed she would have to trust him. 'You know I said I got these scars in a house fire? It was that feller with the knife, Micky Sleet. He set Mum alight.' She could perhaps explain why another time.

'Jesus Christ. Why'd he do that?'

'It's complicated.' As they walked along the wide, busy road in darkness he drew it out of her. She described the moment her father was struck down. As for the rest, the death in a prison cell, she did not know the details. 'Mum got involved. Took her revenge. But it wasn't the end of it.'

'Never is, with people like that. And what about Billy – you love him?'

What could she say? 'Well, I used to. I don't think I do anymore.'

*

Roland Fisk raised the big floor hatch behind the bar. At the top of precipitous steps he flicked a light switch and went step by step into the chilly cellar below as he had done many times before. George Sleet followed, for he was learning the business, and there were barrels to be moved that the cellar man had not moved. The huge subterranean space was paved with ancient stone flags and dug deep. It had once been the extensive larder and food store of the medieval inn, and even, so old-timers liked to say, a smugglers' hide-out with hidden tunnels. Fisk kept his meat safes and cheese cabinets along one side of the cellar, loosely covered with cloth to protect them from dust. Here too were racks of clarets, sherries, ports.

The two men moved slowly and carefully, for the light was dim and the place untidy. Fisk was explaining, checking and measuring. They ducked beneath steps that rose to another hatch, for there were several disused entrances to the cellar. Electric wiring covered in frayed cloth trailed loosely across a ceiling of old ships' timbers, into which were bolted hefty brass hooks of indeterminate use. A few obsolete iron implements, now mere rusting curiosities, lay untidily beyond stacked wooden barrels and a tangle of beer lines. Beyond, the cellar disappeared unused into darkness beneath the inn's stables and neighbouring dwellings.

'Well, George, we done this a few times now, so have a go on your own. See how you get on.'

George checked which barrels were running low. He eased one into position, added finings as Fisk had shown him. Together the pair turned another and lifted it onto the upper rack of a lofty old-fashioned stillage. George attached it to the beer engine, Fisk observing carefully, nodding with approval. 'You've got the hang of it, son.'

'I ain't your son an' I ain't forgot what you done to my Pa.'

'Right enough, George. Sorry. Slip o' the tongue. Must say though, you're better without him. He was no good.'

'Think so, do you?' George retorted. He had had a realisation. He did not need this raddled old man. More than that, if Fisk were out of the picture, his own position would be enhanced.

The pub had closed for the night and they were alone. The live-in staff were far away upstairs. George wondered if he could make it look like suicide. He picked up one of the rusting iron implements that lay on the cellar floor.

Fisk also had a realisation, and was determined not to beg or whimper at the end. 'Yes, George, what a piece of shit your Dad was. Like father, like son. May the both of you rot in hell, along with your stinking brothers an' your whore of a mother.' He then swung a punch and hit George in the face, drawing blood. George really admired his pluck, and conceded to Micky and Em that Fisk had died like a man.

In the refreshment room at Liverpool Street station, Len handed Maud a folded newspaper. 'Here, have a butcher's at the front page.' It was the *Barking, East Ham & Ilford Advertiser*.

Half way down the page she saw a small heading: BARKING PUBLICAN IN TRAGIC ACCIDENT. She read the piece. It ran in a single column with no picture. 'Can I keep this?'

'Course. I brought it for you. I thought you'd find it interesting.'

Maud and Len walked hand in hand to Finsbury Circus, once around the green and back to the station. Afterwards, Maud went home. She unfolded the newspaper. 'Look, Mum, there's something here.' She read the story aloud.

'Roland Fisk, Esq., manager of the Well Smack public house in Barking, was found dead in cellars beneath the historic inn. The body was discovered by a live-in barmaid who told the inquest that Mr Fisk was lying on the floor with a full barrel of beer on top of his chest. A Police investigation was inconclusive. The Coroner noted that Mr Fisk's ribs were broken, and his neck also broken. He concluded Mr Fisk, aged 70 years, was overcome by the weight of the heavy barrel and fell to the floor, striking his head on a piece of ironwork that unfortunately lay there. It was ruled that the head injury was the principal cause of death. Verdict: Accidental death.'

Harriet said, 'Ha ha – accident be blowed! They done him in. Poor old sod.' *And it all happened*, she thought, *because he fancied me.*

'There's more, Mum.' Maud carried on reading. 'The inn's new manager, George Sleet, told *The Advertiser* that he and the staff were deeply shocked. "Mr Fisk had health problems, so did not usually carry out cellar work. He was much liked and will be sorely missed." The funeral will be at Rippleside Cemetery on Wednesday next.'

'Sorely missed! That's them being funny. Your father showed me all over them cellars and tunnels once. Easy place to get away with murder.' Harriet said not another word for some minutes. Then she sighed deeply. 'So in the end one of Charlie Sleet's boys got Ted's pub. That puts the tin hat on it, don' it? I won't never get my old joanna back now.'

*

The young men of the British Union of Fascists were not as easily scared away as Micky expected. Within weeks they had returned mob-handed to the Assembly Rooms, and posted uniformed guards at other East London dance halls, theatres and cinemas frequented by Jews. Their procession through Jewish neighbourhoods having been driven back in the Battle of Cable Street, Mosley's troops now held yet more marches; and these, under police protection, were not driven back. Attacks on Jews in the street, bloody beatings, became the daily routine. Shops and factories, dwellings and synagogues were invaded and wrecked.

As the atmosphere grew ever more frightening, Aaron and Lieba Zuckerman, together with a score of neighbours and friends, decided it was time to leave. They travelled in convoy up Romford Road to Ilford on the edge of London. There they moved into fresh new streets and modern houses beyond Mosley's seething territory.

Yitzy wrote to Maud that it was a much nicer place to live, clean and bright, with good shops, and dances at the Palais and the Ballroom and never any trouble. It was only twenty minutes into town by train. 'Bring your Mum up here. You'd be much happier.'

Harriet could not be persuaded. She preferred to stay in Spitalfields. 'It's safer. Nobody'll look for me down these little streets.' Besides, it would affect her work, for only in Spitalfields could she have her fabrics delivered and finished pieces collected from home.

'Mum,' the day arrived for Maud's important news, 'Len has asked me to marry him.'

'Has he? Well, I'll be blowed! Have you said yes?'

'Course I have. I want to marry him. You said I should! Aren't you pleased?'

'All the same… you ain't goin'a leave me by myself?'

'Well, I can't stay here anymore, can I? Len and me'll need rooms of our own. We'll find you a place near us. We'll chip in with the rent.'

'Oh no,' Harriet shook her head in fear, 'no! Stay here wi' me, Maud.'

'How can I be a proper wife to Len if I'm sharing a bed with you? Where d'you think my husband'll sleep?'

'Wait a bit longer. It's good to wait before getting hitched. Get to know each other first.'

Maud and Len were "betrothed", but could not marry while Harriet insisted Maud live with her. It might have remained so forever, or until Harriet died, if it had not been for obscure events on the other side of Europe.

In his momentous statement on the wireless the Prime Minister mentioned Poland. Maud and Harriet, and Len and his mother, were hazy as to what Poland was or where it lay in relation to, for example, England or France. It seemed that because of something outrageous Germany had done to Poland, Britain was at war with Germany.

*

Dora said, 'Micky, ask me to marry you.' – 'What, now?' – 'Yeah. Ada's marrying Johnny Renvoize. If you an' me marry first, it's better for us, see what I mean?' – 'What about this war they're talking about, don't that make a difference?' – 'That's why you need to ask me now, in case it's for real.'

Dora was not the prettiest Winslow daughter, but Micky had become aware that she had exceptional and useful qualities. She was shrewd. She wanted things done correctly. She insisted on a proper courtship so no fault could be found. He took her to a couple of dances, to the cinema, to a show. They visited each other's parents. Micky began to appreciate that Dora knew the Winslow rackets inside out. In effect, she was Matt Winslow's "right hand man". And Dora realised that although Micky had vision and a tremendous ability to act, he depended on his mother for guidance. He could not manage without a counsellor.

The wedding at East Ham register office was not as Em had dreamed. Only immediate family were present, with a mood of solemnity rather than celebration, as though witnessing a treaty rather than a marriage. Certainly the ceremony was amiable and polite. Smiles were restrained. Hands were shaken. There was mutual satisfaction. Everyone was immaculately turned out, the groom and his brothers in double-breasted charcoal grey suits with a cream carnation, the bride and her sisters in calf-length pink satin, their little brother in a pageboy outfit. Emmeline Sleet and Sybil Winslow wore handsome pleated skirt suits, turquoise for Em, primrose for Syb.

After the ceremony and the signing of the register, the party retired to the adjoining wood-panelled room for a brief reception, consisting of a toast in whisky to bind the vows. The father of the bride raised his glass to the Winslow-Sleet partnership, may it be fruitful and multiply and be very happy together.

Dora's timing was right. Just after the wedding, call-up papers began falling on doormats. Billy and Arthur responded that they were motor vehicle mechanics and repairers, a reserved occupation. So Sleet Motors could remain open. As soon as the war began in earnest, petrol was rationed. Sleet Motors was in a strong position to profit from under-the-counter sales.

Terry truly was medically unfit for duty, so his side of the business was not affected either. Ronnie and George heard about a doctor in Stepney selling fake medical exemption certificates. They each bought one, and did a deal with him – for a 'take', they found other men who wanted to avoid being conscripted.

Micky alone, as the oldest, had not received his call-up letter. He had still not received it by the time food rationing began the next spring. Sales of butter, sugar and bacon were to be strictly limited. Other groceries were added to the list. 'This is startin'a look good,' said Em. 'We'll be in the money wi' this war.' She saw opportunities far greater than the General Strike and Great Crash.

Micky called for a friendly little parley at the Well Smack with Johnny Renvoize and their mutual father-in-law Matt Winslow. The two treated 'Frostie' with fearful respect. 'I reckon there's goin'a be shortages like never before,' he said. 'We don't want to fight over it. We're family now. There's fortunes to be made for all of us.'

Renvoize and Winslow were to obtain from farms and docks, houses, shops and hotels, drivers and warehousemen as much as they could of goods rationed or in short supply. The Sleets would then dispose of everything through a network of traders, sometimes selling goods to the very businesses from which they had been stolen. It worked as a protection racket too – if shopkeepers refused to cooperate, they would be punished. Those that did cooperate would reap rewards.

The Well Smack, as a traditional coaching inn, was classified as a licensed restaurant that could serve meals "off-ration". Its capacious storage cellars and converted stables came into their own, loaded with rationed items. George kept watchmen on guard day and night. From now on, George's Thursday evening meeting with CID officers included a free meal and all the groceries they could carry.

The black market business was set in place, each man knowing his part. Only then did Micky's call-up letter arrive. As a motor mechanic with Sleet Motors he too could be exempt. Politics had never been his topic of conversation, but the fall of France brought out a grim bloody-minded anger. He was very willing to fight. Something in Micky was personally affronted by the ignominious flight of British troops from foreign beaches. In another part of Micky's mind was an idea that to have done military service might prove useful in years to come, mitigation in some future court case perhaps, a feather in his cap. In November, he reported for duty.

*

A siren sounded its rising and falling note of warning. Maud rushed home from work in panic. She shouted to Harriet that German planes were coming in force towards the docks, flying low above the water. Both women screamed as suddenly the air shook. The window glass rattled but did not crack. All that night the sky flickered with colour from riverside fires.

It was a Friday evening in September, more than a full year since the Prime Minister's ominous broadcast. The next day at lunchtime the siren's warning cry again began. Maud urged her mother to please come down to the church – the crypt of nearby Christ's Church had been designated as a public shelter. But Harriet would not go down. There came the din of planes approaching and anti-aircraft guns.

A dull explosion roared. Now the window glass cracked clean across yet still it did not fall from the frame. She saw people were running through the streets shouting for help: a bomb had fallen through a ventilation shaft at Old Columbia Market directly into the cellars, filled with wretches from the flats alongside, sheltering from the raid. Harriet put sellotape along the broken glass and it held.

The next time, it was closer. The window glass blew right across the room, tape and all. That's when all the local children were gathered together and sent away. Neighbours vanished; some were dead, their homes dusty heaps of brick and timber. Families left every day, scared to be near the docks, scattering in all directions, leaving the wreckage behind. Harriet and Maud were among those who remained.

Every morning Maud caught the tube to work as usual, and came back in the evening through a landscape of rubble that changed after every raid. Oxford Street was unrecognisable, especially after the night of bombs that ripped apart Bourne & Hollingsworth and other big stores, John Lewis, Selfridges, Peter Robinson. Many shop staff were leaving, some evacuated far from London. Yet the shops remained open, Union Jacks stretched to cover the smashed facades. It was announced on the radio that unmarried women must now be conscripted into war work and should expect their call-up papers. Even Harriet could see it would be better if Maud were no longer single.

Len was to join the Kings Dragoon Guards, going he knew not where, but apparently in haste. In light of his education, demeanour and the family's army history, in the pressing need of the moment he was made a corporal on the spot.

After the years of courtship, suddenly there was barely time to arrange a wedding, not even time to make a wedding gown. Instead Maud wore a full-length dress of light-blue velvet awaiting delivery to one of Harriet's clients. With some adjustment, it fitted well. Len said she looked quite ravishing.

It was a chilly morning with drizzle in the wind. Len was in khaki battledress with a white blossom in the buttonhole, while the best man, his brother, came impeccable in service dress uniform. Cousin Will, in his battered suit and trilby, stood in to give her away. Len's mother, terrified of the air raids, said she felt poorly and did not come.

Afterwards Len took the new Mrs Blake on the bus as far his mother's house in Manor Park. It was a strange return to the neighbourhood she had fled years before. There they spent an afternoon, an evening and a night in his room. There were no tears next morning, nothing more than a kiss; a whispered *Goodbye, darling*; and one last anxious embrace. Maud caught the bus back to Spitalfields. Len took up his kitbag and made his way to the docks.

At that time, men conscripted from the same district were sent to the same brigade. It was thought good for morale for comrades-in-arms to share memories of the old streets of home. As the surge of recruits assembled on the dockside, neighbours, workmates and drinking cronies hailed one another. The scene was both jolly and fearful. Whatever else lay ahead, there would be novelty, action, a voyage and companionship. Then two men caught sight of each other. Among the familiar faces Corporal Len Blake recognised in the crowd was that of Private Micky Sleet.

6

D olphins frolicked in the blue. On deck, officers enjoyed winter sun and cut-price drinks, amateur entertainments and dances with a cohort of young nurses. In the hold, 'other ranks' lay on bunks deep below the waterline as the ship carried them around Africa. By the time they disembarked in Egypt, the Italian advance had already been stopped and the enemy was retreating into eastern Libya. Even while the men were being given their desert kit, news came of German troops arriving in eastern Libya to retrieve the situation.

The German commander, Generalleutnant Rommel, predicted a swift defeat for the laughably disorganised, class-ridden British. He would crush them, take full control of Libya, Egypt and Palestine and meet victorious Nazi forces marching down from a Europe unified beneath the swastika.

Assessed for intelligence, reactions and fitness, Len was drafted into the Reconnaissance Corps, the "tank-spotters". Into the stony wastes and dry wadis they were sent for days at a stretch to search for enemy positions. They reported back by radio and quit the area before being shot. Len and his men took a carefree view of the danger and discomfort. Tank-spotters, he discovered, were a hardy, good-humoured lot with a knack for fixing engines and solving problems.

Rommel's forces readied themselves to reclaim the lost miles of desert. To confront them, Allied troops were arriving in vast numbers, a kaleidoscope of brigades from across the Empire; Indians, Africans, Australians, as strange to each other as they were to East End eyes; and Hebrew-speaking Palestine battalions and Pioneer Corps eager to meet Nazis head-on; and Czech and Polish units too; as if a coalition of the world was coming together.

With the first shots, Len was raised to the rank of sergeant, his tank-spotting sections now trained as forward observers guiding Allied artillery fire. Among the men newly under Len's command was Private Sleet. He too had made it into the elite corps.

Since that dockside glimpse in England, Len had not seen Micky Sleet. On the ship Len avoided him. After landing, Sleet had been posted to a different area. Now though, he was to be Sleet's sergeant.

Together with Len's new rank came a bundle of confidential reports about his men. Private Sleet, wrote his commanding officer, was a troublemaker who, after several spells of jankers and lock-up for minor offences, had served a period of detention for assaulting a policeman in Cairo after a shameful incident. A pimp, an underage prostitute, a robbery and brutal violence were involved. More details were attached. It was indeed shameful. Nonetheless, added the officer, Sleet had proved an outstanding tank-spotter, fearless and resourceful. Len made a copy of the report in case one day it might be useful.

A little plan formed in Len's mind, a diabolical, unutterable plan, the solution to a problem.

*

Harriet made Maud a pair of green woollen trousers for fire-watching duty. They were practical, cosy and comfortable, a ladylike fit and surprisingly fetching. She also wore woollen stockings and a vest, shirt, pullover, her greatcoat, thick scarf, knitted gloves and a felt hat. Even so, there was no getting warm. She unscrewed the lid from her flask and filled it with piping hot tea.

From a straight-back chair on Bourne & Hollingsworth's rooftop Maud looked over a black void. Oxford Street ran far below, dark and quiet. With a torch beneath her coat Maud re-read Len's troubling letter. She imagined desert wind as something like hot air vents. The landscape, she now knew, was empty to the horizon, more stones than sand, spotted with tough, dust-covered tufts. A rocky, potholed road ran within sight of the shimmering sea, but Len drove on trackless terrain far inland. She now knew about desert sores and that her husband was hungry all the time. Len himself, the man, she found it ever more difficult to picture.

This time, though, he sent a photograph. She shone the torch. He stood in a wide avenue of white buildings with flat roofs. He was tanned, smiling and oddly dressed in open-neck shirt and rolled-up shorts like nothing she had ever seen. Yet he wore boots and thick socks. He looked devilishly handsome, his eyes creased and twinkling.

He wrote that he and the others were 'The Eyes of the Desert', forever wandering in their armoured vehicle. Then came the lines that she read again and again.

The siren began to cry out. Engines in the sky made their familiar, fearful sound. White lines of light fingered the clouds. Explosions flashed, then another, at the end of Park Lane, behind the Dorchester. She saw no fires nearby. Unseen planes passed over. The All-Clear sounded much later, as pale dawn seeped over Oxford Street, dashed with pink.

In the shop's basement, steamy with breath and sweat, her mother lay alongside hundreds of others. Harriet and Maud were now in full-time residence at Bourne & Hollingsworth. They could no longer stay at home. It was impossible for Harriet to work at home, and terrifying too. All the windows were boarded, the street blocked with rubble. The man who collected Harriet's finished pieces had stopped coming.

In the basement shelter the store had installed a breakfast canteen and washrooms. Maud washed and went to her mother. 'Get any kip?'

Harriet shook her head. 'Not much. How was it out there?'

'There was some high-explosives. No fires. This letter from Len, Mum, I never told you everything in it.'

'What d'you leave out?'

'So first of all, Len's been made a sergeant.'

'Why d'you leave that out?'

'I don't know. But here's the thing. He says Micky Sleet is out there with him. He says we're not to worry.'

This was bad news indeed, shocking and inexplicable. Both women feared Len was in more danger from Micky than from the Germans.

*

In Micky's absence, George ran the business. Emmeline, of course, was the real head of the family. Relations with the Renvoize and Winslow mobs were cordial. On the lucrative wholesale black market operation the three families worked as one.

The key to such harmony was Cockney hard man Matt Winslow. Now that his eldest daughter Dora had married Micky Sleet and second daughter Ada had married Johnny Renvoize, the former rivals were pulled together just as Em had planned. Matt knew that if rationing and shortages ever came to an end there would be matters to sort out between them. Until then, he, Micky and Johnny could come out of this war as rich men.

Ronnie Sleet had other ideas. He joked that man cannot live by good odds alone. He wanted high stakes, long shots. He wanted the sharp edge of risk and the thrill of quick rewards. A shortage of police (thanks to the call-up), and pitch-black streets (thanks to the blackout), was a coincidence not to be wasted. He talked it through with Nipper Winslow. 'We need to get hold of ARP outfits,' explained Ronnie.

Matt Winslow adored his only son, Nipper. The lad had a foolish, guileless charm that could bring a tear to the eye. The family knew Nipper was not all he should be. It was hard to say whether he was seriously soft in the head or only slightly touched. Matt wanted to see him settled one day in some safe, uncomplicated situation.

Wearing filched Air Raid Precaution helmets and armbands Ronnie and Nipper cruised West End streets in the midst of raids. While residents cowered in shelters the pair dashed into houses – a door was normally left unlocked so medics could rescue casualties – and made off with cash, jewels, pictures, plate, anything rapidly found and easily carried, driving away before the All-Clear sounded. If any genuine ARP warden should block their path, he could be scared off without difficulty or knocked aside.

The warning siren howled over Mayfair. A policeman stood watch on the corner of Grosvenor Square. Ronnie and Nipper turned into the lightless streets behind the Dorchester Hotel. They slowed by a fine house with a side entrance. Nipper jumped out. He beckoned Ronnie.

Inside, the siren sound was no louder than a crying baby in some distant nursery. The two men cautiously swung a door open. Nipper gasped. Quite apart from a glorious rug and ornate ceiling, a crystal chandelier, polished mahogany and marquetry, oil paintings and handsome marble fireplace, the room was a treasure trove of silver, ormolu and ivory pieces. Glazed cabinets displayed fine porcelain. Against one wall stood shelves of ancient volumes.

'Ruddy hell, look at this flipping lot,' murmured Ronnie. 'Let's get cracking.' He began sweeping every movable not-too-fragile object into a large bag. Nipper did the same.

A high-explosive bomb explodes too fast for the mind to respond.

Only the start of the bang is sensed before timber, brick and shrapnel burst through collapsing walls and ceilings faster than a thundering express train. There is nowhere to hide, and no time. Nipper Winslow was dead before he knew, his helmet blown clear across the room and the contents of his skull mixed with ground glass. Ronnie Sleet lay stunned beneath shattered roof beams, the shredded pages of first editions falling around him like confetti.

Ronnie opened his eyes. A pea-souper of dust swirled above him. His back and chest hurt terribly. Curious sounds became recognisable; whistles, shouts. He could not move, too weak, groggy, pinned into place. 'Nipper?' he said, but Nipper did not reply. The voices became louder as real ARP wardens entered the wrecked house. They understood everything immediately: the victims' coats and armbands were an attempt at ARP uniform. Still clasped in their hands were ripped bags of looted silver and ivory.

The dead burglar was not carrying his National Identity Card, a serious offence in itself. The injured one had a card correctly made out. In the back of an ambulance Ronnie gave them Nipper's details. After all, the Winslows would have to be told. As Ronnie was driven away, the police examined his wrecked car outside the bombed house. It had clearly been used to carry merchandise. Packets of silk stockings and a bundle of meat ration coupons lay on the floor as if they were not valuable. In the morning, detectives looked into Ronnie's medical exemption and went over the car more closely. They wanted to interview every one of Ronnie's friends, family and associates.

*

Len instructed Private Sleet in person to reconnoitre south of El Adem. Micky did not know it, but there was no hope of his returning alive. Len had already received new intelligence that the sector was bristling with German infantry assembling for an assault on Tobruk. Had he been on the road, Military Police would have turned him back. Micky soon radioed that he had 'Jerry in view'. Then nothing.

On the third day Len reported that Private Sleet was officially Absent Without Leave, having driven off without permission. He wrote Maud another letter. 'Your Sleet problem has been solved once and for all.' He did not mention the inexorable Nazi advance. He enclosed a new snapshot.

In London, Maud wondered what was meant by 'solved'. Because there was, after all, more to the Sleet problem than Len realised. She tried to understand the photo. It showed Len and another soldier beside a strange vehicle in a pale featureless terrain of grit and stones. It looked rather like a small tank. Both men had white bandages twined around their arms and legs. That would be for the desert sores, she supposed. Len smiled gleefully at the camera.

*

A hard man is just a man. Matt Winslow could not bear the agony of losing his youngest child, his only son, apple of his eye, foolish, innocent, adorable Nipper. He stood groaning and yelling in his torment, clasped his head, pounded it with clenched fists. Matt did not blame himself or Nipper. He did not even blame the Germans. He blamed Ronnie. It was no consolation that Ronnie was in custody facing a jail term. He blamed George, too – what kind of boss allows his men to get up to that sort of mischief? It would never have happened if Frostie was in charge.

The entire racket had been put in jeopardy by Ronnie's rashness. Matt resolved to wash his hands of the Sleets. When George went to talk it over, man to man, Matt took a swing at him. In his shame and pity George did not even fight back. Nipper's sisters were equally distraught. They loved their brother.

Dora, though, knew which side her bread was buttered. She had married a Sleet and never criticised a Sleet. Besides, during Micky's absence she was living in Em's house and getting on well with her mother-in-law. She was careful not to take sides.

Nor did Sybil Winslow feel it in quite the same way as her husband. Sybil had indulged her son with all the affectionate forgiveness any young rascal could wish for. She wept to think that his boyhood, all the love she had given him, had come to nothing. Nevertheless she knew Nipper for the dissolute good-for-nothing that he had become, sly and lying, thieving from her handbag and his Dad's pockets for cash to waste on his seedy pleasures or lose on the dogs. She saw how Nipper twisted Matt and the girls around his little finger with his pouting, unmanly beauty. To Sybil's mind, her adorable Nipper had been as adorable as an alley cat, and as sharp-clawed.

At Sleet Motors, conveniently close to the police station in Romford Road, two CID officers spoke to Billy Sleet, who in truth knew little about the family's black market business. He told them he personally just got on with the job of running Sleet Motors. They could see that it was so. As it happened Arthur, responsible for the release of petrol (diluted with paraffin) onto the black market, as well as buying and selling "private motoring" petrol ration coupons, was not there when the police called and Billy did not mention him. They asked Billy only if he knew a George Sleet. He said, 'Yeah, I'll find out where he is an' let you know.' The officers were impressed with Billy's frankness. They left their details so he could get in touch. Billy knew it was deadly serious.

An emergency meeting had to be called for that afternoon. Em arrived at the Well Smack with Dora, who took Micky's chair. George, Terry, Arthur and the two women gathered together in the snug. Dora knew to keep quiet and support Em in everything.

'Starting tonight,' said Em, 'we need to learn about them two coppers on the case. Put someone to follow them home after work, to the pub, whatever; find out about their families, their wives and that. Call in some favours from our CID friends. Then, George,' she said, 'in a couple o' days you need to get on the blower. Tell 'em if they don't mind coming over here you're happy to answer their questions voluntary. They'll come, you'll see.'

George welcomed the lean, grey-suited Detective Sergeant May and Detective Constable Bryant, shook their hands warmly, sat them comfortably in the snug. 'What can I get you – drink?'

They declined. 'Cup o' tea, then?' They agreed to cups of tea. 'Milk an' sugar?' George said he would pop out and ask someone to make a pot of tea.

As he left the snug Em entered it. 'Oh, hello there, gents. You the officers what's come to talk to my boy?'

'You Mrs Sleet?' asked Detective Sergeant May.

'That's me. Is it about my Ronnie burgling houses? He's a bad lad.'

'Seems your Ronnie is involved in the black market, an' all,' said

May. 'Stolen goods, forged ration books. You know about that?'

'Oh, dear, yes!' said Em. 'I know all about that.' She sat down. 'Ronnie's your man for a bit of extra meat or butter. Sugar, sweets, stockings for the wife – or girlfriend,' she winked, 'whatever you want, he'll get it.' Bryant was eagerly writing in his notebook.

George reappeared, not with tea but with glasses, a bottle of Scotch and a platter of cold meats. 'Well, well, here we are, gents. Nice pot o' tea on its way,' he explained, 'but I brought this to keep you going.' The two officers looked hungrily at the meats.

Now Dora slipped into the room carrying a second tray. 'Someone wanted tea?' she murmured. She set down the teapot and cups, which remained untouched. Em broke off to introduce her, 'My daughter-in-law,' allowing the policemen to assume Dora was married to George. Dora stood quietly aside, observant.

Em had not finished her remarks to DS May. 'I met your missis, actually, Mr May.' Both officers opened their mouths with shock, May staring and alarmed to the point of fear. 'I happened to be over Chiswick way, down your street,' Em continued easily. 'I bumped into her. She told me you give her some stockings you nicked from Ronnie's car. Well, why not? Makes sense. She had the baby with her. Lovely little girl, pretty. I hope she'll be all right. It's very important that a baby is well nourished. Well nourished. I slipped her some extra milk coupons and wrote her name in. They're in your house now. In the bureau in the parlour, second drawer down.'

'My Christ! What's going on? Mrs Sleet, if you're trying to –'

'Oh, don't you fret, son, it's all free of charge. I ain't "trying to" nothing. Only let's be clear, you better look out for the baby. An' your missis. Some of our fellers can be very cruel. I've tipped the wink to our friends in the force about the forged coupons an' stolen goods in your house. Could be used in evidence if you cause trouble.'

DS May sat up straight. 'Is that a flipping threat? If you lot think…'

'Now, now. Threat?' Em laughed, 'Course not, duck.'

George said, 'Same goes for you, Bryant. We wouldn't want nothin'a happen to your poor old Mum. Nice lady,' he added. 'If we're left in peace, she will be too.'

'Have you been bothering my mother?' The detective constable interjected. 'Why, you fucking bas–'

'Ay, ay – language, Mr Bryant, ladies present!' grinned George.

'Seriously though, come to us for anything. I mean, one egg a week ain't much for a man. Your mum told us you like a boiled egg every day. So we've give her a dozen new-laid eggs this very morning. Promised her a dozen farm fresh eggs every week with our compliments. Anything else will be at the usual coppers' discount.'

The two detectives looked at him by stages outraged, astonished, uncomprehending and furious. They shifted in their chairs, fists clenched. May grimaced, breathing hard, running a nervous tongue over his lips. He stood abruptly as if to restore his personal dignity and the authority of his office. 'Right, you're nicked. I'm arresting you on...' – but Bryant tapped his arm in warning.

'Me an' all?' queried Dora. 'I only brought in the tea.'

'Go on then, May,' laughed George. 'Arrest who you bloody like. See what happens. Like I say, look out for the baby an' the old lady. Tell you who else won't be best pleased – some o' your colleagues.' This was mere supposition on George's part. He said, 'Have Ronnie if you want, though – waste of space. Pin it on him. No one else, see? You'll find causing trouble ain't worth the candle. By the way, if you want any candles...'

Em chuckled throatily as Detective Sergeant May resumed his seat. She picked up her whisky. 'Drink up, lads. Cheers. To good times.'

The police officers raised their glasses unhappily. Dora remained watching, and did not drink.

*

To send a radio signal, an antenna had to be put up so tall it could be seen for miles through field glasses. Micky preferred to send no message just yet. He shot the occupants of the first vehicle he sighted, took money from their pockets and kept their weapons and Soldbüch identity papers. He pressed on, driving further until he spotted an armoured car stationary in the distance. He backed into a hollow, observing through glasses until nightfall. Heavy gunfire was close enough that he could see the flashes. With his compass he made a note of the position of guns by counting the seconds between the flash and the sound.

The vehicle remained always in place, its own antenna raised. Micky supposed it must be in communication with the forward area.

Two men emerged from it carrying tarpaulins; they walked around, cigarettes in hand, then lay on the ground. A third, automatic rifle in hand, remained perched on the vehicle, keeping look-out in the dark. An abrasive breeze started to whisk dust onto Micky's lips and nostrils. The look-out swathed his head and face in a scarf. Taking his knife and rifle and a grenade, Micky walked in the open desert until he was close to the resting Germans.

He threw a small pebble towards the look-out to gauge his alertness. There was no response at all. Micky darted forward. The dozing men on the ground he killed with the knife, first one, then the other, pressing down on their dying faces to prevent any sound.

He clambered onto the back of the vehicle. At this the look-out awoke and half turned in the dark. Micky seized him, punched his face, dragged him to the ground to be disabled and disarmed. He stripped the wounded man and gagged him with his own uniform.

Again Micky gathered their Soldbücher and whatever else he wanted. He clambered into the armoured vehicle emblazoned with its German cross. Inside, to his surprise, a young officer cowered trembling, struggling to hold a pistol with both hands. The man raised his arms in pleading surrender and was glad to be tied rather than shot. There were maps and plans spread, and more papers in a briefcase.

Len received Micky's message in the middle of the night. 'On my way back with souvenirs. Where're you?'

'Meet you at Sullum.' (For so it was called by the troops.) His little scheme to deal with Micky Sleet had failed. He must think of another.

In the balmy darkness of El Salloum docks, Len squeezed into the seat beside Micky. He was carrying a large flask and two metal cups. He expressed no emotion, nor surprise, at the unexpected return of his foe. On the floor behind, the two bound and gagged prisoners squirmed.

'Well, well, well,' said Micky, 'we meet again, Sarge.'

Len pointed his thumb towards the prisoners. 'What you got there?'

'Something I picked up.'

Len was frankly impressed. 'Fancy a cuppa?'

'Yeah, gasping.' Len poured as Micky held up the identity books of the other enemy soldiers he had shot or knifed. 'An' there was these fuckers. Done for 'em.'

'Christ, what, you just left 'em there?'

'Yeah, well, they was dead, or good as. I made a note of the artillery placements.' He showed Len his notebook.

'Fuck me! How d'you do that?'

'Yeah, well, with the old triangulation, like we was taught.'

Len's opinion of Micky was quite altered.

'One of these two,' Micky continued, with a jerk of the head towards the captured men, 'had this.' He carefully put his cup aside and produced the briefcase of maps and documents.

'Ruddy hell.' Len leafed through the papers. 'Christ alive, this is quality stuff. You've done bloody well, Sleet. No, really, you have.'

Each man rolled a cigarette and lit it. Len refilled their mugs. Side by side they stared across the blue-black of the bay under a sky bursting with stars. Dark water lapped the quayside like a whisper.

'Hopin' a see the back o' me, wasn't you, mate?' murmured Micky.

'It's "Sergeant", if you don't mind, Sleet.'

'Shoot me now, Sarge. You won't never get a better chance. Dump my body in the desert.'

'It'd prey on my conscience.' Len's tone was ironic, although he thought it probably would weigh on him to murder Sleet in cold blood.

'I got the edge on you there. Nothing don't prey on me.'

Both men knew that the exchange was mere banter. Each had seen the other kill enemy soldiers without qualms or regret. Each of them would always do whatever the situation demanded.

'Look, Sleet, here's a deal. I'll put your name forward for a medal. I can recommend 'em to overlook your black marks. That's my side of the bargain. In return, you and your family leave my family alone. Make a promise. If you do, when the war ends I'll even help you set up in business, legit.'

'Deal?' Micky chuckled. 'Or what?'

'Or I *do* shoot you, with one of Jerry's guns. Leave you in the desert, like you said.'

Micky snorted. 'You got a good fist, but I could take a gun off you like *that*.' He clicked his fingers. 'A promise don't mean fuck-all. How d'you know I won't shoot *you*?'

Len knew that a promise from a man like Micky Sleet could hardly be relied upon, but also that he would get nothing more. He pressed on: 'I might not have to shoot you, Sleet; there's a hundred ways to skin a fucking cat. I've got the report on what you did in Cairo, when they put you in the nick. D'you want that to come out, in civvy street?'

There was a pause. 'Hm. A'right, put me up for a medal.'

'What about the promise?'

'Yeah, a'right then.'

'No, properly.'

'What's that mean? Like "I solemnly promise to make sure no member of the Sleet family harms or threatens Widder Cotter nor no one in her family." Like that?' he chuckled.

'Yeah, just like that. Say "On my mother's life."'

'You kidding? "On my mother's life"? Now you're playing games. That's fucking daft.'

'Say it.'

'I solemnly promise to make sure no member of the Sleet family harms or threatens Widder Cotter nor no one in her family. On my mother's life, right? So you'll have no cause to show anyone that report. But forget starting a business, I ain't interested in that.' He shook his head at Len's foolishness. 'Anyway, what kind o' business?'

'I was thinking, a printworks, cause I know all about that. Bloke like you could be a real boss. A proper one.'

'Printworks?' Micky was amused. 'Nah, don't bother, mate.'

The Germans were forced back across Libya into Tunisia, where Rommel conceded defeat. From there Len's regiment were shipped at once across the Mediterranean to carry on the fight in Italy, in tougher battles and more difficult conditions. The next photo Maud received showed Len in an army beret, collar and tie and fur-lined jacket. He seemed cold and weary. His eyes and eyebrows were nice, she thought. The narrow moustache had been neatly trimmed. He looked more like a film-star than ever. He still did not explain why he thought the Sleet problem was solved. But if it was, so much the better.

The first letter Micky ever received from Dora let him know that his brother Ronnie had been sent to prison for four years, her brother Nipper was dead from a raid, her dad Matt Winslow a broken man because of it, and she, Dora, acting in Micky's name, was fully in control of the three families with the blessing of his mother, Em.

Dora's second letter found Private Sleet in central Italy. *Sorry to send bad news*, she wrote, *about your dear Ma.* Emmeline Sleet was dead, killed in a disaster at – and here several lines had been crossed through with the censor's broad black pen. *I'm sorry, love, more bad news*, the letter continued, *a bomb destroyed Sleet Motors and killed poor Arthur.*

She gave the dates of his mother's and brother's funerals. Both had already taken place. *Everyone sends condolences. I hope you are alright. Except for the motors, business is good.*

*

'We can have the winders done now, put everything back to rights,' Maud told her mother. 'The Government's giving five hundred quid for repairs.'.

Harriet said she did not believe the Government would give them anything. 'An' there's still the Sleets to worry about, war or no war.'

'Oh, don't be daft, Mum. Len wrote that it's all finished with the Sleets.' These days she often felt exasperated with her mother.

'He don't know that for sure,' argued Harriet, 'an' nor do you.'

'Len said they came to an understanding.'

'Misunderstanding, more like.'

'Come out to the tea party, Mum.'

'Nah, you go.'

Maud went out alone. There were tables in the roadway, flags, a gramophone, singing. After dark, curtains were left open to celebrate the end of blackout. Bonfires blazed on bomb sites, women and men dancing in flame-light.

Try as she might, Maud could not feel celebratory. She felt worn out, angry. She walked as far as the Tavern at Aldgate, where she and Yitzy used to play. The pubs were staying open late tonight. She ordered a shandy. They said it was on the house.

A piano still stood in the corner. 'May I?' – 'Course you can, love. Give us a tune.' She played just as she did then, and pictured Len standing at the back, pint in hand. Was he in shirtsleeves somewhere, collar undone, celebrating in a bar? Did he have his arm around a foreign woman? Had the war really stopped, or was it still going on?

Wives assumed husbands would soon be home again at the table with them and in the bed. It was not to be. For more than a year Len remained away at an army camp in Northern England. It seemed the longest year of the entire separation; the hardest to understand. How indifferent the authorities were to peoples' feelings. At last he was "demobbed", took up his kitbag and caught the overnight train to London. In the middle of the next morning, he stepped out of little Manor Park station. A slight breeze urged breaking clouds gently eastward. He paused in Romford Road and wondered at the sublime loveliness of ordinary things. Nerves taut, he turned down a narrow street of ordinary terraced houses to the ordinary terraced house where his wife and mother were waiting to hear the door knocker.

Against Harriet's pleas and warnings, Maud had moved her things into Len's bedroom.

Everyone looked much older than they expected.

'Hello Maud, hello Mum,' he said. His mother replied, 'Hello, son. Good to see you.' It was he who went forward to embrace.

'Hello, Len,' Maud said calmly, 'want a cup of tea?' He nodded. 'Please, darling.'

She had not seen him for over six years, nor he her. She wanted to be courted all over again, taken to the pictures and to a dance, have him buy her a drink. She wanted to be six years, ten years younger. He wanted only that the war had never happened.

She discovered that he was very quiet; she had forgotten that he was thoughtful and considerate but never talkative. He learned about his wife that she would not sit quietly, she must chat. She learned that he was a Socialist, and he learned that she was a Tory. They had never talked about politics. It had not mattered before and they must not let it matter now. They walked hand in hand. He did take her in his arms and kiss her. It seemed foolish at their age. She was thirty-nine, too old, they felt, to start a family. 'It don't matter, love,' he said, 'we're together now, we'll make a go of it, just the two of us.'

The baby was born early the following summer. It was a few weeks before the National Health Service started, so Len had to pay Forest Gate Hospital one and six. They named her Elizabeth, a precious, skinny little thing with dark hair. The birth was recorded, her identity card and ration book issued. For the time being, she would sleep in a cot at the foot of their bed.

ELIZABETH

Born May 1948, Forest Gate, London E7

1

Micky Sleet sat upright and drove without a word. His bright moonlight hair was impeccably oiled and brushed this morning. Along Barking Road, up High Street North, a left turn onto Romford Road and he arrived at the cemetery gates. As if actually attending the funerals he had missed, he wore an immaculate black suit with his medals displayed. Beside him in dark grey hat and coat, Dora held in her arms an immense spray of red roses and white lilies. Her pregnancy was hardly visible. On the back seat lay a bunch of red carnations.

Micky laid the carnations on his brother's grave, tenderly placed the roses and lilies on his mother's. *In Loving Memory.* Without expression he read the engraved slabs.

Arthur Sleet... died 17th January 1943 ... much missed brother and son.

Emmeline Sleet, died in the Bethnal Green Station disaster, 3rd March 1943 ... beloved wife and mother.

Micky was the least sentimental of men, and disdainful of emotion. Yet he was not entirely unemotional himself. He knew anger and desire, he knew ambition, longing, vanity and obsession. Now he discovered grief and desolation. He felt the hollow space within himself where had dwelt his shrewd, forgiving mother. On her guiding hand he had depended in this vexatious world. *Rest in Peace.* Micky could not progress without an adviser; he knew that. Dora was at his side now. She had already stepped into that role. With Dora's counsel, what could he not achieve? Inwardly he glimpsed life as it might be, should be, a basking golden meadow in the distance.

Micky knew that even with Dora's help he would never arrive at a place of golden meadows. That much he would not achieve. More clearly he saw tanks in the desert rolling forward, their purpose only to advance, to win the fight today. When Dora told him she was expecting, *then* he understood! He too lived only to win today's battle. He would send his *child* onto the field of victory! He would stop at nothing to achieve it. It's what his parents would have wanted.

'I reckon, Dora,' he said, 'now we're goin'a be a family, Pa should be lying here beside Ma. We'll get a licence to move him.'

'Where's he buried?' she asked.

'In a prison graveyard. I want him here with the rest of us. A family plot.'

Dora was intent on a move "out to Essex". She eyed fine Edwardian houses in Romford Garden Suburb and the airy modernity of the grander, greener new private estates. She wanted to enjoy the fortune they had made from the war, and, especially, find somewhere decent for their baby to grow up. She argued for Emerson Park in east Romford. It was 'class', and far enough away from the town's famous brewery that its sickly tang probably would not reach – not that Dora minded, personally, the yeasty whiff of beer-making. Micky refused. He might consider a farm or a secluded country house. He could not see himself living in a street of houses, no matter how opulent. Dora insisted. She wanted to live among 'quality'. Micky reasoned it would be in his interest to let Dora have her way. She chose the house herself and paid cash.

*

Occasionally the air-raid siren sounded at midday. It was just for practice, and always the hallelujah of All Clear. Every morning when Maud awoke it seemed a miracle that Len's large, warm muscular body in its flannel pyjamas lay safely beside her. All the peculiar details of his virile masculinity were revealed to her now. The intimacy was tender and thrilling yet unlovely, distasteful even; hair in the basin, the shaving brush, his white underwear, the essential nightly embrace before falling into sleep. Len's rough-textured jackets and trousers in the compact wardrobe pressed hard against her silk and cotton. She discovered that not only was her husband quiet, too quiet, but that while sitting quietly he was not idly daydreaming. He was a schemer, planning ahead, clever, careful and calculating. The most incomprehensible thing was that this unbelievably handsome, capable man had chosen her. While he readied himself for work and she made his pot of tea and gave Liz her feed, she would have offered thanks to heaven if she only could; might even have wept with gratitude if she were that way inclined.

After Len left the house, she cleaned and dusted, boiled and mangled the laundry, shopped and cooked, fed and washed baby Elizabeth. She found herself being treated as a maid by Len's mother who, she admitted, could not cope on her own. With Elizabeth on her lap, Maud then sat on the bus from Manor Park to Spitalfields, there to wait on her own mother. Such chores and errands were the ordinary lot of women. She saw that all around her there was grieving for those lost, and bomb sites, ruined streets, maimed neighbours and rationing. For herself there was untroubled gladness. She knew that others suffered while she did not.

From the papers and the wireless and Pathé News she knew, everyone knew, about momentous happenings in foreign lands, the tumult, revolutions, assassinations, new nations, new flags, new anthems played. The Empire was no more. Len marvelled that foreign soldiers who fought beside him in the desert as British troops – the Palestine Brigade, the Indian divisions – were now the armed forces of independent nations. It was momentous at home too, what with the National Health and Nationalisation. And the Old Age Pension – no sooner had she stopped work because of the baby than the Government chipped in with twenty-six bob a week for her mother!

Len was cheerful. The Socialists were in power, he had his job back, he was sparring again at the boxing club. Most of his old colleagues had survived the war. He was captain of the firm's darts team and won a silver cup. He and Maud were getting on well and he adored baby Lizzie as she adored him.

Maud dreamed of playing piano again, which was too silly to be worth mentioning. Len had more sensible dreams: he applied to the council for a home of their own. Their name went on the list with hundreds of thousands of others, the whole population of East London's bomb-damaged houses and shared rooms. All knew that vast modern estates were being built for them "in Essex", in that mysterious green land far beyond Barking, further out even than Dagenham. All knew and were waiting to hear.

*

Deposited in metal scales like those at the greengrocer's, Miss Elizabeth Blake was weighed in pounds and ounces. Stretched out on a wooden board like a length of fabric at the draper's, she was measured to the nearest eighth of an inch. Elizabeth did not rail against these indignities. She stared about at dozens of other babies, able to focus on them for the first time and astonished by the sight. They looked back at her in equal amazement.

Maud was also astonished, because among the women waiting with their prams at the new NHS maternity clinic was a face from long ago. 'Not you is it, Effie? My God! Well, I never!' Her old friend seemed to have become quite prosperous, wearing a good dress and hat, not the housecoat and headscarf of the other women.

'Blimey, Maud, long time no see!' She peered at the infant. 'This one yours, then? What a sweetie!'

'This is my little Lizzie, five months.' Maud cradled Elizabeth to be admired. 'But Ef,' – she looked at the baby in Effie's pram – 'not *yours*, is it?' It would be odd if it were, Effie being even older than herself.

Effie chortled. She pointed to a young woman nearby, willowy and fair. 'That's *my* baby. Name of Flo.' That too was odd, as Flo looked to be in her mid-twenties. Yet hardly that long had passed since Maud and Effie were girls themselves, dancing at East Ham Palais.

'So, Effie, when did you get married, then?'

'Oh, I ain't married. Flo's dad is George Sleet. Brother o' that Billy you was keen on, remember?'

Maud stared, instantly afraid and confused. 'Oh, I ain't forgot him,' she replied evenly. That was certainly true. She still glanced into Sleet Motors, rebuilt as a modern showroom, every time she passed on the bus, searching in vain for a glimpse of Billy. 'You live with George Sleet, then, do you?'

'Nah! George's got a wife, an' three kids by her. I won't hear a word against him, though. He pays for everything. What about *you*, Maud?' she asked. 'You just upped an' left! Where you living now? You hitched up with a feller?'

Maud thought, *Mum was right about Effie. She's no decency at all.* 'You must o' heard about that fire attack on our house before the war? And someone got shot?'

Effie pursed her lips and raised her eyebrows. 'Yeah, I know who got shot an' all – George's brother Terry. An' I know who pulled the trigger, Maudie.'

What bad luck running into Effie! 'Yeah, well, before that – did I ever tell you? Mum an' the Sleets've got history. It's something serious. She had to stay clear of 'em, didn't want 'em to find her. Only you went and told George our address, that's what you did, Ef. That was the trouble. So Micky Sleet's come round and he's tied Mum up and set light to her. That's literally what he's done, Ef. He's not right in the head, that bloke. Mum's been hiding ever since. Nervous wreck, she is. I have to visit nearly every day, poor soul.'

'Maud, I swear I never knew.'

'For God's sake don't tell George you've met me here. Don't tell Flo neither.'

'I won't tell no one. I can promise you that, Maud. Where did you an' your Mum go?'

Hearing this question, Maud wondered why she had been so willing to believe Len's airy assurance that the Sleet problem had been "solved".

'I can't say, Ef, 'cause she don't want no one to know.'

'I'm so sorry, Maud. I am. Silly to ask after all this time, only is there anything I can do to make it up to her?'

'Tell you what, there might be. You know the old pianer at the Smack? If it's still there, that's Mum's. Can you get it for her?'

'Yeah, a'right. I'll see if George wants rid of it. By the by, if there's anything you need – off ration an' that – I can get it for you. Ask me or Flo.'

The baby boy whimpered and Effie picked him up, chucked his chin. His colouring was as fair as a freshly laundered sheet, with endearing whisps of cotton-blond hair.

The two infants reached out, staring at one another in tender curiosity. Their innocent fingers touched.

'Talking of Micky,' said Effie, 'this little chap is Micky an' Dora's. Dora is Micky's missis.'

There was a moment's shock. 'You saying this is Micky Sleet's baby?' Maud had assumed the child was Flo's.

'That's right. Flo is his nanny.'

'Your daughter works for Micky Sleet?' Maud was gripped with a nauseous, sweating realisation. By coming to the maternity clinic, which she must, where her address was known, she brought danger to her herself and her mother, to Len and his mother, and, worst of all, to baby Elizabeth.

'The little darling's named for his granddad, Charlie Sleet. Ain't you, Chaz?' she cooed, 'say hello to Lizzie.'

Effie pushed open the door of the Well Smack pub and went straight to George. 'Anything?' he said. She handed him a purseful of notes and coins, and a list of what had been requested.

'You know who I met at the clinic today, George? You'll never guess,' she said. 'That Maud Cotter, only she's married now, name of Blake, Maud Blake. She talks posh an' all – putting on airs, stuck-up cow. Got a little baby.'

'Really! I'll be damned. Turned up again, has she? What about her mother, the widder?' he asked. 'That's who we're after.'

'Still a hundred quid on the table?'

'Might be, if you know where to find the widder.'

'One of the clinic nurses give me Maud's address. Maud visits her mum nearly every day, she said. See what I mean? By the way, her mum wants the old joanna. Says it belongs to her.'

'Ha ha! Does it, now?'

Their cars drew up outside the Smack like a display at the Motor Show. To gawping passers-by it was a spectacle of fabulous riches and no doubt criminality, Micky's cream Jaguar XK, Terry's black Bristol 400, Ronnie's yellow and white Sunbeam Talbot 90. Billy came along last in a roaring red MG.

There were noisy greetings, hands vigorously shaken, loud laughter, backs slapped, pecks exchanged. Micky's powerful form was sleek in an immaculate striped suit, Dora's sturdy bulk contained within a business-like skirt and jacket; louche, preening Ronnie cutting a sharp figure in check suit and cravat. Cigarettes were passed around. Into the cheerful room George wheeled a trolley of beef sandwiches, fruit cake and whisky. With him came George's young son cradling a soda syphon. The lad looked about with sneering defiance. Micky gave him half-a-crown.

When the boy had gone glasses of whisky and soda were solemnly raised to the memory of Emmeline and Arthur. Then to business: it was not Micky who spoke, but his wife Dora. The other men were surprised. It seemed that because she had run things on his behalf during the war, Micky was allowing his wife to continue as an equal partner.

'Flour's off ration now,' she said, 'clothes'll be next. They say fuel a come off next year. When it does, we'll feel the draught. We knew it'd end one day,' she reasoned. 'The war's over, so it had to happen.'

Terry argued, 'Stuff'll be on short supply for years yet.'

'Even so, we need to raise our sights,' said Dora. 'You don't want to go back to piddling little rake-offs from races an' cards an' two ounces o' this or tuppence o' that.'

The others sat rather stunned, looking at her as if unclear what could be better than living on rake-offs.

'I wouldn't exactly call it piddling,' responded Ronnie. 'It all adds up.'

She glared back. 'When rationing ends, that's what I'm talking about. Things'll be in short supply, like Terry says, but it won't be like now, will it? You don't want to go back to ducking an' diving, turning over shops, scrabbling over garden walls, do you? You're too old for that malarkey. We're in the money now. We want to keep it that way. We got to build on it. We need to invest before others beat us to it.'

George understood. 'An' do what?' He liked Dora's approach.

'We're goin'a get professional, tidy up the bookmaking, give proper odds. All the local riff-raff need getting rid of. Every bookie in this manor's got to work for us. We don't want to lose our partnership wi' Renvoize an' Winslow. We got a keep it going, spread ourselves out into parts where the stakes is bigger.'

George nodded. Ronnie too was thoughtful.

'An' Terry,' Dora turned to face him, 'it's time to move on from tatty old knocking-shops, slapping cheap tarts about. We want smart new clubs done up nice, glamorous girls, places where blokes can drink, relax wi' mates, have a flutter, snooker tables, watch a proper show in comfort an' privacy. All under one roof, see?'

Terry objected, 'My girls ain't cheap. I don't slap 'em about 'cept wi' good reason.'

Micky responded curtly, 'Yes, you do.'

'I like the way my shops're run. You telling me how to do my job?'

Micky stared. 'What would Ma say if she could hear you talk like that? Wasn' it her an' me set you up with the job in the first fucking place? Those ain't *your* shops, Tel – they're ours. Any more talk like that an' you'll be out. I fucking mean it. Out.' He grinned charmingly and his brothers laughed, treating this last remark as a joke, unsure what it meant.

Terry chuckled nervously. 'A'right Micky, keep your flipping hair on. Thing is, I ain't got it in me to run a smart club. I ain't got the education.'

Dora said, 'We'll have someone on front of house for you, Terry. There'll still be tarts, only posher. You'll enjoy it. Only no more slapping girls about, right?'

Terry shifted uncomfortably in his chair.

Micky revealed, 'The other thing I'm thinking about is house property. See 'em all over – Bombed-out houses, bomb sites, derelict places. They're dirt cheap. What's funny is, the council will pay us to repair 'em – there's grants. Do 'em up an' let 'em out, that's the way to do it. Rents. Best racket o' the lot.'

Amidst the men's uncertain response Dora raised a glass to the good times coming, and the others joined her.

George mentioned another matter. He said, 'You'll never believe who's popped up. Ma said she would one day. It's Widder Cotter. Effie bumped into the daughter. Goes by the name of Mrs Maud Blake nowadays. Remember that bloke wi' the right hook, at the dance hall in Stepney before the war? She married him.'

'Well, well.' There was a considerable stir.

Ronnie asked, 'Get an address?'

'Just the daughter, but she visits the mother every day, she says. We still interested?'

'Course we are,' came Terry's answer.

Micky said nothing. He caught Dora's eye. George's news and Terry's answer were unwelcome.

It so happened that neither Micky Sleet nor Len Blake had ever discussed their secret meeting at El Salloum dockside. Micky always had a piquant tale at the ready when asked to explain how he came to be decorated for courage behind enemy lines. To Dora alone had he mentioned the deal, the threats and promises made on that sultry night in the Western Desert.

Micky had not told Dora everything though. She did not hear about robbing a Cairo brothel where he had had sex with an underage girl. He did not reveal that Blake knew all about it. He did not explain the leverage this gave Blake. Not that Micky was ashamed – these things happened. It was just that it would go against him if anyone found out. It would damage his standing. It would diminish the prestige of his war service.

What Micky told her was simply that Blake promised to help him in exchange for his family not being harmed: in other words, 'protection'. He said Blake in his turn warned that if Micky didn't keep his side of the bargain, there would be a heavy price. Micky said he believed it; Blake was a clever bastard, there was no knowing what he would or wouldn't do. It was sort of protection both ways.

Dora was especially interested that Blake offered to help her husband in business if his family were left in peace. She had given Micky her opinion that it would be sensible to keep Len Blake onside. He said he thought so too.

Dora interjected. 'To my mind,' she said to the brothers now, 'put it behind you. This revenge malarkey makes no sense. You might end up wi' twenty years inside. All for what? Just a feeling.'

Billy cleared his throat. He had not spoken so far. Dora had hardly even referred to him or Sleet Motors in her future plans. 'Ma used to say, focus on business, not feelings.'

Dora said, 'She was right about that! Besides, your Pa would o' been dead by now anyway, so why worry?'

Billy nodded, 'That is wise words, Dora.'

'To cap it all,' George grinned, 'she's asking for the pub's joanna. Her property, so she says.'

Amid their scornful chuckling, Terry cried 'Bloody cheek! She can forget about that for a start.'

'Effie wants a ton for finding the address,' George added.

Micky shook his head, 'No. We said we'd pay for the widder's address, not the daughter's. Anyway, we ain't interested. Let's take Ma's advice an' put it behind us.'

Terry rapped the arm of his chair, indignant. 'You forgot what she done to me?' This was acknowledged with sympathetic nods. 'Ma never said put it behind us. She said leave it till the time is right. Well, now it's right.'

Micky said, 'No, it ain't. I'm telling you, don't none o' you do nothing – not to the widder, not to the daughter. Leave 'em be. I mean it.'

'No!' Terry banged the arm of his chair. 'She never put a bleeding bullet in you, Micky, did she?' he bellowed. 'An' *that* was all down to you! Look at the fucking state of me. She had Pa topped an' she crippled me, an' you fucking sit there saying I ain't to do nothing about it!'

Micky turned with gritted teeth. 'Shut it, Terry, control yourself, or you'll be in an even worse fucking state than what you are already. I'm warning you.' This time there was no smile and no laughter. This was the good old Micky they knew and respected.

*

Maud's contented mind had been overturned like a market barrow. Dread and fearful imagining beset her. Micky Sleet would find her at the maternity clinic. He would harm the baby, hurt them both. Or he need only force one of the nurses to give him her address. He would come to the house. She confronted Len bluntly: 'What made you say the Sleet problem was over? You sure about that?'

Len paced the room clenching and unclenching his fists. It grieved him that he had put Micky Sleet forward for a medal with only an empty promise in exchange. He should have shot him when he had the chance. In the cold light of home he recalled Sleet himself saying a promise 'don't mean fuck-all.' Sleet had even mocked him, saying that he too, Len, would be disposed of in due course.

He replied to Maud that he was not sure anymore. She said, 'I'll move back to Mum's for a bit. Maybe I can register Liz at a clinic down there.' – 'No, don't. We mustn't run away at the first sign of danger. We have to think.'

There was little sleep that night. In the darkness Len sat up. 'You awake, love? No, you're right. Take Liz to your Mum's first thing in the morning.'

However, it was already too late.

Terry grilled Effie. 'What time o' day does she visit her mum?' – 'She never said.' – 'Give us the address then, love.' – 'What, for nothing?' – 'No, there's half a ton in it. Strictly between us, right? Keep shtum or I'll cut your tongue out, get it?' Effie gave him Maud's address straight away and he counted out the banknotes.

Terry was damned if he would be told by Micky. With his damaged body, Terry did not usually drive a car. Bella, his nurse and girlfriend, normally did the driving. The passenger seat had been specially adapted for his comfort. However, this morning he would drive by himself. He did not want any witnesses.

Running a brothel, Terry was used to late nights. At three o'clock in the morning he sat down to his usual plate of bacon and eggs and glass of Scotch. He rose from the table and put on his black trilby and black coat. Terry did not have Micky's love of fire and flames. He favoured a different sort of burning. In his pocket was a phial of sulphuric acid. In the other pocket was a razor, in his belt a knife, inside the coat his loaded Colt 45. He would prefer not to shoot her. Guns attract attention. It was more pleasant to imagine how long and how much she would suffer with the acid. The roads were empty at that hour. He drove to Manor Park and stopped at the top of the street, there settling back to watch and wait.

At six in the morning he saw Maud and Len leave the house together. She was carrying the baby in her arms. They hurried up to Romford Road, joined a queue and boarded a bus. Terry stayed at a good distance behind, slowing the car at every stop.

He kept Maud and Len in view as they alighted and walked to a street of boarded-up dwellinghouses and shuttered old Jewish shops near Spitalfields market. He stopped at the corner of a side road to watch. They reached a door and went in without knocking. Presumably Maud had a key.

Terry considered his next step. Of course, he could not be completely certain that they were calling on Widow Cotter. If this *was* her address, perhaps it made more sense to wait until she was alone. No doubt he could easily break the door open – he was not agile or fit, but powerfully built and strong. He pictured being inside. There would probably be a narrow hall and a flight of stairs. He might need both hands, so would have to manage without his stick.

Even as Terry pondered, Len emerged and strode away. After a few minutes, Maud also came out and walked down the street. He smiled with quiet amusement. They had left the baby inside with the old lady! Here was unlooked-for opportunity! Terry fingered his razor, felt the phial of acid. He would strike at the baby too, put the fear of God into the whole damn lot of them *and* give Widow Cotter the hiding she deserved.

*

Maud and Len turning up like that, without warning, so early and on a weekday, surely meant trouble. Harriet's first words were, 'What is it – baby all right?'

'Fine, Mum. Put the kettle on. I see the street door is bust.'

'Some poor sod broke in looking for somewhere to sleep out of the rain. What brings you here at this hour?'

Harriet listened grimly. Whatever her fears and reservations, she welcomed them. Maud could sleep in the bed with her, she said, tight squeeze though it was. In truth she was delighted by the thought of sharing her bed with her daughter again. They could rig up some sort of cot for baby Liz in the same room.

'I'll be all right on the settee,' said Len. He thanked her warmly. 'I'm off to work now. Back about six.' He kissed them and was gone. Maud settled Elizabeth in an armchair among blankets. She said, 'I'll pop over to the market.'

Harriet distrusted their complacency. As soon as Maud had left, she took Ted's pistol from the carpetbag under the bed. Fearful and alert, she glanced out of the window: a few parked cars and vans. *They might think I'm a silly old bat, but I know Micky Sleet better than they do.*

Almost immediately Harriet heard the broken street door creak open and a slow, irregular step coming up the stairs. It was someone trying to be quiet. The steps reached the first landing and stopped. Without doubt Maud and Len had been followed. There was a long moment of silence. Suddenly her door was thrust wide open and through it barged a big, heavy, silver-haired man, infirm and unsteady, with a savage cut-throat blade open in his hand.

It was not as he expected. Harriet stood holding Ted's pistol with both hands, pointing it directly at his chest. She was much older than he had realised, at least seventy, and very frail.

Harriet recognised him. 'Thought it would o' been Micky,' she said. 'I've saved a bullet for him. You come back for another one?'

He saw how she struggled with the weight of the weapon. If she did not fire at once, he would be able to take it away from her. He must keep her talking, tire her.

'I want to make you an offer, Missis.' He showed her that he was closing the razor and putting it away inside his coat. Beneath the fabric his fingers rested on his handgun.

'I don't want no offer from you.'

'Micky says he wants to do a deal.'

'Tell him the answer is no.'

She could hardly hold the gun, let alone take aim. With a quick, startling move Terry was bringing out his Colt. Rather wildly, Harriet simply pulled the trigger of Ted's pistol. The recoil wrenched her right wrist and shoulder and forced her several yards across the room. She had no idea where the bullet had gone.

The deafening bang and the baby's shattering scream happened in the same instant. Terry was thrown against the doorframe, losing his balance and dropping his pistol. He could not bend to pick the gun up. To his astonishment, blood flowed from the side of his chest. He was dizzy with pain. Still the baby screamed like a whistle, sharp as pins in his ear.

He stumbled out of the room, staggered half-slipping down the stairs, trailing blood. As if in a dream or nightmare he managed to reach the car door. He started the engine and drove away slumped over the steering wheel, intending to make it to East Ham Hospital.

Blood soaked warm through his clothes onto the leather seat. He could not see or breathe. He could drive no more and knew he needed immediate help. A strange instinct caused him to veer off the road to stop at the entrance to a church. A place of hope, salvation, redemption; of life and death; someone here, so he believed, would come to his aid. He opened the car door and fell dead onto the paving.

2

A gangster shot dead at an East End church during the morning rush hour was news all over London by midday. The victim, according to early editions of the *News*, *Star* and *Standard*, was known to local police as pimp and racketeer Terence Sleet, aged forty-one. Police were unable to say whether it was a "gangland killing". Despite the busy location and time of day, no witnesses had come forward, perhaps afraid of reprisals.

In his pockets was found a phial of sulphuric acid, Mr Sleet's notorious hallmark. He was known to favour this cruel liquid. Blades were also found. Apart from that he had nothing on him other than plenty of cash. His girlfriend told police it was extremely unusual for Mr Sleet, who was handicapped owing to a previous shooting, ever to go out on his own, especially by car. She could not imagine what he was doing, but she doubted that he had been attending church.

Micky's reputation was immeasurably strengthened. The three families, and many others besides, "knew" who had done this. It was all explained by George – Terry argued with Micky the day before; he refused to do as Micky asked and Micky warned him of serious consequences.

A man who would murder his own brother was terrifying, maybe mad; and never, ever, to be trifled with. The police also suspected Micky, but found no evidence against him. Micky had an alibi. He was asleep in his bed with his wife. She confirmed it was so. No one believed that, and they were full of praise for Dora's steadfast loyalty.

That evening the *News*, *Star* and *Standard* printed fuller reports on the slaying. Len read the story on the train. When he arrived at Harriet's, he held up his paper. 'You heard about this? One of the Sleets has copped it.' To his horror he then learned what had really happened.

Harriet told him, 'You and Maud was followed here, love. The feller comes in here just like that. He says to me – he says, Micky wants to do a deal. But when I've said I ain't interested, he's pulled out a pistol. Well, what could I do, Len? I've shot him first.'

'You *what*?'

'With Dad's old pistol,' Maud explained. She told Len what happened next. By the time she returned from the market, Harriet was resting calmly in an armchair, baby Liz tranquil in her lap. Everything seemed in order. Except, Terry's handgun lay amid a ghastly pool of crimson on the floorboards.

'My God.' He glanced around but there was no sign of blood in the room.

Maud said, 'No, well, I thought I better clean up before it dried. Before anyone saw.'

Harriet interjected, 'I told her, don't touch his gun – you'll leave prints.'

'I picked it up with newspaper,' said Maud. She told him how she had placed Terry's handgun in a paper bag, taken a mop and pail, a brush and cloth, and set to work. Several buckets of scarlet water were poured into the gutter outside.

After hearing this account, Len sat pensive at the table. '*Do a deal?* I wonder what he meant by that.' Maud set down his stew and mash and a cup of tea. 'What you thinking?' she asked.

He shook his head. 'Just thinking.' Neither of the women spoke as he ate, nor did they do more than glance at one another in anxious silence as if waiting for some response from him. When he had finished and pushed the plate away, he stood and put his hat and coat back on. 'Going out for a bit.' He took the paper bag with him.

'Chuck it in the river,' Maud suggested.

'That's not where I'm going. Don't wait up for me.'

'Be careful, love.'

Len strode fast to Bethnal Green boxing club in the murky evening. Terry's pistol in its paper bag he shoved to the back of his locker. From the club he hurried to the tube station, changing at Mile End to another train crammed with weary silent passengers pressed together in a fog of acrid smoke. Station by station the train squealed and rattled to Barking, Len all the way upright, thoughtful and prepared.

It was a five minute walk from Barking station. He pushed open the swing door into the Smack's crowded public bar. There was a din inside; the place seemed to be thriving. He asked the barmaid, 'Landlord in, love, or manager?'

George wore a colourful waistcoat and tie. Len saw the man's resemblance to Micky; the size and bulk, the slicked hair like sugar icing and eyebrows of the same strange colour. There was no sign of mourning a lost brother.

'Sorry for your loss, mate,' said Len. 'Know where Micky is?'

The genial publican's smile became a puzzled grin of recognition. 'Hello, hello, if I'm not mistaken it's the man with the golden right hook. Married the former publican's daughter, we heard. Micky's here now as it happens, me old china, but he's not to be disturbed under no circumstances.'

'Well, go and disturb him. Say I've got something for him. Something he doesn't want.'

George nodded. 'You're a brave man, or maybe a foolish one.'

At that moment Micky and Dora were in seclusion with Matt and Sybil Winslow and Johnny and Ada Renvoize. Despite the presence of wives and glasses of drink, it was not a social occasion. Dora was outlining the role of the other families; what they would do within their neighbourhoods. No one raised a murmur of objection. The Winslow and Renvoize families were in awe of Micky, more afraid of him than ever since the news this morning that he had killed Terry. Micky was keen to preserve the illusion. He did not say he had done it, only that he did not want to discuss it. Terry had it coming, he told them – he admitted nothing. They listened respectfully.

George knocked and opened the door; he apologised for the interruption. 'Micky, it's that feller Blake. Won't take no for an answer. Says he's got something you don't want.' Micky left the meeting intrigued. It seemed an odd, fortuitous coincidence that Len Blake should turn up at this moment.

'Hello, Sarge, long time no see.' Len refused a drink. Micky urged him to a quiet corner. 'What you got that I don't want?'

'A warning,' Len answered, 'and a little story about who shot Terry Sleet.'

For once Micky was taken by surprise. 'Oh yeah. Who was it then?'

'Me,' said Len.

Micky's surprise increased. His eyes darted around. 'Don't piss about.'

'I happened to stop by my mother-in-law's this morning. Guess who showed up, just like that, while I was there? Your little brother. He bust in pointing a gun saying you sent him to do away with the lot of us.'

'That's a lie. I never sent him.'

'So I shot him with my own pistol. I put him in his car and he drove off. Seems like he's died on the way.'

'Not a true story, Sarge. Why would I send a bloke can hardly walk, why was you holding a shooter in your hand at that very moment, an' why was you there in the first place? It's a fairy tale.'

'Something else I've got is Terry's gun. I've put it somewhere safe.'

'Don't believe that neither. What kind of shooter did Terry have?'

'Colt Automatic, like the Yanks in Italy. The 45.'

Micky nodded. It was the correct answer. He said, 'Honest to God I never sent Terry. He came off his own bat.'

'Don't play the fool, Sleet. That's not the deal we made. It was your job to stop him.'

'Well, he's brown bread now, so you can forget about him.'

'Not good enough, Sleet. That's the last time you give me any grief. I'm keeping Terry's pistol. Any more trouble and I'll use it on you and Dora *and* the little boy.'

Micky scoffed. 'You never would. You'd hang for that.'

'No,' Len nodded toward the bar, 'your brother George would. The law gets a tip-off and the murder weapon turns up in the cellars of this pub. Where people will remember there's already been one dodgy incident on George's watch. My mother-in-law knows more about what's underneath this place and how to get in and out of it than anyone living.'

Micky could believe that. 'What about the old conscience, Sarge, didn't that used to trouble you?'

'I got over it. Family comes first.'

'Well, I ain't having it, Blake, not a threat like that.' Both men were calm and quiet. They could have been discussing the price of beer. I can send someone to take out the whole lot of you. Finish this once an' for all.'

'Think so? Terry just tried that.'

Micky nodded slightly. 'Give us a bell tomorrow night. We'll sort something out.'

'Oh, by the way, see that old pianer there?' Len added. 'My mother-in-law wants it back.'

'Fuck off, Sarge.'

Micky returned to his friendly business meeting in the snug. Wary of being followed, Len walked a mile before running to catch a bus to Spitalfieds. Harriet and baby Liz were in bed.

'What you been doing all this time?' Maud asked.

He said, 'Nothing.'

'D'you get rid of the gun?'

'I hid it.'

Later, as they undressed for bed and stepped in and out of the bathroom, Micky told Dora frankly what Len had said. 'Terry went round to Widder Cotter's an' Blake just happens to be there. It was him shot Terry an' now he's threatening to shoot you an' me an' the baby if he has any more trouble.'

Dora was dismissive. 'Is that what he says?' She slipped her sturdy figure into a silk nightdress. 'It's just talk.'

'No, it ain't. I know this bloke. It's not vengeance. It's to solve a problem. That's how he thinks. Not sure he'd shoot a baby though. It'll be hard to get rid of him. He's tricky.'

'Why get rid of him? How does that fit with our plans? You need to mend fences with him. Tell him "sorry". Do him a favour.' She advised Micky to warn his brothers that anyone who laid a finger on Harriet or her family would meet the same end as 'poor Terry'. There was something else. 'Micky, you told me Blake said he could help you in business. Was that all talk an' all?'

When Len phoned, Micky assured him that Harriet would be left alone. 'Promise you that. An' if you want to send a van, she can have her joanna back.'

A terrible joy, as when a prisoner steps free, overwhelmed Harriet at the prospect of seeing her piano again. Len and a gang of his workmates heaved it up the stairs, she and Maud and little Elizabeth calling out advice and encouragement. Harriet clapped with glee as the instrument reached the landing and lumbered awkwardly across the floorboards into her dayroom. There was nowhere to stand the thing. She declared that her sewing machine may as well be pushed aside as she could not use it these days, with her weak eyes and arthritic hands. The longed-for piano was eased into position.

'What about a tune then, Mum?'

Harriet sat at the keyboard. Strangely, her mind was blank. Her little audience waited. She touched the keys with a hesitant, painful hand, sounded one delicious, jazzy chord. She turned away without playing.

Maud was perturbed. 'What's wrong, Mum?'

'No, you play. I can't just now.'

Maud began a Duke Ellington number, singing 'Now the stars are in your eyes, doo-dee-doo, dee-dee-doo, I'm beginning to see the light.' Impulsively Len joined her in song. Harriet held Elizabeth in close embrace, moving in time to the music. She planted kisses on her grand-daughter's head, and the baby reached up to touch Harriet's face, wet with shining tears. For all of them it was a blissful moment.

When everyone had gone, leaving Harriet alone, she took her seat again at the piano. She glanced up at the framed photograph of Edwin and caught his eye. 'Now, where was I, Ted?'

As she began, Harriet heard loud conversation and laughter around her, men and women in the bar, the bright, fast notes of ragtime, a voice behind ordering a drink. She continued where she had left off without missing a note, fingers quickly moving, silent above the keys without touching them...

Little Maud did not come barefoot into the bar with her urgent warning. Charlie Sleet did not burst through the door. There was no yelling mob, no interruption, no fight, no firebrands. No Great War.

Ted pushed a pint across the zinc. Harriet made music. Life at the Well Smack inn carried on as before.

Maud found Harriet dead on the floor beside the piano. Lying there, twisted awkwardly, in death she seemed a discarded puppet, pitifully worn out, her large NHS glasses fallen half across the lined smoker's face. Apparently it was heart failure. The body was driven to the cemetery to lie with Edwin.

*

Of course, people must be told. Maud leafed through her mother's address book. Harriet had hardly seen anyone for years, not even her family. Aunt Gina had passed away. Still believing herself to be a bringer of bad luck Harriet had lost touch with her old friends.

It's strange, thought Maud, who remembers you at the end. They all came, those that were still alive, in their hats and coats, the great cousinage of Hayes, and wept as she was laid in the ground. The Zuckermans were there, Aaron and Lieba in their sixties, correct, reserved, dignified, smartly dressed in black. Yitzy, calling himself Isaac now, was distinctly middle-class, well-to-do, half bald. Maud and Yitzy's paths had vastly diverged. Isaac said he was a chartered accountant with his own firm in Ilford. As always he devoted himself to work. His brothers ran the confectionery business. His manner as gentle as before, he wished Maud every commiseration, kissed her charmingly on both cheeks and shook Len's hand.

Maud told him about baby Elizabeth. He said, 'That's nice! We've got a little boy, Jacob.' – 'That's a lovely name. How old?'

'Just over a year.' – 'Oh! Same as Lizzie. You still play the clarinet, Yitz?'

'Sometimes, for fun. I hope you kept up your piano.' – 'I've just inherited Mum's piano, as it happens.'

'Good, good. Come over one day, both of you. Eva would love to meet you.' – Maud thought it unlikely. She would feel out of place. She said, 'That would be nice.'

One of those still alive was Cousin Will, strong and upright in his old age. Maud asked if he could give a short eulogy. He had always loved his cousin Hattie, he told the gathering. He remembered her so full of life. She had a rough time of it after losing her husband. Well, Hattie and Ted could rest together in peace now. It was the end of an era, he said.

*

As well as the piano, Maud inherited her father's pistol and cosh, three shabby armchairs, two frayed rugs and the three-quarter bed. She had nowhere to put them. For this reason Len and Maud moved into rooms a few doors along the same street. It was the usual arrangement, a house shared. This, though, was one of the larger corner houses. Once upon a time it must have been, they all agreed, the home of 'a better class of people'. Theirs were the upstairs rooms. On the ground floor were a mother and daughter, one whose husband had died in the first German war, the other in the second.

In their new quarters, Len, Maud and Elizabeth still had no front door, but they did have a bedroom and a little private living room across the landing, even their own scullery, and their own bathroom cubicle with a toilet. Maud pondered her situation. And she realised something extraordinary. She was liberated, liberated from her mother and therefore (so she assumed) from the Sleets. In truth – she knew it was reprehensible – what she felt was relief. Maud had been finding her mother's company tiresome. Nor did she have to keep taking the tram to Spitalfields anymore. Instantly the realisation yielded to the sharp prod of conscience. She was selfish. She was neglecting her mother's grave. She felt ashamed of herself, especially as the cemetery was less than a mile away.

For Len, it was not so. He did not feel liberated. Micky Sleet was always in his thoughts. Had the death of Harriet ended the diabolical pact between them? Micky was wondering about this, too. With Widow Cotter gone, was the threat to his wife and son lifted? But of course Len Blake still had Terry's gun. Micky called Len and said he wanted to have a chat.

'Overtime tonight, love,' said Len. That was quite normal. Apart from his overtime, there was often Union business and nights when he played darts, or went to the boxing club after work. Maud saved up the ironing and darning for those long evenings. This time she did something different. She hurried Elizabeth in her pram along Romford Road, pausing to buy a small bunch of carnations at a corner shop.

The earth on Harriet's grave was still piled with flowers from the funeral. She gathered up the bouquets that had faded, tidied the others. The task soothed her. She resolved to come more often. Maud lay down her fresh blooms and spoke softly. She said: 'Hello Mum. I'm so sorry I haven't been to visit. And Dad, I'm really sorry.' She gazed at the soil beneath which lay the body of her mother, and below that, her father.

Elizabeth looked on from among her blankets in the pram. As burial grounds often are, the place was tranquil and pleasing. There was birdsong, and a murmur of traffic. There were few people about at this hour. A bell would be rung soon and the grounds locked. Ahead she noticed a man standing with head bowed beside a new grave. With shock Maud recognised him: it was Billy Sleet. She wondered what to do, whether to leave. But he turned and saw her.

The greeting was innocuous, a simple hello. Absurdly she felt a tremble of youthful love. She could see in his eyes, the quick breath, that he felt it too; the excitement and pleasure.

She had not spoken to Billy since they were sixteen, on that unhappy morning at Wanstead Flats. They had talked then about running away together, free as birds. He had made her a necklace and she kept it still among her treasures. Years afterwards came that brief sighting at Stepney dance hall, when Len saved Billy from a razor. Since then, nothing, despite always hoping to catch sight of him.

'You're looking well, Billy. Haven't changed a bit.'

He laughed sweetly. In fact he looked his age, the silvery hair combed over a balding crown, a slight puffiness around rosy, hairless jowls.

They were both forty-one years old. 'You too, Maud.' He nodded at the pram: 'Effie told us you had a kid. Come to see your mum's grave?'

She nodded. What a traitor Effie was! She'd promised she wouldn't tell anyone!

'Pa was moved here to lie wi' Ma an' Arthur. The new one's Terry.'

'Oh, your father's here, is he? Which is his?'

She left the pram on the path to stand beside Billy. She gazed fascinated at the ornate gravestone of Charlie Sleet, whom she had seen strike her father with a piece of fiery wood in the bar of the Smack, the blow which had carried him off. Their whole story was in these graves.

'Fancy a stroll?' said Billy.

'Did you marry, Billy – find someone?'

'No, Maud, there's no one else. Don't worry, I'm used to it.' He shot her a wry, sad grin.

She could see how it was. 'Remember when we wished we had no names? You didn't want to be a Sleet.'

He nodded ruefully.

'You know Shakespeare?' she asked.

Yes, he had heard of William Shakespeare.

'Shakespeare said a rose by any other name would smell as sweet. You ever heard that one?'

Yes, he was familiar with the saying.

Maud said, 'You know what's wrong with that? A rose can't have any other name.'

'That's what we found out,' he said. 'Once a rose, always a rose.'

At the end of a row they turned onto another path, strolling beside the back wall of the cemetery.

'Look!' She grasped his arm.

A few yards ahead was an incomprehensible and astounding sight. Her husband, Len – not at work, then! – was sitting on a bench with Micky Sleet. The two men were deep in conversation.

Len and Micky had arranged to meet in a place where they might have come across each other by chance. Len first showed Micky the shared plot of *Edwin Cotter, Esq. and Harriet, his beloved wife.* 'Well, Sleet, you got your medal and she's dead. You can't hurt her anymore. So that's the end of it between us.'

'Think so?' Micky led Len to the graves of his parents and brothers. 'Here's my Pa, who your wife's mother took from us. Here's Terry, who *you* took. No one's paid for that. See how it is, Blake? No one paid.'

'They deserved it, Sleet. *That's* how it is.'

'What do you deserve, sending me into the desert thinking it'd kill me?'

The two walked from their family graves to a bench at the back of the grounds. Len asked, 'Anyone with you?' – 'No. You?' – 'No. My wife thinks I'm doing overtime.

'Listen, Blake, back at El Sullum I made you a promise an' you made me one,' began Micky. 'Remember?'

'Like I say, you got your ribbon, and she's in her grave,' responded Len at once.

'Back then, you said I could be a real boss. You said you'd help.

That was part of the deal. Don't tell me you've forgot?'

'You weren't interested in that part.'

'Don't laugh, Blake, but I want to do it after all. I want your advice. Don't tell no one – it's between us.

'What d'you mean, a real boss?'

Micky pursed his lips. 'No, just tell me what *you* meant.'

'What about your side of the bargain, Sleet?'

Micky gave a nod. 'I ain't forgot. If anyone gives you or your family any aggravation, I'll take care of it. Long as they live. You help me, I'll help you. You hurt me, I'll hurt you. That was the deal. Help me wi' this, Blake, an' it'll settle up all the old scores between us.'

'All right, so what d'you want?'

'Tell you what I *don't* want. The papers wrote that Terry was an East End villain known to local police. He sounded like fucking *nothing*. I don't want that said about me.'

'If you mean to be an even bigger villain, Sleet, I can't help with that.'

'Don't be daft. That's just dogs fighting in a cage. I want the good life. The best life.'

A trace of amusement passed over Len's face. He could not bring himself to say it was a lost cause. 'Depends what you mean by the best life.'

'Don't get philosophical wi' me, Sarge, or I'll chop your bleeding head off.'

Len said, 'Look, me and the wife rub along, got enough to pay the bills, bringing up a kid healthy and happy. *That's* the best life, Sleet. There's nothing better.'

'It's *little*. You want a *little* life.'

They heard voices. There on the path stood Maud with Billy Sleet beside her. She was holding his arm.

'Well, *that* ain't a good start, is it?' murmured Micky. 'We'll have to talk another time. Work over Covent Garden way, don't you?' Len nodded that he did. Micky said he knew somewhere suitable near there, at Seven Dials.

The encounter in the cemetery was tetchily explained as they walked home. Maud said she had met Billy by chance, that was the honest truth. Billy had been at his parents' graves, and she at her parents'.

They had got chatting, reminiscing, that was all.

Len said that was exactly what had happened to him. He finished his overtime and on the way home popped into the burial ground to visit Harriet's grave. He met Micky there completely by chance.

Maud knew Len would never visit Harriet's grave on his own. 'What were the two of you talking about then?'

'I asked him if they'll leave us in peace now your mother is gone.'

That was not how it had looked to her. 'What did he say?'

'He promised we'd be left alone, only he didn't want you meeting Billy or even talking to him. It's best to do as he says, love.'

That was most definitely not how it had looked to her. Nevertheless she replied, 'I promise I won't see Billy again. And *you* ought to keep well clear of Micky, if you want my opinion.'

'Oh, I will, love, don't you worry about that.'

3

S even Dials was a squalid, run-down area in those days. It takes its name from an old junction of seven lanes between Soho and Covent Garden. At the meeting point of the lanes stands a tall pillar bearing six sundials. As its shadow turns with the passing hours, the slender pillar itself and the circular junction where it stands become the face of the seventh dial. Here Len waited until he saw Micky approach and beckon. Len followed along a stinking alley, passing derelict yards, disused storehouses and the rotten masonry of empty dwellings. They stopped at stone steps descending to a heavy basement door with a grille. Len had never before seen such places. He had not even known the alley existed.

Eyes peered through the grille. 'Wotcher, Frostie, me old china,' came a cheerful voice from within, 'long time no see. Who's the other bloke?' – 'Just a bloke. A friend. Open up, mate.'

A key turned in a lock to let them pass, and turned again behind them. Len looked about. They were inside a cavernous space of bare brick and flagstones under an arched roof. Here stood a makeshift counter, a snooker table and small groups of frighteningly muscular men all of whom stopped speaking to welcome Micky with great deference. As if in imitation of the lanes above, rooms and narrow corridors radiated from the central space.

Micky asked at the counter for a couple of bottles of mild. There was a darts board on the wall. Len had learned that he could impress other men with his skill at darts, and so it proved.

'What is this place?' he asked. – 'Well,' shrugged Micky, 'it's somewhere private for a drink an' a chat, ain' it?'

'No, I mean, in days gone by.' – 'This place? I believe it's part of the old brewery what stood above.'

'Is it like a private club or something?' – 'What is this, *Twenty Questions*?'

Len asked nothing more. They sipped their beer and played darts quietly, chalking up the score, their cigarettes on an overflowing ashtray. Len won by a big margin. Match over, they moved to battered armchairs in an alcove.

Micky said the Sleet family was rebuilding some premises in Stratford as a smart modern striptease bar, to be called Break. He explained that the Sleets, in partnership with the Winslow and Renvoize families, had for years made a good living from a variety of sources – protection, pimping, blackmailing homosexuals, betting, the black market and so on. Yet Micky still felt himself to be, as he called it, a fucking nothing.

'To get down to brass tacks, when you said I could be a proper boss,' said Micky, 'what did you mean by that?'

'I think you got it in you, mate. Divide the Sleet business in two,' advised Len. 'You on one side. All the rest on the other side. Keep your side clean as a whistle. Set up a firm of your own, above board, arm's length from trouble.'

Micky finished his drink. 'How, though? What do I need – a solicitor?'

'No, it's an accountant you want.'

'What, a bent one?'

'No, a clever one. Leave it to me. And for Christ's sake keep away from places like this.'

*

Isaac Zuckerman – Yitzhak – stood at his office window meditating upon the domes and balconies of Ilford Town Hall, observing the pleasing effect of streaming rain on its pale stonework. Down below, men and women struggling with umbrellas in the squally wind dashed around huge puddles. What on earth could Len Blake want to see him about on such an evening? He had said only that he could not explain on the phone. Then Yitzhak actually spied Len on the busy pavement below, a lean, well-built upright man in hat and coat approaching with dignified stride, unbowed by the downpour.

Len found the doorway marked *I. Zuckerman and Co.* opposite Ilford's famous department store, Moultons. Uncarpeted stairs led up to an exceptionally plain, unpretentious office containing a desk, two chairs, a filing cabin, coat stand and paraffin heater. A simple calendar on the wall was the only decoration. Evidently a showy office was not part of the appeal for Yitzhak's clients. The two men greeted one another with a handshake.

'Hello, Zuckerman, thanks for staying late to see me.' Len carefully shook the water from his hat and removed his raincoat, hanging them on the stand.

'What a filthy night! What can I do for you, Blake?'

When Len had explained, Yitzhak shook his head. 'Why on earth are you involved with this madman? He tried to kill a member of your family. His father tried to kill *my* family. I wouldn't touch him, if I were you.'

Len agreed that Micky Sleet was a madman. Of course it was impossible to tell the whole story. He could not go into his reasons, the mutual threats. 'I'm doing it for Maud. It must be a good thing, mustn't it, to help a man go straight? It would help Maud put the past behind her.'

Yitzhak conceded that point. 'As it's you, Blake, I'll see him, but it's not my usual line to deal with such people. I won't do anything underhand or illegal.'

'So much the better.'

Not three weeks later, as December began to bite and the first Christmas decorations were pinned up at Moultons, Len brought Micky to Yitzhak's office.

It had been a still, hazy dawn and icy cold. Patches of dense fog hung stagnant in the side streets. There was an eerie quiet in the air when Len reached the print works at Covent Garden. The smog started in earnest before midday, thickening like skeins of moist, mustard-coloured wool trailing from the sky, piling in masses across roadways, over rooftops, gradually blotting out the daylight, slowly edging into every corner, knitting tightly between buildings, seeping like tendrils through keyholes, vents, loose windows, beneath doors, staining the air inside rooms.

During the lunch break Len stepped outside the works to look. An acrid stink stung his nose and throat. Boys and girls were feeling their way along the street, sent home early from school. Conductors walked ahead of buses, tapping the kerb with long poles, holding lamps or flaming torches to guide the drivers. The headlights of fearful cabs made no impression on the shroud before them.

By the time he left work the fog had become 'a proper pea-souper'. It was very dark and oddly silent, all sound muffled. Len could not see the road beside him, finding his way to the tube station guided by a voice shouting from the entrance. He was due to meet Micky at Ilford. No doubt, he thought, things would be easier at Ilford, which he half imagined as nearer to clean countryside and the blowing, bracing sea.

Yet at Ilford the blanket was just as dense. He called out from the station forecourt, 'Micky Sleet!', his voice seeming to die away inaudible. Like a figure in a film, Micky stepped forward from the gloom and grasped his shoulder, peering. 'That you, Blake?' They could hardly see one another, nor make out the pavement at their feet. As the two men set off, Micky walked with confidence into the gloom. He took Len's arm and guided him. They hurried with handkerchiefs at their mouths to stop the bitter taste of the air.

Yitzhak was shocked to see them. 'You walked here in this!'

The two men stood in his office, lit cigarettes and inhaled as if the smoke were oxygen itself.

Micky said politely, 'Thank you for making the time, Mr Zuckerman.'

'Not at all. Did you know, Mr Sleet, that your father tried to kill my father? He thought we were Germans. Caused a lot of trouble to a lot of people, that did. A lot of misery. We're not Germans, by the way.'

'I know that story,' responded Micky, unruffled. 'Is your father still alive, or has he passed away?'

'Still alive, thank God.'

'Well then. Mine's dead. Murdered when I was twelve years old. I'm not here to talk about that. Let's get on.'

Dora understood the new situation perfectly. It was harder to explain to George. 'You're a bleeding traitor to your own fucking flesh an' blood!' he yelled at his brother, fist clenched. 'All what belongs to the fucking family, you're saying belongs to you. You said we need to invest. That ain't investment. That's daylight fucking robbery.'

'Shut up, George. Stop an' *think*,' Micky retorted. 'Listen, from now on, everything's in *your* hands, the club, the spielers, the girls, the lot. The rackets, the ration books, all of it. Run things how you want. My company *owns* the club. But what goes on *inside* it is *your* business an' I don't want to hear about it. This is *better* for you.'

'Still want a slice of the takings, though, I suppose?'

'Well, George, you got to pay the club's owner a fair percentage, stands to reason.'

'You just said *you* own it!'

'No, I never. I don't own nothing. I don't own a brass farthing. Break Entertainment Ltd owns the club.'

'What the bloody hell is Break Entertainment? Don't take me for a mug. Who owns that, then – you, I suppose?'

'No, no, no, Georgie,' Micky gritted his teeth in the effort to get his brother to understand, 'like I said, Sleet Properties own it. Sleet Properties own everything. I just take my drawings from the firm.'

'*Drawings*? What are you, a flipping artist? I tell you what y'are, mate, a flipping *con* artist. Well, you ain't goin'a con *us*. We see what you're up to, robbing your own kiff an' kin. We see you.'

'George, George, it ain't like that! You'll have the biggest take of any of us. I'm only a director at Sleet Properties, that's all I am.' For this was how Yitzhak had set matters up for him. 'I won't be coming to no more meetings at the Smack. I'm making you boss of the manor, George. I'll come along one more time to make it all square with the families. We'll drink to it, then I'll scarper. I'm outside everything. Me on one side of the line, you on the other. Can't you see how handy that is for both of us? We can help each other. No one has to know.'

George was prepared to be mollified. 'How does that work, then?'

'For crying out loud, I been telling you! I've got people at the Town Hall to help with licences, an' coppers who'll turn a blind eye to trouble. You do me favours, an' I make sure favours get done for you. Break Entertainment is opening another club in Southend an' one up Clacton way.'

'Where's the dough coming from for *that*?'

'Bank loan. That's the art of it, mate.'

'Bank loan!' George sneered. 'Ain't that the stuff you give back plus ten per cent?'

Micky chuckled. 'Funny enough, you never pay it back. You just give 'em their cut. It's Sleet Management Ltd borrers the money, not me.'

George snorted, mocking. 'Fucking trickster.'

'An' there's Sleet Motors, obviously.'

'Oh no, mate, *oh* no. Not the garridge. That's Billy's pigeon, always has been.'

'No, George. I set up that motor business with Ma when I was a lad. You're too young to remember. It was a bomb site from the first war. No word of a lie, I even saw the bomb go off. Blew me off my feet. Me an' Ma literally built that place with our own bare hands. It was my idea, so she put it in my name. It's in the paperwork.'

'What, Billy's garridge is in your name? You clever bleeder.' There was a note of admiration.

Micky chuckled. 'Billy can carry on running it if he wants, no problem.' He buttoned his coat, tucked in his neck scarf. 'Well, George, it's a new era, ain' it?' He reached out to his brother and the two men shook hands. 'As of now you're head of the Sleet family. I'll be off. Happy New Year to you an' the missis, an' your nipper.'

'Likewise, Micky. All the best.'

'Be lucky.'

'Yeah.'

Dora urged Micky henceforth always to wear a black suit and crisp white shirt, with silver-grey silk ties matching his hair. She portrayed him as a rough diamond with the Midas touch and a heart of gold, who had served King and Country and won a medal for bravery. He gave generously to a charity for widows and orphans of fighter pilots, and to another for wounded veterans of the desert campaign. They invited him to fund-raising events. He cultivated his old friends at the police station and on the council, men who even now were afraid of him.

*

Up the road was a corner shop. Maud gave Elizabeth thruppence for half an ounce of tea and two ounces of biscuits. She looked out as the adorable slip of a thing hurried so diligently, concentrating hard, repeating the order to herself, clutching the coin in one hand and the ration book in the other as she skipped along the pavement.

From the window she watched as three older boys waylaid the little girl, stopped her in her path, forced her fingers open and took the thruppenny bit. Maud rushed downstairs and out of the front door as fast as she could, running along the road yelling furiously. She was too far away. The boys ignored her. Maud recognised them, uncouth tearaways. She knew the family, a troublesome lot. She regretted shouting; it might cause Elizabeth more problems. The lads turned from their crying victim and sauntered away with a sneer and a gob of spit.

That evening, over his dinner, Maud mentioned it to Len. After the meal he walked up to the telephone box and mentioned it to Micky.

People do not always know they are being protected, nor what price they pay for protection. The citizen is not aware of the part played in his or her day by, for example, the armed forces or GCHQ. So also Elizabeth did not know that Maud's protective gaze followed her along the street. Nor did Maud know that she too had protection.

Micky's men came the same night. It was a small thing, a token, an opportunity to show that the arrangement was not mere words. The boys were pulled out of their house and beaten in the road for all to see. 'Lucky for you it was only thruppence,' their father was told. The men emptied the father's wallet and drove away with his week's wages. Their mother wept and hollered on the pavement. Maud and her neighbours watched from bedroom windows. She called to Len to come and see, but he did not.

It was as though he knew already. A silly feeling. How could he? She had a vague notion that Len knew a lot of things about which it was better not to ask. There were areas of life that he considered his business and not hers. He would not talk about the war, about his work or what was in his wage packet. Len was amusing, loving, hard-working, dutiful and generous. He was many good things. He was quite extraordinarily handsome, had a ready smile and was always willing to lend a hand to anybody. Yet he was not forthcoming.

She supposed he was what they call *the strong, silent type*. Before going back to sleep, she dared to ask: 'Those men who beat the lads for taking Lizzie's thruppenny bit – how did they know about it?'

'Someone must've told them, love.'

*

With confectionery freed from rationing at last, Elizabeth celebrated her fifth birthday with a cornucopia of sweets, chocolate and cake. Maud and Len gave her a picture book about the new queen who shared her name. Large colour-plate "coronation books" were the gift of the moment, as were tea sets decorated with portraits of the young monarch and her prince. She pored happily over pages of tinted photographs of Her Majesty and the royal family, their crowns and palaces, halls and gardens, uniforms and swords, carriages, ribands, jewels, crests, shields and ensigns.

On the great day itself bunting fluttered at every window and gate. There was no school, although unfortunately it was too cold and wet to play in the street. For many adults too it was a holiday. Len, a doubtful monarchist (though no republican), went to work as usual. As soon as he left the house, Elizabeth helped her mother make sandwiches for later. When they had finished, mother and daughter sat down together to study the coronation dress ("a dream in white satin") in the newspaper before changing into their own best frocks.

They carried the sandwiches along the road to Grandma's house. Other neighbours excitedly arrived, bringing chairs into the back room where a rented television set had been placed on a tea table. The marvellous object was made of shiny brown Bakelite resembling polished wood. Everyone had seen television sets in shop windows. This was the first time any of them had been in the same room as one, let alone watched a broadcast. It was nervously switched on to warm up in good time for the menfolk to make adjustments to the vertical and horizontal hold and position the aerial. The screen was fully nine inches across, with a magnifier like a glass bubble fitted over it.

Elizabeth peered at the tiny picture as the royal procession began. Straight away she recognised the Queen, pretty and smiling, with the Duke of Edinburgh inside a quite fantastic carriage drawn by four pairs of pale horses. Beside each pair walked men in fabulous livery, and on each nearside horse sat a rider. It surprised her that somehow she knew that the people and horses on the little screen were actually normal-sized. Like in a photo.

Ceaseless cheering seemed to scare the animals. Elizabeth stared in disbelief at ecstatic faces in the crowd, grown women yelling and waving with mad abandon. Never before had she seen anyone, child or adult, behave in such a way. She wondered what would happen if the horses bolted and killed some of them. Would the coronation carry on anyway? But the horses were always brought quickly under control.

Even with the magnifier the image was hard to see, the flickering black and white lines unclear, occasionally vanishing into a blizzard of buzzing interference. Yet the assembled family and neighbours were enthralled, constantly reminding one another that it wasn't the same as a film, they were looking at real events taking place at this very instant! One said it was like meeting all kinds of people you normally never would meet. One said it made the world feel bigger somehow. One said a television was like a periscope that could see for miles. One said it was a new age.

Lady commentators with tremendously posh voices, of the type sometimes heard on the wireless but nowhere else, described Her Majesty's dress and jewels. The fairytale carriage arrived at Westminster Abbey and a lady commentator said 'A splendid scene there awaits her,' which quickened Elizabeth's interest in language. A gentleman's hushed, reverential voice took up the story as the Queen continued slowly on foot inside the majestic church. At the most solemn moment of ritual, when the Queen was unjewelled and stood humbly in a white robe, many in Grandma's back room began to weep and choke with emotion. To restore their equilibrium, Maud's sandwiches were brought out, and a cake, and endless cups of tea.

'Will the Queen have tea?' Elizabeth wondered aloud. The answers were 'Shush!', 'Maybe later' and 'Glass of sherry more like.' Suddenly with a blast of trumpets the National Anthem struck up. Now wearing a crown and a gown of 'shimmering cloth of gold lined with crimson silk' (according to the lady commentator), the Queen joined a slow procession out of the church.

The back room television audience hesitated; should they stand for the National Anthem? 'Well, would you when it comes on the wireless?' the question was asked. The answer was, most did. 'It especially seems the right thing,' explained Grandma, 'when you can actually see Her Majesty.'

They watched as thousands of soldiers, to the clamour of bells, cheers and bands, marched with the Queen's golden carriage to Buckingham Palace, where she stood on a balcony with her family. When at last they went inside Elizabeth supposed Her Majesty must have said 'I ain't half famished.' Which was true, because (according to a lady commentator) 'Their Majesties will now enjoy a late luncheon, including a new creation called coronation chicken.'

Maud put it to Len, 'You know what, it would be nice to have one of them television sets. I heard you can get them on the never-never, six guineas down and a pound a week for two years or something.'

'I don't know, duck. The wireless licence is three quid a year for a television. You really think we'd watch it?'

'There's kiddies' programmes, variety shows, football, the news, all sorts.'

The next Saturday fortnight, all three of them travelled by bus to the famous Harrison Gibson department store in Ilford, there to sign a hire-purchase agreement for a television. Maud had never been inside such a shop. Her heart beat hard at the sight of richly upholstered three-piece suites, dining tables and modern gramophones. She could just imagine herself sitting on such a sofa watching her new television.

On the same morning that the television was delivered, the postman brought a manila envelope marked *County Borough of East Ham*. It was addressed to Len. Therefore Maud did not open it. She stood beside the door and handed it to him the moment he came in.

Len read the letter twice then raised his eyes to hers. 'They've got a place for us, love, a proper house. There's a new estate over at Hornchurch Aerodrome, in Essex.'

'Where the Spitfires flew from?' she asked. – 'That's the one.'

'What's it called, the estate?' – 'Elm Park, it says here. It's even got a tube station, on the District Line.' He handed Maud the paper to see for herself.

'Well, *that's* good. Only where will Liz go to school?' – 'We'll find out all these things.'

'She won't have any friends.' – 'Why not? Hundreds and hundreds of families are being moved there.'

*

As if coming into fabulous riches Maud paused wonderingly in the narrow hallway. Here she stood and turned to look all around, grasping the Yale key in her clenched fist. For the first time, she had a front door of her own. Disbelieving, exultant, disconcerted, afraid too, she passed slowly from room to room in a waking dream: *two* bedrooms, a real full-size bathroom with a geyser, a proper separate toilet; a quite amazing 'through lounge' leading to a fabulously modern kitchen.

Walls and ceilings pristine with fresh white distemper! A whole upstairs *and* a whole downstairs, and none of it shared with strangers! She wished her mother could have lived to see it.

Len was equally pleased. Of course, it was not heaven on earth. They had moved into an immense building site of half-constructed streets. There were no shops, no buses. For their groceries Maud must walk a mile, taking Elizabeth's old pushchair to bring the shopping home. And the party wall was thin. On the other side of it a man and woman shouted at each other and slapped screaming babies and toddlers.

As soon as any group of houses was habitable, new families arrived to occupy them. Most of the men were quickly taken on at the Ford motor factory in Dagenham, which was ready and waiting for them as car production expanded in step with the house building. Over the months, lawns were laid and gardens cultivated. Len covered the party wall with sound-proofing. A bus service started. A parade of shops was opened near the house. Maud noticed a few familiar faces from Manor Park. The noisy family next door emigrated to Australia on the ten-pound scheme. Len and Maud became friendly with Ernie and Babs Parkes, across the road. Ernie worked at Ford's and Babs at the new greengrocers. They enjoyed a drink and a laugh just as Len and Maud did.

As for Elizabeth, she had no thoughts about the move, except that it was certainly strange at first having a room of her own. Ernie and Babs' daughter Kate, the same age, became Elizabeth's closest companion. The two played on building sites, secretly mocked other children, discussed girlish fashions such as stirrup trousers, jested together and went to each other's houses for orange squash and jam sandwiches.

Len left the house every morning at six-thirty in his mackintosh, suit and tie, hatless in the modern style, with a sandwich in his briefcase. Ernie came out of his door at the same moment, his sandwich and pac-a-mac in a holdall on his bike. He too wore a suit and tie, with a cloth cap and bicycle clips. With cheery nod to one another, Ernie joined the stream bicycling towards Ford's while Len marched with the army of foot-soldiers to the tube station.

Life was good. Len continued at the boxing club and the works' darts team. Maud found a part-time job at a Co-op in the new parade, and a second part-time job playing piano for a ladies' Keep Fit club one evening a week. In the kitchen she kept a budgie in a cage for company, and called it Chippie. At the weekend Len and Maud laboured companionably in the garden. They gave a big Christmas party every year, jolly affairs with dancing, singing, screeching laughter and crates of beer like the good old times. They finally bought the three-piece suite Maud wanted, and a Ford Anglia car as well, and had enough left over for a fortnight on the south coast every summer.

Although the telegram was addressed to Elizabeth, the young man in a peaked hat handed it to Len. To receive a telegram at all was extraordinary but that it be brought to a caravan at a seaside holiday park in Bognor Regis gave it absurd importance. Her form teacher had sent the message. Len laughed with disbelief as he read and re-read the slip of paper with its laconic pasted-on text. In a puzzled whisper he announced, 'Blimey, who would've thought it? You've only gone and passed the Eleven Plus, Lizzie.'

4

At the start of the new term all the others moved on to the Secondary Modern. Elizabeth watched as they walked together each morning, larking about in their own clothes, while she stood alone at the bus stop in her painfully distinctive bottle green tunic dress, white shirt and school tie, blazer and correctly positioned beret. Some taunted her gently as they passed. Elizabeth stayed on the bus as far as Romford County High School.

She was the only one from her class. Her very best friend, Katie Parkes across the road, remained her very best friend and only confidante. Yet like Adam and Eve realising that they were naked, even they perceived a difference between them where none existed before.

The first thing Elizabeth learned at 'big' school was that she did not fit in there either. It took just a few minutes to see it. The other girls had more confidence, straighter teeth and better hair. Nicer skin, too. They spoke in a different way, moved in a different way and laughed in a different way. Gradually she discovered that none of their fathers worked at a printworks, nor at Ford's nor the Gas Works or the Forest Gate sweet factory or the Murex alloy makers, not even as managers or clerks. None of their mothers was a shop assistant. Slight, diffident, with her accent and NHS glasses, Elizabeth felt awkward at school and awkward at home.

Over in Emerson Park, Charles Victor Sleet was a spirited, sneering boy with a savage streak who had no desire to go to the boarding school chosen for him by his father. Nor did Dora want him to be sent away. She advised Micky, 'They'll learn him Latin an' Greek an' that, but the toffs'll see right through him. He'll be an outsider.'

'It's good to be an outsider. Gives you an angle,' Micky opined. But Charles made sure to fail the entrance examination. Micky's angry response was that the boy must be crammed with private lessons and sit the Eleven Plus. If he passed, he would be given a horse and riding lessons. If he failed, he would be given a whipping and his weekly allowance halved.

Charles replied that he did not want a horse, he wanted a drum kit. Nevertheless, scared of his father, he worked hard with his tutors. The cramming paid off and Charles took up a place at Romford's boys' grammar, the Royal Liberty School. Micky, grimly proud, rewarded him with a horse *and* a drum kit.

Before the end of his first year, the ungrateful Charles asked for a banjo as well. 'Banjo!' Micky was so disgusted he could spit. Dora suggested, 'What about a guitar?'

Charles said, 'The band's got a guitarist already.' It turned out the precocious Charles had started a skiffle group at his new school.

He did no homework, tormented his teachers, became one of the tearaways, the troublesome youths, jack the lad, amusing, disreputable, on the edge of being expelled, admired by the other boys for a rakish insolence. He too did not fit in with the rest.

Before the end of her first year, Elizabeth casually remarked that human reproduction and all about periods had been 'done' at school by the biology teacher. Maud was extremely pleased. She would not, after all, need to explain that (in the words of her own mother) a woman's body is a burden to her. She had been steeling herself to tackle the subject.

'She say about sex?' – 'She told us when a man loves you and you want to have a baby, it's called conception.'

'Oh Gawd. Did she tell you about being careful and not getting into trouble?' – 'Not exactly.'

'Did she tell you about the Urge?' – 'No, what's that?'

'Men's sex drive. That's the thing a girl does need to know.' – 'Oh.'

'I hope she told you about cramps and that?' – 'Not really.'

When it started, Elizabeth showed her mother the blood on her knickers. Maud hugged her daughter and gave her a packet of sanitary pads. She said, 'Hide them in your bedroom. Don't ever let Daddy find them.'

Elizabeth 'kept her head down' at school. She made a few friends. Every evening for four years, Elizabeth sat on the sofa doing her homework as Maud made tea in the kitchen with the radio chattering.

As 'O' levels approached, she started to take her homework to Romford Library. It was silent there, the atmosphere tranquil and studious.

*

In the fifth year, when many would soon be leaving school, the headmistress gave Savoir-Faire lessons. Introducing people to one another was role-played, how to hold a knife and fork, and a wine glass; how to stand up and sit down, and curtsey, and get in and out of a car without showing anything. Most of the other girls already knew these things.

The school's careers advisor asked each girl what type of jobs interested her. Elizabeth said the law. The advisor thought, in that case, the women's prison service might suit her. It was something you could do without 'A' levels. Elizabeth had no intention of becoming a prison officer. On the library shelves she discovered the weighty *Directory of Opportunities for School Leavers*. Teaching, nursing, the retail trade and social work, she read, were the four careers open to women. All four could be happily combined with being a wife and mother. There was other, simpler work for respectable girls, such as typing. She turned to the section on going to university. *Employers today are prepared to pay for qualified men. The opportunities for such men are many.*

It was not clear from the wording that women may also go to university. Elizabeth knew they could, because most of the school's teachers were graduates. The headmistress routinely swept along the corridors in her college gown. Elizabeth tried to find out if women had ever taken law degrees. It seemed that they had. She would like to be a lawyer. She was resolved not to be a prison officer, at any rate.

Still less did she have any intention of becoming an actress, though she loved amateur dramatics and always landed a role in the annual school play. She learned her lines, did not feel nervous on a stage and gave a convincing performance. It was the era of experimental productions, Shakespeare in modern dress, in modern language, fancy dress, undress; new interpretations of old themes; unexpected sets.

After the 'O' level exams, Elizabeth's name appeared on a list of pupils chosen to play in a joint production by fifth and sixth-formers of Romford County High and the Royal Liberty School. Elizabeth demanded that her name be removed. She said she did not want to act in front of the Royal Liberty pupils and parents. Her friends said she should: she would meet boys. Her English teacher said she should: it would develop her speaking skills. Her parents said she should: it was a step up in the world.

The play was *Whiteoaks*, by Mazo de la Roche. Elizabeth was cast as the cantankerous centenarian who wonders to whom she will leave her fortune. In the end the money goes to her rebellious grandson, Finch, played by one of the Royal Liberty's best actors, Charles Victor Sleet.

In the final weeks of term the two met often for rehearsals. Elizabeth knew a few boys, friends of friends, brothers of classmates. Occasionally she found herself chatted up and snogged at parties where drink and dope were on hand. But Elizabeth and her friends were serious and quiet. She liked thoughtful, intelligent boys. Charles Sleet and his crowd were the sort of 'idiots' she avoided. Yet something drew them together, as if there were an understanding. He became quieter and more serious in her company. She became more devil-may-care. And he was good at acting.

Charles said, 'You like am-dram and that, don't you?'

Elizabeth admitted that she did. 'I go to the National Theatre a lot,' she said.

'*Do* you?' He was full of eager questions. 'Where is it? What you seen?'

'It's called the Old Vic. You go to the Embankment and cross the river. I see practically everything at the Saturday afternoon matinées. I just saw a play by Peter Shaffer. It was fantastic.'

'Blimey, you're keen. Must cost you a packet!' – 'Not really. I work for a hairdresser on Saturday mornings, so I've got enough to go to the theatre in the afternoon.'

'You work for a hairdresser?' – 'Yeah, on the estate. She gives me ten bob to wash ladies' hair and take their curlers out.'

'Wow.' He looked at her open-mouthed. 'Can I come to the Old Vic with you next time? I'll treat you.' – 'All right.'

He asked, 'You ever go to the local theatre, you know, the rep?' – 'But there isn't a theatre in Romford, is there?'

'Not Romford. The Queen's Theatre in Hornchurch have a drama club for sixth-formers.' – 'Oh! You go to it?'

'No, but I will if you will.' – 'All right, then.'

The performance of *Whiteoaks* went well. Elizabeth's dark hair was permed and greyed with talcum powder. She dressed in a white cotton nightdress and bedroom slippers. Charles played in his normal persona as a vain, showy rocker with a silver-blond Elvis hairdo.

In the audience, Maud's attention was fixed on Elizabeth. She did not follow the story, had no opinion of the acting and hardly glanced at the boy. She had no interest in the cast list. Len noticed that the boy's name, as printed on the flyer, was C. V. Sleet. He folded the slip of paper away. He cast his gaze around and saw Micky and Dora at the back among the other parents. Of course he made no comment; Maud would be terribly upset if she saw him. Micky cut an impressive figure, though, a powerfully built man of late middle years in a black suit, strong and severe in bearing, with thin, strangely colourless hair somehow matching the rigidly inexpressive features of his face. Micky's eyes met his. There was a shake of the head. *Least said soonest mended*, seemed to be the message.

Micky was not proud of Charles's acting talent. He was frankly disgusted by the direction his son was taking. Acting! He had hoped for a smart lad who would take to manly pursuits. The Royal Liberty had a Combined Cadet Force with a military uniform and silver badge; that was more the sort of thing. Boxing was something he could have taken up. Instead, he liked music and acting! There was a horrible, effeminate quality to it all. For God's sake let his boy not be queer.

At the Queen's Theatre drama club a good-humoured company of actors taught stage-struck teenagers how to project voices, memorise lines, speak clearly and play a role. Afterwards, some of the youngsters stayed to drink coffee, talk and practise among themselves. Elizabeth and Charles moved away from the rest to the unlit back of the empty auditorium. Out of view, they chatted quietly and held hands and kissed on the lips.

There was certain amount of fondling, unbuttoning, reaching awkwardly inside clothing. It was thrilling and strange, secretive, intimate and intriguing. They fell rapidly into dizzying, heart-pounding obsession, excited to be near one another, look at one another, touch one another's hair, faces, hands, to taste the taste of a lover's mouth.

They began to 'go out together'. His friends knew she was his girlfriend. They embraced with long, long wet kisses on park benches and in bus stops. Even to themselves it seemed an odd match. Other than their love, they had so little in common.

Hours apart became an agony of looking forward eagerly to their next meeting. Yet all they did was kiss and talk, talk and kiss. They discussed teachers, school, friends, their favourite groups, the latest records. They talked about their 'O' level results. To the surprise of her teachers, Elizabeth had eight good passes. Charles scraped through five. Both would be moving up into the Sixth Form after the summer holidays. They talked about their families. Charles said he lived in Emerson Park.

'Oh! Are you rich?' – 'I don't know. Maybe.'

'What does your dad do?' – 'He's a businessman. He owns lots of companies and stuff, mostly property and leisure. What about you?'

'Dad's a printer and Mum works in a shop. We live on the Elm Park estate.'

'Oh! Are you poor, then?' – '*Poor?* No! They're both working! And Dad's got the best job of anyone in our road – I think. Mum only goes out to work so she can have some money of her own.' She had no idea if this was true.

'D'you want a ciggie?'– 'All right.' She pulled her first cigarette from his pack and he showed her how to inhale.

Into her ear, his lips in her hair, he whispered, 'I love you.' She held her breath. He said, 'You're special to me, Liz. More than anyone.' It was true, he thought about her all the time, wrote her name again and again on his exercise books. 'I love you too,' she whispered in return.

'Only with you am I the real me.' – 'That's how I feel, too.'

'I don't want no one else.' – 'Me neither,' she said.

'You're like a diamond that was hidden, the prettiest and most precious and most lovely priceless thing, and it was me that found you.' – She flushed, proud and embarrassed, a little breathless. 'That's lovely, Chaz.'

They clung in close embrace, mouths together for fully ten minutes, each tongue slowly caressing the other. When they parted he said, 'I want to give you a special treat, Liz. Did you see the Beatles at the ABC in March?' – 'No, it was a week night. My parents wouldn't let me.'

'The Beatles are coming back to Romford on the sixteenth. They'll be at the Odeon.' – 'I know.'

'Do you want to see them?' – 'No, well, the cheapest tickets are 5/6d.'

'Well, then, can I take you, Lizzie? We won't have cheap seats. We'll have the best.' – 'I must ask my parents.'

'They won't mind. It's on a Sunday, and we can go to the early show.' – 'I'll ask them.'

Over tea at the kitchen table, blushing and nervous, she said, 'A boy asked if he can take me to see the Beatles in Romford. Is it all right?' It was an important moment for Elizabeth. Until now she had managed to keep it from her parents that she had a steady boyfriend.

'Course it is!' Maud was pleased for her. The date and time were fine too. 'Who's the boy, anyone we know?'

'You don't know him. He goes to the Royal Liberty.'

'Oh, does he!' Maud was frankly delighted to hear it. Len, more wary, asked, 'What's he like, this boy?'

'Really, really nice. His family live in Emerson Park.'

'Oh!' Maud raised her eyebrows. 'Does he know where *you* live?'

'Yes. We've been seeing each other for a while.'

'Have you! Well, well, you dark horse!' smiled Maud. 'What's his name, dear?'

'Chaz. Or Charles. He was in the school play. That's how we met.'

'Charles what?' asked Len.

'Charles Sleet.'

Maud let out a shocking sound, a gasp of pain. At once she stood up and moved away from the table, grasped the sink for support. 'Ye Gods, are we never to be free of them!' With this, she ran from the kitchen. Elizabeth stared uncomprehending.

'Darling, we have a problem with that family,' said Len. 'You see how upset Mum is.'

The girl was almost indignant. 'What problem? He's *my* friend, not yours! You don't even know them.'

'Oh yes, we know the Sleets. They've been around for years.

They're no good. It'll make Mum ill if you see this boy.'

'Ill! Why?'

'Put on your coat, darling. You and me're going for a walk.'

'A *walk*? Now? I don't want to go for a walk, Dad!'

'Just round the block so we can talk in private. Put your coat on.'

They strode away from the house. He began. 'It goes back to the time of Mum's mother, Nan. Very, very bad things were done to Nan by...' it did not seem right to mention Charles Sleet's father by name, '...by the Sleet family. They're wicked people, evil, and I don't want you involved with them.'

'Wicked!' she scoffed. 'What bad things?'

'I'm not going to say it. Not until you're older.'

This made Elizabeth think he must be referring to rape. 'Come on, Dad, tell me. I'm not a child.'

He went on, 'When it happened, Mum arrived just in time to rescue Nan. Neither of them ever recovered. Mum still hasn't. She has nightmares about it.'

'What does that have to do with me and Chaz?' retorted Elizabeth heartlessly. Against her will she stopped walking and began to weep. 'What about the police?' she asked. 'Was it... was something done to Nan that's against the law?'

He stopped to face her, touched her arm with pity. 'Yes, seriously against the law. Sorry, pet, Mum can tell you more when you're older. You've seen the burn scars on her hands and legs. One day she'll tell you how she got them. But the police wouldn't help. No one was prosecuted. They were paid off by the Sleets. Hand in glove with them. Sometimes the cops and the robbers are on the same side, Liz. That's why if you carry on with the Sleet boy it'll break her heart. Listen, I want you to go home, make Mum a nice cup of tea and tell her you've thought things over and she doesn't have to worry. Everything will be all right. Now I have to phone someone. I'll be back in a tick.'

'I can't split up with him, Dad. I can't.'

'Do as I've said, Liz. Go home, now.'

Elizabeth tore away from him and ran back with tears of rage, all the way saying the name aloud to herself, 'Chaz, Chaz, Chaz, I love you, Chaz, Chaz, Chaz, I love you.'

Len walked to the phone box by the parade of shops. As it

happened, Charles himself answered the call. Len pressed Button A and asked for Micky. He next heard the raw croak of Dora. 'Micky's out. Who's that?'

'Hello, Mrs Sleet. Len Blake here. I must speak to him, it's urgent.'

'Why, what's up?'

'End this little romance between our kids or I'll tell them everything there is to tell about your husband. Some that even you don't know.'

'What romance?' She knew nothing about it. Dora was desperately afraid of anyone stirring memories of the old Micky, spreading tales of events she wanted forgotten. She asked, 'What does your girl know at the moment?'

'Nothing.'

Micky did not normally eat his breakfast with Charles and Dora. This morning he was waiting for them in the kitchen. 'Right, son,' he said, 'pack your bag.'

Dora remained tight-lipped. Last night she had given him Len's message. He spent over an hour on the phone before coming to bed without a word.

Charles thought he must have misheard or misunderstood. 'Pack my bag?' he grinned. 'What bag?'

'I want you to learn the business.'

'Dad, not now, I have to leave for school in a minute.'

'You ain't going to school no more, son. We've opened a new club in Liverpool. You'll do a spell behind the bar, then in the office. In September you go to college in Liverpool to learn business studies.'

'Dad, that's crazy. I'm not interested in business studies. I haven't applied to a college in Liverpool! Where would I live?'

'That's all sorted. I've got you a place at the college. We've a good man up there. He's goin'a teach you the ropes. He'll find you good digs. His missis will look after you.'

'Dad! What about my friends, my band?'

'Don't argue. Pack your bag.'

Charles was close to rage, close to tears of frustration. 'No, I'm not going.'

'Don't come it with me, son, or I'll knock your ruddy block off.'

'But… I've got a girlfriend here. I haven't told you about her.'

'Yeah, we know. The Blake girl. There's plenty o' smashing girls in

Liverpool, you'll see. I'm taking you up there this morning. Get cracking – we're leaving in half an hour.'

Early in the journey Micky warned Charles against trying to contact Elizabeth. 'It'll be the worse for you, an' for her. If you try to use friends to pass on a message, it'll be the worse for them.'

The one message that did get through was sent to the drama club: *My love, my dearest darling Liz, I have to stay up here a long time. I'm not allowed to write to you. Please don't look for me – it's dangerous. I think of you every minute of the day. I'll always love you, no one but you. Always just us forever. Chaz.*

It was disappointingly brief, and "up here" the unhelpful sole clue to where he was. On Sunday, after the drama club – which it was in any case pointless to attend without him – Elizabeth walked to the Sleet's house in Emerson Park to confront Charles's parents. 'Where is he?' she demanded in the hallway, 'Why can't I see him?'

'I'm sorry it has to be this way, dear,' said Dora with rare tenderness. 'Charles don't live here no more. He's gone away.' She truly felt sad for the innocent girl.

'Dad says I can't see Chaz because of bad things you did. What did you do?' A rather menacing figure in a black suit, Charles's father she supposed, stood in the long hallway behind, watching.

'Go home an' forget about us, dear. Bad things was done on both sides,' replied Dora, 'an' it's too late to put it right now.'

*

Elizabeth did not confide her misery even to Katie Parkes, since Katie had left school and had a proper job in a typing pool and a serious boyfriend of her own, and grown-up wages, and was indeed awfully grown-up. While she, Elizabeth, seemed to herself locked in interminable childhood, under the thumb of parents and teachers.

Maud could not quite understand why Charles had immediately vanished from the scene as if on cue. Len said it was a mercy that the boy had left the area, and certainly she agreed. It pained her though, dismayed her terribly, to see how Elizabeth became withdrawn.

Elizabeth did not find the right moment to ask her mother what exactly had been done to Nan, and by whom. In any case it did not matter anymore; nothing mattered anymore; the harm was done. Charles was gone, she did not know where, nor how to contact him.

She studied, never raised her hand in class, never went out with boys, never mentioned Charles. Nor did she watch television with her parents, staying in her room, wandering the entire canon of Victorian, Edwardian and 1920s literature, or lying on the bed listening to Radio Caroline and daydreaming of Charles's embrace before sleep.

Elizabeth had one hope. She returned to the careers advisor to ask which of the new universities would be best for a degree in Law. She had a notion that the new universities were being built especially for people like her. She was told, 'Forget about law. You need a lot of money to go into the law. In any case, male colleagues would make it impossible for you. They'd place obstacles in your path. Look, Elizabeth, face it, you're not a Helena Normanton or a Rose Heilbron. Apply for sociology. It's useful in the women's professions and you're more likely to get an offer.'

Whether that meant an offer of a university place or an offer of marriage Elizabeth did not ask. Presumably both. She went to the library to find out about Normanton and Heilbron, of whom she had never heard. It was an inspiration, especially, to read that Helena Normanton, the first woman barrister in Britain, was a working-class girl from Forest Gate. Just like herself! In fact, everything about both women was an inspiration.

*

Quite suddenly, parents, teachers and the bus to Romford were unimaginably remote and half-forgotten. The transformation occurred in an instant. Elizabeth could not remember it happening. She was not the only girl studying Law at University College London. Her tutor spent tutorials with an eye up their skirts, but he also offered his students glasses of sherry; or at lunchtime, chianti and slices of pizza made by his wife, none of which food or drink she had heard of before, together with worldly conversation and erudite good humour. Such sophistication she had never known. That she had been offered a place here astonished her constantly, just as it had astonished her teachers. In the busy, traffic-filled streets, in legendary Gower Street, in Tottenham Court Road, in Russell Square and Euston Road, she thrilled to the sublime thought *This is where I live!* She sat reading course books on the floor of Dillons bookshop, travelled strange worlds within the walls of the British Museum, ventured into the Greek grocer's in Goodge Street among its crates of unfamiliar produce. In soaring freedom she idled in the Georgian squares and gardens of Bloomsbury, each enclosed by terraces of tall houses, the long unbroken lines of their windows, balconies and railings perfectly exquisite, and everything glorious in the colours of Autumn Term. At one lofty dwelling she paused with fascination; for up these steps, behind this sturdy door, in the years of her triumph the great Helena Normanton had lived. No doubt she gazed out of these very windows, and indeed Elizabeth pictured her standing there, looking down.

The student grant was almost entirely used up by bed and board in the women's hall of residence. She made sure not to spend more than a shilling a day, preferably only sixpence. In the bedroom next door, her new friend Hilary was a Literature student from a family of Buckinghamshire gentry. Hilary was thrillingly eccentric and immensely sociable, habitually clothed in an iridescent green gown and elaborate hats adorned with feathers. Hilary was not constrained by a student grant. She invited countless friends and acquaintances and fellow students to her room for roasted coffee served from a percolator, or cups of maté or eclectic herb teas, but no drugs, which – it was part of her eccentricity – she emphatically opposed. Records were stacked on the Dansette and played all evening as, in Home Counties accents, politics and philosophy were argued with tremendous vehemence, Vietnam, the military-industrial complex, anarchism, ecology, pop art, women's liberation. *There can be no freedom while the State remains! Why can't we do what we dream of doing? We live all our lives without joy!* Amidst the febrile talk, liaisons and sleeping arrangements were made.

At the end of term Maud and Len came in the car to collect Elizabeth. Her attitude towards them had softened. She certainly did not forgive them for parting her from Charles. Even so, life had moved on. She showed them around, took them to see Jeremy Bentham, the clothed, padded relic sitting in its glass-fronted cabinet. 'That's not a waxwork,' she impressed on them, 'it's really him.' They were suitably disgusted.

Nothing could be stranger than hearing her father call for help. At the start of that first vacation it happened. On Saturday mornings Maud would take Len a cup of tea in bed before she left for work at the Co-op. He would then read in bed until half-past eight or even nine o'clock. On this morning, as usual, Maud brought his cup of tea and went out to work, slamming the door behind her.

At half past eight this morning he called out, 'Lizzie! Quickly.'

Elizabeth went into her parents' bedroom. Len was sitting on the side of the bed in his pyjamas. He said, 'Get the doctor.' He did not seem unwell.

'Why, what's the matter, Dad?'

'Doctor,' he repeated.

She ran a couple of streets to the surgery, which was also the doctor's home. He returned with her at a brisk pace. After just a few moments with Len, the doctor asked Elizabeth to call an ambulance. 'And get your mother to come home.' Elizabeth ran again, to neighbours who had a phone.

Maud and Elizabeth travelled with him in the ambulance, Len awake and saying nothing. He held Maud's hand as the bell rang crazily through the streets to Oldchurch Hospital in Romford. On the way he fell into a deep sleep. He was wheeled unconscious into Accident and Emergency. Curiously, considering the haste to bring him, nothing was done when he arrived. A nurse said calmly, 'Come back tomorrow at visiting time.' For such was the rule.

From a pay-phone in the hospital corridor Maud called Len's mother and sister. The following afternoon at the start of visiting time they all arrived together – Len's mother and sister, wife and daughter. By then, he was already dead.

'I'm sorry,' said the nurse, 'he died during the operation.'

Len's sister Audrey alone reacted. 'Don't care a jot, do you?' She threw her handbag at the nurse and shouted, 'It's not fair.' The other three women looked at her startled. The nurse handed the bag back and said, 'He had a brain haemorrhage. I'm sure the doctors did their best.'

In her shock Maud remained composed. She said, 'May I see him?' The nurse shook her head, 'You won't want to, after the operation. Better to remember him as he was.'

As people do, with controlled calm Maud dealt with every formality.

She sat on the bus to Romford, registered the death, enquired about probate. Mindful that his wages would end next week she phoned Len's place of work to ask about his pension. She arranged the funeral for two weeks later at Manor Park Crematorium, close to Woodgrange cemetery where her parents were buried. She placed an announcement in the Romford Recorder and East London Advertiser.

Len Blake had been a popular sight locally, his tall, spruce figure marching to and from the tube station each weekday. He was respected for working industriously on his house and garden at weekends. He was an admirably fit man, laconic, always helpful. The suddenness of the death shocked the street. Half a dozen neighbours joined the family in procession to the crematorium. Ernie and Babs Parkes, with Katie, were among them. Katie embraced Elizabeth with heartfelt commiseration, and on the instant their old friendship was reawakened. Katie said she was married now and living in Grays, further along the Thames estuary. She gave her phone number. 'Call me,' she said. With a simple nod Elizabeth showed that she would. Even Len's workmates were given time off to attend. Isaac Zuckerman came along too, with his son, Jacob.

Maud shook Isaac's hand, their grasp lingering. 'Hello, Yitzy. Thank you for coming. How did you hear?' It had not occurred to her to inform him after all these years. She should have, she realised, for old times' sake.

Isaac had seen the notice in the paper. 'We only meet at funerals, it seems. I'm so sorry, Maud. He was no age. It's such a shock. He seemed so fit and well lately.'

The remark surprised her. It sounded as though Yitzy and Len knew one another and had recently been in touch. She did not understand how it could be so. He handed her a card of sympathy from his parents. She asked, 'How are they?'

'Pretty good, considering.'

She introduced Elizabeth, who was not in a mood for pleasantry with strangers. He in his turn introduced Jacob, who politely offered condolences. Jacob was slim and slight, a couple of inches taller than his father, with dark curling hair tumbling attractively over his collar.

Isaac said, 'I always liked Len. One of our fans in the old days, at that pub in Aldgate. Before the war, remember?' – 'Oh yes, that's where I first saw him. Seems like another lifetime. Izzie on clarinet,

Miss Maud at the piano.' She smiled sadly at the recollection.

Elizabeth had not known that her mother played gigs in an East End pub. It seemed impossible.

Jacob was scrutinising her. He said, 'Hey, aren't you at UCL?' He told her he was doing Politics and Economics there. 'I've seen you in the Union building.' They stepped away from the others.

Elizabeth replied that she was studying Law. 'Not sure if I'm going back. I can't leave Mum on her own.'

'I expect your father would have wanted you to carry on.'

Suddenly they heard Maud's raised voice, indignant and fearful. 'What's *he* doing here? Come to spoil everything.'

Elizabeth was astonished to recognise Micky Sleet, whom she remembered from her visit to Charles's house. He wore a black suit with medals displayed. The big man seemed unwell, gaunt and pale. She could see her mother was scared of him.

Yet Micky addressed Maud quietly: 'My condolences, Missis.' He turned to shake Isaac's hand. 'Hello, Zuckerman.'

Isaac explained, 'Mr Sleet is one of my clients.' It was another perplexing surprise for Maud.

'Why have you come?' Maud challenged him.

'To show my respects. Blake was my sergeant in the war. I need to make sure the old bugger really is dead an' buried. Ah no, not buried,' with a short chuckle, 'ashes to ashes in this place, ain' it?'

Elizabeth was yet more amazed. Her father had been in the army with Chaz's father!

'You're not welcome,' retorted Maud.

Micky leaned forward and urged her to listen. He murmured, 'Don't know if he ever told you. I made a deal with your husband. I promised him protection for you an' the girl as long as you live. That stands even now he's gone.'

'I don't want anything from you, Sleet.' A deal! Her husband certainly could keep things to himself!

'Makes no difference what you want. This is between me an' him. Anyway, I'm not long for this world myself.'

'How so?'

'Doctors give me six months. It's cancer.'

'Good.'

'Careful, Missis,' Micky grinned, 'I'm not gone quite yet.'

5

Maud sat on the sofa turning the pages of Woman's Weekly, not reading. She switched between television channels, not watching, not listening. It did cross her mind that she was being taught about the loneliness of her own mother. Punished, even, for not caring about it. Her mother had to manage without a TV for company. All widows grieve; she had not understood before how bad it is. There was also the feeling of unfairness – she had married late and been widowed early. Spending every evening on her own, she definitely did not like that. Still, plenty of others had it just as bad, or worse. Like her mother.

The most soothing thing, she found, was gardening. She would announce to the budgie, 'Well, let's just go and do something in the garden, shall we, Chippie?' The cheeky creature cocked its head to listen when she spoke, squawked and whistled its agreement and pecked at its reflection in a little mirror. The budgerigar was, she sometimes felt, her only friend, sticking by her through thick and thin. She wondered if the bird missed Len.

To cap it all, within the year the dear little thing itself died. There was no warning. Maud came downstairs as usual, put on the kettle and uncovered the birdcage. The creature lay motionless, as endearing and colourful as in life. She opened the cage door and touched gently with a fingertip. 'Oh, darling, not you as well!' Her beloved pet had become an inanimate object.

She went out to the garden shed, took a trowel and dug a hole. Into it she laid the tiny corpse with sorrow and solemnity. There seemed to be nothing appropriate to say. She said, 'Dear, good Chippie. You've been a lovely friend. I hope they have budgies in Heaven,' and with the trowel filled the hole with earth.

She did miss the little bird; he had been someone to talk to. She went full-time at the Co-op, serving and stacking. Frankly she loved the job, chatting with the other girls. As for the rest, well, she must get used to it. In case of another emergency, she had a telephone installed in the front hall. The instrument stood on a cabinet with the four London directories inside. One of the first to call her was Dora Sleet.

Dora's plan now, as soon as Micky's cancer had carried him off, was to sever every link with those who knew his past, including Maud Blake. She must tie every loose end and free young Charles entirely from that history.

'Hello, Mrs Blake. Got your number from the operator. Can I ask, d'you happen to know where Terry's gun went? Terry, my brother-in-law.'

'That the bloke came to kill my mother?'

'Yeah, but like I told you, it weren't us sent him. He come off his own bat. You got his gun?'

'It was in my husband's locker at the boxing club. They've give it me in a cardboard box, still in the paper bag where he put it. You want it?'

'Yeah, soon as you like.'

'What'll you give me for it?'

'Ha ha!' Dora's throaty chuckle came down the line. 'You're quick! How much d'you think it's worth?'

Maud regretted asking. The thought of haggling with the Sleets sickened her. She wanted nothing to do with them. 'No, on second thoughts, you can have it. I'll bring it to you somewhere. Let's just draw a line, shall we?'

*

'Miss Blake?' A rap at the door and the warden's voice. 'Visitor downstairs.' Elizabeth wiped her face with a towel and ran a brush through her hair. Lost in a fog of depression, as if weighted by burdens too heavy to lift, she found a way to struggle from morning to night and from night to morning.

Elizabeth had not been to any of Hilary's gatherings this term. Through the wall she heard laughter and debate, The Who, Dylan, Jimi Hendrix, *Strawberry Fields, A Whiter Shade of Pale*. 'Sorry, Hil,' she would say, 'essay to write.' Nor to the Dramatic Society, nor Monday night jazz in the Union. Hilary hugged her and tended to her with kindness, brought nettle tea and oat biscuits.

The visitor downstairs was someone she recognised from her father's funeral, a fellow student. The last thing Elizabeth wanted was to be 'pursued'. She could not deal right now with the fancies of a young man. He had a tender, kind look about him. The dark, loosely curled hair was longer than before, a cascade. He was in open-neck shirt, sloppy summer trousers, scuffed suede shoes. He said, 'Hiya, Liz. Jake Zuckerman.'

'Oh yeah. Hi.'

'You OK?'

'Yeah, yeah. Jacob, please, you don't have to worry about me.'

'It's Jake. Feel like a walk? It's nice out.'

'Not really. Where?'

'Nowhere. Maybe just down to Russell Square.' He studied her weary face. 'Come on.'

Jake's cheerful insistence appealed to her somehow. Elizabeth stepped out of the women's hall into the street. He was right, it was a beautiful day, the air silky and fresh, the sky milky blue. She felt unmoved by it, perfectly willing to return to her room and be left in peace.

'Look!' He persuaded her to notice how sunlight caught the Georgian façades, how it accentuated their neat lines. The sight rather surprised her. The whole street had been built as a single harmonious work.

They walked, not fast, from one green space to the next, Gordon Square and Woburn Square, Russell Square. There they paused, but did not turn back. The trees were in full leaf now, groups of students lounging on the grass in the shade. Elizabeth admitted to Jake that she was finding life difficult. 'I'm upset about my dad.'

'Ah, yes, you must be. But you're doing your reading, your essays?'

'I don't know. I feel a sort of panic at the thought of it. At the thought of everything, actually.'

'Have you talked to the women's tutor?' he asked.

'I don't want to be offered counselling. If people are unhappy they should go to their room and cry.'

'Is that what you do?'

She replied with a shrug. 'Yeah, maybe. My neighbour Hilary is good to me, anyway.'

'Really Liz, go to the doctor. They'll give you something.'

'What, advice?' They passed through the British Museum with not a glance at the cabinets of foreign treasures arrayed around airy halls. Outside again, Elizabeth said, 'Let's go this way,' and led Jake to an unremarkable red-brick factory building in Long Acre. High across the front wall *Engraving* was painted in faded white letters. 'Here's where Dad worked. He spent more time here than with us.'

'Probably not a choice he could make.'

'No, he loved it here, camaraderie, workmates. He was a Union official, and captain of the works darts team. This was his world.' Suddenly her eyes were wet, but she dried them at once with quick fingertips. 'I wanted to make him proud of me, and now he never will be.'

Jake protested gently, 'I'm sure he was proud of you, Liz. And your mum, she must be proud.'

'No, I picture him how it would have been on graduation day. Mum doesn't get it, what a university is. She literally only learned the three Rs and sewing. Nothing else. I think Dad kind of understood.'

'How's your mother coping?'

'Seems OK,' Elizabeth answered indifferently. 'She's got a full-time job. Gets on with things, never complains.'

'No, well, they don't, do they, that generation?' They skirted a series of Covent Garden yards stacked with wooden crates and boxes, kerbsides littered with cabbage leaves, straw and paper wrappings, discarded fruit that they agreed looked quite edible. However, they did not bend down to sample any, for in every breath was the market's cloying pungency, its scent of rot and fermentation.

Newspaper vendors were clipping up the afternoon billboards. *"Act of War"*, read one, in quotes. They announced in large capitals that Egypt had closed the Suez Canal to Israel. Jake said nothing; he guessed Elizabeth had no interest in the matter.

He offered her a cigarette and lit it from his own, which she felt as a most intimate gesture. *Did* he fancy her? There's usually something of that with boys.

'Jake,' she asked, 'why did you come to see me?'

'Dad asked me how you were. He always says your family did so much for our family years ago. Saved their lives, he says. I think he means when his parents arrived from Russia.'

'Saved their lives! I don't know anything about that.'

Reaching the wide Thames they peered over the embankment wall and contemplated the bright view before them, a new concert hall on the other side, small ships moored, old brick warehouses, the OXO Tower, the Houses of Parliament away to the right. To Elizabeth the scene was suddenly magically alive, overwhelming – a counterpoint of mundane and majestic, ineffably wonderful. Two barges passed in mid-stream, seemingly harmonised. A corps of pigeons turned gracefully, wings raised. An exquisite breeze blew over the swirling grey water and touched her hair.

Quite suddenly she began to cry. Jake was shocked, completely unprepared. He touched her arm helplessly, as far as he dare go in offering comfort. 'Liz...'

She turned and grasped him, and rested her head upon him. 'Sorry.'

'No. It's fine. Let's sit.' And he led her to a bench under the plane trees. He said, 'Tell me anything.'

'Nothing to say. But just because I was really angry with Dad, that didn't mean I wanted him to die.'

Jake absorbed this odd confession. 'No, of course!' He wanted to comfort her and show tenderness. 'You know, Liz, even if you *had* wanted him to die, you did not kill him. His death is not your fault.'

'I do know that, Jake. Not everything in the human mind is rational.'

'What happened? Why were you angry?'

'There's a guy, and I really, really love him. My parents didn't approve. My dad and his dad got together to break it up. He was literally sent away, I think it was up North somewhere. No one will even tell me where. Haven't seen or heard of him since.'

'Bloody hell. Why? Who is he?'

'I'd better not say. He's from Romford, used to go to the Royal Liberty. It might be someone you know.'

Jake accepted this with a sympathetic move of the head. 'I don't know anyone that's gone away.'

'I don't want to talk about it.'

'That's fine, I understand.' They sat in grim silence until he suggested, 'Feel like a cup of tea?'

She said, 'I could murder a cup of tea. Thank you for bringing me, and listening to me.' At the tea stall outside Charing Cross station a poster supporting Israel was being pinned up. Elizabeth asked, 'What will happen?'

It appeared she was interested after all. He replied, 'A miracle is the only thing that can save us.'

'You don't believe in miracles, do you? Are you religious?'

'*Believe* in them? No!' he laughed. 'Not religious at all! But the Jews have *always* depended on miracles. That's our whole story. Miracles are our secret weapon. Maybe the only weapon in our armoury.'

She smiled, unsure if what he said was irony or jest. She said, 'Well, that sounds pretty religious to me!'

With twinkling eye he assured her it was not. They stood in the narrow street holding cheese rolls and mugs of tea. She appeared to be in a better mood. 'What did you say you were studying?'

He reminded her, 'Politics and Economics. I'm hoping to go into politics. As an advisor or a strategist, maybe with a think tank if I can. What about you,' he asked, 'want to be a lawyer, right?'

'Barrister. That *was* the plan. Not sure now.'

'Where you going to live in second year?'

'Might be dead by then.'

'Me and my girlfriend, and some friends, we'll be sharing a short-let house in Camden.'

'Oh, you've got a girlfriend!'

'Yeah, Abi Klein, doing History. Come in with us, if you like. It's only about a pound a week.'

'OK then.'

*

The crowd at Speakers' Corner on Saturday March 6th, already huge and more arriving, was almost entirely female – women young and old, in thousands, dozens of banners and placards raised. A few men stood among them, presumed supporters of the women's cause. Though springtime, it was wintry cold, a day of woolly hats, thick sweaters and scarves, jeans, gloves and duffle coats. Elizabeth arrived with Abi and Jake. The three had become close friends. During her two terms on Valium, with Jake's help and encouragement Elizabeth had returned to her course work, started seeing people again, joined the marches and demonstrations, went to parties and gigs. They stood waiting by the park gate, where Jake had arranged to meet an old schoolfriend.

Abi and Elizabeth looked around in awe. 'Have you ever felt, do you ever feel,' wondered Abi, 'that until now women have been nothing but spectators in this world? Men are everywhere, we're nowhere. Everywhere men's faces, not women's; men's voices, not women's. Doing things, pontificating, giving instructions. Like they're the players and we're the reserve. We have our "womens' work" to get on with, serving and smiling and being skivvies. Am I exaggerating? It was men they sent to the moon, not women – *obviously*. Judges, doctors, politicians, priests – that's them too. The people driving trucks, delivering mail, mending leaks, fighting wars, reading the news – that's them. We're on the sidelines. Do you have that feeling, Liz?'

She nodded. 'It's no exaggeration. Women can be bus conductors, I suppose. Never in the driving seat.'

'Yes, it seems women may conduct buses, but not orchestras. I want to see women's faces! In politics, in sport, in everyday life, everywhere. And conducting orchestras.'

Elizabeth agreed most ardently. 'But do you ever ask yourself if there *are* things... to help the species survive, a natural division of labour? I mean, are men and women so different *for a reason*?'

'Let's give everyone an equal chance and find out.'

The great and good of the Labour movement were preaching through crackling loudspeakers, their message hackneyed and inappropriate. Stationed around the edges of the gathering stolid men of the far-left offered leaflets and journals. There was the usual chanting, *What do we want...When do we want it*. But this time it was different, intoxicating, no mere protest, no ordinary demonstration, no simple march. Nor could this be decided at the ballot box.

Banners displayed the names of countless *women's* groups. There was a refreshing freedom from femininity, a black humour in the melée, witty banners that spoke of unfunny reality. One woman had built a small prison around herself and moved about thus encumbered. A lofty makeshift crucifix held high was hung with a headless female torso – a dressmakers' dummy – a Woman of Sorrows with wifely instruments of subjugation: underwear, housework gloves, shopping bag, apron.

Jake's friend arrived, skinny and alert as an alleycat, hippie-looking with a mighty cascade of dark brown hair and a long red beard, a vividly embroidered Afghan coat and threads of glass beads twined around his throat and wrist. Jake introduced him to Elizabeth, and her to him, as 'another lawyer'. She thought he looked an improbable legal adviser. The shifting crowd began leaving Speakers' Corner towards Oxford Street. Now that they were on the move, Elizabeth found herself alongside Jake's friend. 'What was your name again?' she asked.

'Bernard – Bernard Kassin.' He was talkative and smiling. He told her without being asked that he had returned from India and was sharing a squat in Hackney. He talked of an ashram, a beach, a commune.

'Are you *really* a lawyer?' she asked, doubtful.

He chuckled at her scepticism. 'Yup, BA Jurisprudence. Did my articles at the new Law Centre in East London. You know about Law Centres? Free advice and legal work for the local community.'

'Yeah, I heard about them. Sounds great.' As for herself, she said she was saving for the barristers' vocational training, bar school. 'I can't save enough. I have to rob a bank or something.'

'Well, if you get caught, give me a call. So, do you think men should be on this march,' he charged straight in, 'or should it be women only?'

'It's nothing to do with what sex you are! Plenty of men fought for women's equality, and plenty of women opposed it. Why are *you* on it?'

'Because I hate to see anyone disadvantaged, or taken advantage of. Men have been taking advantage of women since the year dot.'

'I think lots of men took part in the Women's Strike for Equality in New York last year, didn't they?'

'So they should. After all,' he argued, 'it's not *women's* equality, is it? If people are equal, they're *all* equal, right? That's maths. It's common sense. On the other hand, *are* men and women equal? Are any two people equal? Human beings are not congruent triangles.' He spoke eagerly, smiling with the somewhat fervid pleasure of discussion. 'Equality's been bandied around for centuries about like a great big nothing – it doesn't mean anything at all. It's *liberty* I march for.' He was emphatic, expansive. 'Liberty for all! Liberté, egalité, sororité. Equal pay – that's nothing, a given.'

She wished he would remain sensible and serious. 'Let's have equal pay and take it from there. What's needed is legislation. You're not against a few laws, are you? You're a lawyer!'

He laughed, scornful. 'I see my role as *defending* people from the law! Liberation is *not* about law, is it? How could it be? The people will not be granted freedom, they must free themselves. *Everything* must be different, at work, at home, in the courtroom, in the bedroom, in the mind. You can't legislate what people think.'

'When we have equal pay everything *will* be different.'

And so they continued. In spite of herself she started to enjoy this friendly parrying with Jake's friend. She liked him. The weather became bitingly cold, and the mocking looks from the pavement of Oxford Street were nearly as icy. It even began unseasonably to snow, and the road quickly whitened as Elizabeth called out to bystanders, 'Join us, join us.'

A woman called back, 'When hell freezes over.' But on an impulse she stepped into the march alongside them. 'Votes for women!' she yelled comically.

Elizabeth clapped with delight. *Finally,* she thought, *Hell is freezing over.*

*

With a shopping bag slung from one shoulder, Elizabeth sauntered unhurried through crowded, sweltering Camden towards the street market. Almost before she knew it her hand had darted out to grab the sleeve of a young man as he passed. 'Chaz? You!'

He turned, thrilled and incredulous. 'Lizzie?'

Despite the novelty of a moustache, it really was him! If she had been a few seconds earlier or later, or on the other side of the road, they might have missed each other.

There on the pavement they kissed in a long, longing embrace. They made an unlikely couple. Elizabeth's dark hair hung down below her shoulders. Petite and slender, she was in a light-as-air batiked smock over a loose, ankle-length cotton skirt, Indian sandals on her feet. Her face had a fresh, natural bloom, without colouring or cosmetics; her eyes too were bright and fresh. Charles had become a powerfully built young man with strikingly fair hair flicked charmingly over his eyebrows, his cheeks, his collar. He wore a smart suit of sorts, the jacket tight with wide lapels, the trousers revealingly tight (though flaring wide below the knee over chelsea boots). A tight pink shirt was likewise wide collared, with a kipper tie. As their lips parted she asked, 'Not married or something, are you?' – 'No! You?' – 'No.' They laughed with relief.

He gazed in wonder. 'Wow, look at *you* – you've changed. You a women's libber?' He pointed at her badge.

She cheerfully admitted it. 'And *you*, Chaz! So *straight!*' She was gleeful. 'What are you doing here?'

'I had a meeting with council planning officers. Just going back to my car.'

'You've got a car now, of course! Planning officers! What was the meeting about?'

'I presented a proposal for a warehouse at Camden Lock. There's a terrific space we could use.'

'What did they say?'

'No go. Camden Lock is due to be demolished. There's a new motorway coming through, the Inner London Box. Did you know?'

Elizabeth did not know the details. She understood that her own address was in a street of perfectly good houses scheduled for demolition. He said, 'Yeah, the whole area will be flattened. *You* don't live round here, do you?'

'Yes! Just up the road. It's a shared place, short-let community housing. Come round now. You might know one of the guys – Jake Zuckerman. His dad is your accountant or something.'

'You're *living* with Mr Zuckerman's son?'

'No, not like that! Sharing. Jake's got a girlfriend. Where have you been, Chaz? Were you up North?'

'Liverpool.' Charles said he was back in London now, in his own flat. 'I heard you were away at university.'

'No, I was in London the whole time, at University College. I've got my law degree, Chaz! I'm saving up for the professional training, "bar school", they call it, to be a barrister.'

'Wow! Do they let hippie chicks become barristers?' Charles grinned.

'I'm not a hippie! I haven't dropped out. I'm trying to drop in!'

'You going to wear one of them wigs on top of your hair?'

'Not at this rate,' she grimaced. 'I can't start bar school till I've saved enough. It's not only the course itself. You need a stash to cover food and rent for a couple of years, and the smart clothes. The way it's going, I'll never make it.'

'You're working, though, you've got a job?'

'Evening barmaid at a pub, modelling for an art college, proof-reading for a publisher, gardening, house cleaning, whatever. I can't save enough. I need at least a thousand pounds.'

'You'll never make it like that, doing bits and pieces.'

'Oh, that's just the start. When you become a barrister you have to rent your place in chambers before you have any income to pay for it. You need cash in the bank.'

Charles did not want to go to her house. 'Let's go somewhere and talk.'

They sat on the grassy crown of Parliament Hill on Hampstead Heath. Around them groups of young people sprawled passing joints from hand to hand, lips to lips. In the distance someone played a saxophone. Couples embraced on the ground. Charles had not been here before. He marvelled at the vista across London. The elegant dome of St Paul's Cathedral he found with ease, uncertainly picking out landmarks south of the river and to the east.

'Maybe you can work and study at the same time,' he suggested.

'Not with the Law, Chaz. The training takes too much time. Until the war all barristers were gentlemen. I mean *proper* gents – gentry.' She explained the arcane world of the Bar that she had yet to penetrate, the four historic Inns of Court, the twelve formal dinners, finding chambers in which to pass twelve months under a pupil master. She did not mention every difficulty – for example that (in those days) pupil masters might demand a hundred guineas or more to take on a pupil. She did not want to bore him with details.

'After the war,' she said, 'along came the Eleven Plus and GCEs. At last ordinary kids could go to university and get law degrees. Rough boys and girls from the Essex marshes rising up like noxious airs in the nostrils of those gents. But gents have a clever weapon to keep ordinary kids away, called pounds, shillings and pence. Without plenty of that you can't beat them nor join them.'

'Funny to think,' Charles reflected, 'if it wasn't for the war there probably would'a been no Labour government, no Eleven Plus, no baby boom, no us. What would it be like if there had been no Adolf Hitler? It's the old unforeseen consequences.'

'And if it wasn't for the *First* World War, would there even have been a girls' grammar school for me to go to?'

'Well, there was, and we'll find a way to do this, Liz,' Charles assured her. 'I'd give you a job at Sleet Properties, except my mother wouldn't allow it. She doesn't want us to see each other. I can find you something cash-in-hand in one of the clubs, if you don't mind that sort of work. It's casual but the money's good. She wouldn't have to know.'

'Is she the boss?'

'Till I'm twenty-eight. I can take over then, but only if she approves. Any case, it's her has all the contacts. Trouble is, she won't seize new opportunities.'

'Like what?'

'She wants to push up rents. The colour bar has been good for us, see. Housing that our people thought wasn't good enough, migrants are crying out for. Can't get anything else, see? I want to get rid of all that property and go into student housing, purpose-built. All these new universities and not enough decent places for students to live! But Mum says no. And snooker halls and strip joints, that's finished. I want to turn them into music places, discos, dance clubs. People want to dance, right?'

'I suppose.' She smiled at his eagerness. 'Still prefer a good play, myself.'

'Ha! Choose a play, then, and I'll take you. Anyway, when you grow up it's all play-acting, isn't it? Dress up and say your lines. No one knows who anyone is under the make-up and the costume.'

She loved him for thinking of that. She said, 'Don't find me a job, Chaz. It would kill my mother if she ever found out I was working for the Sleets.'

Charles stared into the hazy distance over the city. The humid air was preparing a downpour. The saxophonist had finished playing. 'Look,' he said eventually, 'why don't I just *give* you what you need? I can let you have a grand soon as you like. No strings.'

She gave a small laugh and shook her head. 'No! Not really, Chaz.' He must realise, she thought, that it was impossible. 'Because,' she hesitated, hopeful that he would understand, 'I'd be in your debt, wouldn't I? Not being funny, Chaz, but I'd be under an obligation. I do love you, but I don't want to be trapped in a situation.'

'This is *us,* you and me, Liz! We're already in a situation. We're going to be in it forever. Anything I give you, it's to make up for past wrongs, whatever they were.'

Charles's flat was in an old-fashioned West End mansion block two streets north of Oxford Street. With heart beating hard Elizabeth reached an ornate entrance. *How strange that he was so close to me all this time*. It felt unreal to press a buzzer and step inside. A 'cage' lift creaked up two floors with maddening lack of haste.

At the top, there stood Charles, waiting, smiling, gaudily bright in close-fitting tee shirt and loons. As soon as his door clicked shut behind them, they embraced and kissed, excited by privacy and secrecy and freedom. He led her along a corridor to a large sitting room.

'Wow, the rent on this must be costing you a packet.'

'No, it's all mine. Come and look round.' Charles's flat had clearly been grand a long time ago, the fittings still stylish, the mahogany and upholstery a little battered. He had proper things, real things of his own, a double bed with clean sheets and blankets, a wardrobe hung with suits and shirts, a complete set of crockery, matching towels, even a cocktail cabinet containing bottles of whisky and gin and a soda syphon. Her own possessions give or take a dozen law books, would fit into a few carrier bags, her bed was a foam mattress on the floor under Indian bedspreads. A bottle of spirits was something she had never owned. He seemed terribly grown up in her eyes, and she not at all.

But this moustached man, this fashionable man, he was Charles, she reminded herself, her darling Chaz. He reached to the back of the drinks cabinet and drew out a tightly folded square of silver foil. He said, 'Liz, there's something I need to tell you.' – 'What?'

'About not being married.' He opened the foil; inside was a dark fragment. He began preparing a joint. – She laughed, 'Don't say you are married, after all!'

'Not married, love, but engaged. And it's, like, all settled.' – 'Fuck. Who to? D'you love her?'

He grimaced, shrugged. 'Look, Liz, I didn't know you and me would ever meet again, did I? Her name's Nicola Meyrick. She's at Sussex Uni. The wedding's straight after she graduates.'

Elizabeth repeated the name. 'Nicola Meyrick. Does she come here, have sex in that bed with you?'

'Yeah, well, it's either that or do it on the floor. Doesn't mean I love her the way I love you.'

'Can't you break off the engagement?'

'That would be scary. A lot's riding on it. It's business. You know Meyrick Construction, the building firm? Bob Meyrick is Nic's dad. It's all arranged between my mum and her family. They would kill me. Skin me alive.'

She laughed again, unamused. 'Not literally, I hope.'

'You never know.' He gave an anxious chuckle. 'Don't worry, Liz, whatever happens you and me will still see each other. This is what's real – you and me. It'll be our thing. We'll keep it to ourselves. It'll always be just us.' He finished rolling a joint, lit it, inhaled deeply and handed it to her. At last he breathed out. 'You on the pill, Liz?'

'Yep.'

'Not a virgin or anything, are you?'

She laughed. 'No!' She recalled the various occasions at university, odd, barely credible couplings, not especially pleasant, rather messy and surprisingly brief. She prepared herself to do something similar with Charles Sleet.

It turned out to be incomparably different with him. There was no haste. There was exquisite tenderness. There was affection and sheer joy. In body and mind, heart and soul, she felt fulfilled – happy and in love.

'Don't tell anyone,' he said, 'like Zuckerman or someone, in case it gets back.'

*

Six stops on the Northern, seven on the Central, and twelve stations above ground on the District Line. The journey to Elm Park usually took about two hours. Elizabeth always made sure to have a book with her. The pages lay open as she debated inwardly what to tell her mother about Charles's offer, or whether to tell her at all.

They passed the evening with supper on their laps, the television monopolising the room. Maud adored variety shows, a slick compère, a perfect chorus line, a breathtaking magician or juggling act, a madcap comedy routine. Her favourite programmes were *Come Dancing, Sunday Night at the London Palladium* and *The Black and White Minstrel Show*. Elizabeth found all three crushingly boring. She hated the minstrels. 'How can you watch this, Mum?'

'Don't you like it? They're very talented. I'll turn it off if you like. There's *Benny Hill* on the other side.'

'No, it's OK.' Elizabeth made no mention of Charles.

As it happened, in the morning Maud opened the subject herself. 'I had the most awful dream last night, or nightmare, rather.' This was a surprise, as Elizabeth believed her mother was not the type to remember dreams, let alone discuss them. 'Oh dear. What about?'

'It was about that man Sleet.' It did not occur to Elizabeth that her mother was not referring to Charles or Micky. 'You and me and Dad are here, in this house. We've locked the front door and windows. Only we forgot the back. Suddenly Sleet and his son come charging in the back door.'

'His son?' Elizabeth sat riveted. What horrible, bizarre fantasy was this? 'What happened?'

'So we've run upstairs for dear life and the two men have set the downstairs alight. They make a bonfire of our precious things. I lose sight of you and Dad in the smoke, and you don't answer when I call. So I'm roasting and choking, and woke up scared out of my wits.' Maud grimaced with embarrassment. It was the first time she had ever told anyone of her nightmares, other than Len.

'Blimey, Mum, that's awful. I wonder what it means.'

'Probably I was too hot in the night.'

'But it's incredible, because I met Charles Sleet in the street only the other day.'

'Oh no, you never, did you? Don't still have feelings for him, do you, love?'

Elizabeth saw that her mother was repelled by the thought. 'No, no, don't worry about that, Mum. Only I told him I'm saving up for bar school, and you know what? He said he'd give me a grand towards it.'

'My God! Don't take it, love. Don't take anything from them, darling. He'll want something in return.'

'He said it's to make up for past wrongs.'

Maud retorted with spitting scorn, 'A grand! He doesn't know what he's talking about.'

'But Mum, I want to get on with becoming a barrister. I need the money.'

'I wanted to be a milliner, pet. Only my mother, Nan, she couldn't afford the premium. I had to give it up. I never became a milliner. Things didn't turn out so bad. I met your Dad, and we spent some happy years together. People say follow your dreams. I say forget about dreams and grab what chances come along to be happy.'

'That's good advice, Mum.'

6

'How would it be,' Charles dared to ask his mother, 'if me and Nic changed our minds? If we…'

'What, not get wed? Why's that, then?' Dora interrupted, 'Cold feet, or involved with someone else? Not still stuck on that Blake girl, are you?'

'No, course not! It's just I don't love Nic.'

'Love's a lot of nonsense, boy. Marriage ain't a box of chocolates. Not everything is sweet. I never gave no thought whether I loved your dad, but I knew he was the right bloke for me. We understood each other an' we was ready to do whatever it took to make it work. That's what I call a good marriage.'

He shook his head. 'Yeah, I know, but I don't want to settle down right now, Mum.'

'You have to, Charles. Nicola's a nice girl, educated, arty an' that. You'll get on well. She's a good-looker, nice figure. No man could ask for more in that department.'

'Not saying Nic isn't nice, but…'

'No, son, you ain't backing out. We can't afford to make an enemy of Bob Meyrick. Anyway, what about *her* feelings? You not thought about that? *That* ain't fair.'

Nevertheless he shook his head. 'I'm not marrying her, Mum, that's that. I just won't.'

'Sorry, Charlie, you're marrying Nicola. Her mum's people are top drawer down in Surrey, an' her old man's firm needs a partner like Sleet Properties. An' *we* need something like him. He's built estates up and down the country. Play your cards right an' his business can end up in our hands. Be sensible about it. If you *ain't* sensible, son – well then, remember till you're twenty-eight I can cut you out of the firm with not a bloody farthing.'

'Mum, you've no call to get nasty,' protested Charles. 'Dad wouldn't't've wanted that.'

'Oh yes he would. Your dad had big plans for you, Charlie, an' I promised him I'd make it happen. In the end you'll thank me an' you'll thank him. You'll see.'

'All right, I'll marry her,' Charles replied in anger, 'but only if you don't keep standing in the way of my ideas for the firm.'

*

They were shown to a table pretty with gingham, sparkling glassware and a pink rose. Large framed prints hung on the wall, landmarks and landscapes of France, the Eiffel Tower, Mont St-Michel, Rouen Cathedral, the Baie des Anges. The dinner *à deux* was in celebration of Elizabeth being called to the bar. Twin champagne flutes were cheerfully touched together and raised to her success. 'Thank you, my love.' She smiled across at him.

Charles pleased her as much as ever, his impressive physique within a pale summer suit, the silvery mane swept back, the rakish demeanour gloriously appealing. Elizabeth was far from hippie-ish these days. She might be thought glamorous tonight in a dress of turquoise seersucker belted with satin. Her dark hair was loosely tied . She'd changed into high heels.

Elizabeth placed her order, *lapereau aux cèpes*. Charles asked for the *poitrine de porc et boudin avec purée de pommes de terre*. She chose a bottle of red Château Simone. Still an advocate of tasty, wholesome brown rice and vegetables, Elizabeth had also learned a great deal about food and wine at Inns of Court meals and outings with fellow law students. A dozen times, eating her formal dinners in the Great Hall, Elizabeth had inwardly thanked her old headmistress for those Savoir-Faire lessons. To fit in and succeed she had needed to remake herself, carefully studying the gentlemen around her, picking up pronunciation along with the soup spoon and the fish knife. She had passed on to Charles some useful tips on reds and whites, Burgundy and Bordeaux, Loire and Rhine, sherry and port, how to eat an oyster, crab or lobster, artichoke or asparagus, what to do with elbows and hands, knife and fork, bread, plate and napkin. These lessons Charles had studied well.

The wine was tasted and poured, the dishes served. They agreed that everything was wonderful and delicious. However, the mood was strained. Charles's wedding was imminent.

'We'll keep seeing each other,' he promised. – 'Your wife won't like that!'

'We can still be friends.' – 'How's that going to work?'

'No, but we must always be friends, Liz.' – Elizabeth looked over unhappily. 'Yes, of course.'

She said brightly that her next step must be to find a pupillage at one of the barristers' chambers. Charles talked about his plans for the growing Sleet enterprises.

When the bill came, he took banknotes from his wallet, great quantities of them. The grey-haired *maitresse d'* smiled knowingly and wished them a *bonne soirée*.

Rather drunk, Elizabeth hung on Charles's arm as they walked towards his flat. 'Might Nicola turn up?'

'She's out of town. It's our last chance.'

*

Elizabeth's heels clacked down the uncarpeted steps of 15 Parchment Buildings. The clerks had treated her with contemptuous deference, apologising that it was impossible for the chambers to take on members of the fair sex as there were no ladies' facilities on the premises. 'Good luck elsewhere, Miss,' was their smirking farewell. She was not furious, nor despondent, nor yet resigned, but ever more determined.

She sensed that they objected not only to her sex. No one has a better eye than the English for placing their fellows on the rungs of social class. Despite her suit, handbag and cultivated tones, the clerks recognised at once what Elizabeth was and was not, and from what place she had emerged. They probably thought she was "getting above herself".

Every chambers she entered seemed a Wonderland of odd creatures, grotesques and caricatures, and she the bewildered Alice. Not everyone within their doors was male. Bluff and affable, middle-aged and squarely built, and dressed indeed as a man, one "lady barrister" invited the young novice into her office for friendly woman-to-woman advice. 'A female pupil wouldn't be right for me,' she apologised. 'We girls don't want to look like a separate team. We must stand our ground among the lads.'

'I understand. Do you think my background goes against me?' enquired the innocent.

'Not a bit of it. Being female is *such* a handicap – such a *curiosity* – that one's origins are hardly noticed. You could try Barnaby Rouffley-Wright, at Compass Court. You could learn a lot from him. Very senior, good advocate. But don't get within arm's reach. It's not just him. Chaps will be all over you in any case. No holds barred, literally. Lewd comment is just the start. Try to look serious, bookish, humourless. Careful with drink, a lot of drinking goes on. If men think your boyfriend will get riled, they might leave you alone. Have you got a boyfriend?'

'I – don't know. I don't think so.'

'Ha ha! Well, I'm sure you could find one in ten minutes if you put your mind to it! What's your special interest? You'd better say family law, because that's often the only thing open to ladies. That's what we're here for. It frees the men to take the better paid work. Way of the world, I'm afraid.'

Elizabeth confided, 'I'm interested in the dishonesty of the police. Corruption.'

'Oh, my goodness!' Her friendly adviser gurgled with amusement and shook her head. 'Never a good move to question the veracity of the police. Doesn't go down well with judges, nor with juries, and it's rather beyond our calling. Our purpose is simply to earn a living. If a constable tells a few fibs to put crooks away, well, that's his business, not ours. And it's all for the good, isn't it?'

'I'm interested in the officers who keep crooks *out* of jail. Collude with them. Line their own pockets with the proceeds of crime.'

'Oh dear, no! That's not something lawyers can tackle. If you want to change the system, politics might be better for you. Were you hoping to go into politics?'

'No, but I know someone who is.'

Elizabeth made her way to Compass Court to meet Mr Rouffley-Wright. The portly, clever-looking man welcomed her into his rooms with beaming pleasure. 'Come closer, Miss Blake, let's have a look at you!' Without a moment's delay he reached a quick hand under her skirt, slid it up her stocking to the naked flesh above and swiftly drew one fingertip along the satin between her legs. Elizabeth recoiled and stepped back, pushed his arm away. 'Ah, now *that's* what I call taking silk,' he guffawed. 'Don't mind, do you?'

'I rather think I do mind, sir.' She was incredulous at his effrontery, which he seemed to think would pass without comment.

'Ha ha! Well, that's the name of the game. Better get used to it, my dear, if you want to make a go of things. Quid pro quo, as I believe you lawyers call it.' Again a robust laugh, with an offer of a glass of whisky. 'I like a bit of spirit.'

'I'm sorry, sir, it's frightfully good of you to see me, but frankly I don't think it would work between us. My boyfriend would object. He's a jealous type, bit of a short fuse, cavalry officer. No hard feelings, I hope.'

'Talking of *hard* feelings –,' he joked. 'Ha ha! No, of course not. I apologise. Always *come* to me – ha ha ha ha ha ha ha ha! – if I can help, give you a leg up, you know.'

His Honour Lord Robyn Hedgesparrow-ffinch, head of chambers at Compass Court, was not perturbed by Elizabeth's remarks about Rouffley-Wright. 'He behaved improperly towards me, sir.'

'By Jove! What did he do?'

'Touched me in an ungentlemanly manner. Assaulted me, actually.'

'Did he indeed?' he chortled, 'I'll be damned. Cheeky chap!' His appreciative eye flicked down and up her figure. 'Well, I don't know anything about that. Never heard a word against him. Excellent advocate and a first-class rugby player. Good man in a scrum, and a trial can be awfully like a scrum sometimes. No place for shrinking violets. Not a shrinking violet, are you? Not lodging a complaint against him, are you?'

'No, sir, certainly not! But I wouldn't feel comfortable in his room with the door shut, if you take my meaning. Is there anyone else?'

'Try our Chester Smallchance. He's a youngster like you. Modern ideas.'

She knocked on his door. Chester Smallchance was quite a different sort. Not a youngster at all, though young in heart perhaps, Elizabeth placed him well into his thirties, fit and alert, busy and business-like. 'Which branch of law are you especially interested in, Miss Blake?' – 'Family law, sir.'

'Ah! Nothing else?'

'Well, yes. Crime.'

'Good!' He made it plain that he could use a pupil to ease his workload and would be happy to teach a clever young woman everything he knew. In the first six months of pupillage, the pupil followed her pupil master throughout the working day. She sat in on client conferences and witness interviews and court hearings. She did a great deal of research and paperwork for Smallchance, reading briefs, drafting opinions and preparing cases for trial.

Elizabeth got to know her new colleagues at Compass Court. Hedgesparrow-ffinch, for example, was a collector of first editions. Rouffley-Wright was a lover of racetracks and played the stock market. Smallchance was extremely knowledgeable about art. From all of them she learned a great deal.

In the "second six", a pupil may take a few cases of her own, be heard by a judge, and even earn fees. Elizabeth started with straightforward applications to a judge in chambers, costs hearings, pleas before venue, committals. It was true, no one took any notice of her accent, but they were startled to see counsel in a dress. She was given the least rewarding cases, shoplifting, taking of vehicles, criminal damage by rough kids of the type she loathed and had been avoiding all her life. She spoke up for them now, heartrendingly eloquent on their mitigation and their tragically missed opportunities. Instead of the expected youth custody, she won them probation, discharges, even dismissals. Lord Robyn Hedgesparrow-ffinch, head of chambers, praised her successes. He offered her a tenancy – a permanent position at Compass Court.

Smallchance was delighted for her. 'Well done! Do you know any solicitors who might send you a brief or two of your own?'

In truth she had hardly met a solicitor in her life. Although there was, she supposed, Jake Zuckerman's friend, if he remembered her. Elizabeth phoned the Law Centre in East London and asked for Bernard Kassin. He did remember her. 'From the women's march?' – 'That's me.'

*

Bernard wanted to help Elizabeth, sending her a succession of briefs in theft, mugging, pickpocketing and burglary that were going to trial. He was pleased with the results. He found a few thornier cases for her, and still he was pleased. After more than a year, something much, much bigger turned up. She made her way to meet Bernard and his client at Pentonville Prison.

Elizabeth often had a quick word with Bernard before and after a hearing. The relationship was cordial but professional. He had changed since the women's march, nearly to the point of being unrecognisable. The cascading hair was now respectably collar length, the beard trimmed. The beads had vanished. He had different glasses, too, and in court wore a plain grey suit remarkable only for its dullness. He was still terribly thin and animated.

The client's name was Ray Meldew, a paunchy middle-aged man, jowly and bald, arguably villainous-looking, on remand for armed robbery. He had preferred to go to the Law Centre because he thought ordinary solicitors were in cahoots with the police. Elizabeth and Bernard talked with him in a locked interview room. Mr Meldew was surprisingly witty though terse, with a curious accent half Cork, half Cockney, at times incomprehensible. Their conference over, Meldew was taken back to his cell. His barrister and solicitor were politely led through metal gates into the busy road outside. Rain fell steadily from a slate sky, the tarmac and pavement shining wet.

From her briefcase Elizabeth pulled a folding umbrella which Bernard, taller of the two, struggled to hold over both of them as they hurried to a bus stop. She said, 'So Mr Meldew's whole defence is that he's been fitted up and verballed by a gang of bent coppers. He doesn't seem to have much else. Can we prove it?'

Bernard replied, 'We need to talk.'

Elizabeth said, 'Are you free right now?'

He said he was free now. However, the subject of Meldew proved too sensitive to discuss on a crowded bus. They sat side by side on the smoky, steamy top deck. Bernard chattered instead about other things. He said he had lately got a mortgage. 'I'm buying a little house near Victoria Park. The People's Park, they call it. Love it round there, always a lot going on. Good music scene. What are you into these days?' he asked.

'I don't know. I… hardly ever go out. Too busy working.' She could kick herself for giving such a lame reply. 'What about you?'

'Jazz, especially. Anything from Jazz Age to John Coltrane. I love proper jazz: New Orleans, big bands, swing.'

She smiled at his enthusiasm. 'My mother's got a terrific collection of old 78s like that.'

'Really? I'd love to see them one day.' They stepped off the bus platform and walked through a gateway into the Inner Temple.

In those days, before the Crown Prosecution Service came into being, it was the job of the police themselves to bring prosecutions. They engaged prosecuting counsel to place the damning evidence before judge and jury, who would then hear the defence counsel's version of events and so aim for the elusive truth. For the case of *Regina vs Raymond Meldew*, the police chose the eminent barrister Mr Barker Fuphel for the prosecution.

As always Elizabeth put on her costume and learned her lines. She was in control of her appearance, her argument and her nerves. However it was alarming to find herself, a junior junior, pitted against such a senior senior. He greeted her with a salacious wink and eyebrows raised in happy surprise. In her white wig and black gown and dress, standing as tall as her frame allowed, she spoke slowly and distinctly, ever mindful never to drop a single *h, g,* or *t.*

The clerk of the court read the charges against Mr Meldew; that he and others unknown did rob a bank in Stratford, in possession of firearms with intent. When asked how he pleaded, Mr Meldew, standing in the dock, replied angrily, 'Not effing guilty, em ah?' The clerk prompted him to respond with either *guilty* or *not guilty*. The mumbled riposte sounded very like *Feck aff all o' yous.* A ferocious scowl did not endear him to the judge or the twelve men and women staring from the jury box.

'My lord,' explained Elizabeth to His Honour Judge Adikios with an unctuous smile (for judges sitting at the Old Bailey were to be so addressed), 'my client is saying that he pleads not guilty.'

For long hours Mr Fuphel put the case against Ray Meldew. He described in detail the robbery that had taken place, and the part played by Meldew. He called as a witness an underworld informer, a man as hard to pin down as a spider's web, who said it was a known fact that Ray Meldew was in on the Stratford bank job. The way Mr Fuphel told it, Ray Meldew had confessed to the crime under questioning. In addition there was a great quantity of banknotes in a holdall at Ray's house, and no one willing to confirm his absurd alibi that he was at Charlton Lido having a swim.

On the second day, from the witness stand Detective Inspector Scallop, the officer who had led the investigation, read his signed statement, faithfully taken from his police notebook, which included Meldew's admission of guilt. A big, broad man, wide-faced and large in the belly too, Scallop had the bearing of one who lets nothing stand in his way. He spoke at a measured pace, in a plain working-class accent, at a good volume. He was impassive, confident, with a brutish respectability. He was, above all things, credible.

Detective Sergeant Whelk, a creature cut from similarly hefty fabric, came next to the stand to read his own statement, which robustly endorsed the words of DI Scallop. In this time before CCTV, DNA testing and recorded interviews, the word of such policemen was as near as jurors could get to the Gospel.

Elizabeth rose to her feet. She admitted at once that Raymond Meldew was no innocent. 'I daresay there's hardly a sin Mr Meldew hasn't committed, my lord. But one sin he did not commit is the robbery for which he is on trial.'

She called Inspector Scallop back to the stand and asked him to read again from his statement. It seemed a false, puzzling step – she was allowing the prosecution's most convincing witness a second opportunity to state his case. She asked if he had written those notes himself, and where and when they were written. She held up her copy of his statement and pointed out to the judge and jury various misspellings and errors of grammar, the word *receipt* written incorrectly, confusion between *to* and *too*, and an apostrophe wrongly inserted into *yours* in one paragraph, but not in the next.

'Miss Blake, you are not, I hope,' interrupted Judge Adikios, 'impugning the officer's statement owing to a mere spelling error?'

'Far from it, my lord. The point will be clear shortly.'

She now called DS Whelk and asked him to read those lines from his own statement. She referred the judge and jury to the fact that Whelk's wording did not vary in even the smallest particular from Scallop's. Even the spelling mistakes were preserved, and the misplaced apostrophe in one paragraph but not the next. Furthermore Whelk, it turned out, had written his statement in the same room as Scallop and at the same time.

'I suggest,' she said, 'that Inspector Scallop ordered you to copy his notes, and no doubt told you to deny that any such thing occurred.' At which, Sergeant Whelk did promptly deny it. Elizabeth would have said more, but Judge Adikios interjected, 'You are not suggesting that the officers are lying, Miss Blake?'

'Absolutely not, my lord. That will be for the jury to decide.'

'You've made your point, Miss Blake. It's nearly four o'clock. Let's adjourn until tomorrow.' The Court rose with a sense that if that was Elizabeth's best point, she was on a hiding to nothing.

In the morning, Elizabeth called her next witness. 'Please state your full name.' It was Archibald Belling Cameron Douglas Efghi, a professor little known to the world at large but renowned in the world of Philology. After a slightly soporific preamble about ingliding diphthongs, yod-dropping, th-fronting, syntax, local vocabulary and double negatives, Professor Efghi responded that he could state with certainty that the supposed confession bore not the slightest resemblance to Mr Meldew's distinctive speech patterns.

Mr Fuphel challenged Professor Efghi as to his certainty, and the unflappable academic agreed that *certainty* was not the right word. 'Better to speak of probabilities. To put it another way, there is not one in a million chance that Mr Meldew made that confession.' Prosecuting counsel Barker Fuphel dismissed the professor's evidence as the idle speculations of an ivory-tower eccentric.

After a recess, which Ray Meldew spent in custody and Elizabeth in the canteen, Elizabeth resumed her case. 'May I say at this point, my lord, that following his arrest Mr Meldew asked his solicitor to take a sworn statement concerning his whereabouts at the time of the robbery. Unfortunately DI Scallop chose not to allow the solicitor to speak with his client, so the statement could not be made.'

'The officer was perfectly in order, Miss Blake, as I'm sure you know,' responded Judge Adikios (for such was indeed the law at the time). 'A police station is no place for a solicitor. Please proceed.'

'Absent the statement the defendant wished to make, I call Mr Benny Bigg.' Another villainous-looking character was brought in by officers. The new witness confirmed his name as Bennett Bigg and his current address as Pentonville Prison. With a disconcerting grin to the defendant and a wink at the judge, he swore to tell nothing but the truth. Elizabeth asked him where he was at the precise moment that a bank in Stratford was being robbed by masked men armed with sawn-off shotguns.

'At Charlton Lido. You know the pool down there is heated? Did you know that? Well, it is. We went down together, me an' a few mates. I remember the date 'cause Charlton played Watford, an' I'm sure you know what happened in *that* game!'

'Now, Mr Bigg, who were these mates of yours?'

'What, you want names? All of 'em? Well, there was Diesel Dick, Jack the Choke, Percy Squibbs an' Ray Meldew, if that's what you want to know. I never said before because that bast... that feller Inspector Scallop threatened me if I step up on Ray's behalf I'll go in the frame with him. He's threatened all of us the same. To be perfectly honest with you, now I been sent down for a long stretch on another matter it don't make no odds no more what Scallop says. If they was sworn under oath Diesel an' Choke an' Squibbs'd back me up.'

Barker Fuphel reminded the court that Mr Bigg was a professional criminal. He queried how it came about that Bigg gave his address as Pentonville Prison. Bigg was challenged, cross-examined and stood his ground.

When His Honour Judge Adikios adjourned the hearing he agreed to allow Meldew out on bail for the rest of the trial if a surety could be found. He set the bail bond high, at five thousand pounds. As it happened, Ray's wife, Molly, was in court and offered to be his surety. The judge scrutinised her doubtfully. 'Ah, madam, do you actually *have* five thousand pounds?'

Molly Meldew made a throaty gurgle of contemptuous amusement. She held up her right hand for all to see. 'There's five grand on me fingers, ducky.'

Barker Fuphel's closing argument rested on the question as to who was most believable. One could choose between the preposterous inventions of two proven liars like Ray Meldew and his comrade Benny Biggs, as unscrupulous a pair of rogues as ever saw the light of day, or the sworn testimony of two police officers, finest of men, with unblemished records, giving their all to keep such wrongdoers off the streets.

Elizabeth's final word to the judge and jury was that it was not the job of the police to keep a man off the streets unless it was *beyond reasonable doubt* that he had committed a crime. There was nothing *but* doubt in this case, she said. Indeed she *doubted* whether the police had any idea at all who robbed the bank at Stratford, and *doubted* that they had even bothered to look. She very much *doubted* that Detective Inspector Scallop had been entirely frank in his account. She reminded the jury that Ray Meldew had no need to prove anything. He need merely swear that this particular sin was one he did not commit. And she for one believed *that* to be nothing but the truth.

The jury returned their verdict. Elizabeth and Bernard shook the hand of the astonished, liberated Ray Meldew and wished him luck. Bernard said, 'If you know anyone needs help, Ray, tell them to give me a tinkle. I won't be at the Law Centre anymore. I'm starting my own firm.' He gave a card to his satisfied client. 'Kassin and Co. Here's my new number.'

Elizabeth politely refused Barker Fuphel's offer of a drink in the Magpie and Stump. Instead, she set off on foot with Bernard. He remarked thoughtfully, 'I think you just proved Scallop lied under oath, didn't you? He's not going to like that.' After a moment he said, 'It'll bring in more work. Meldew has pals, lots of them.' And after another moment, 'You deserve a glass of champagne or a massive joint or something.'

'I'm not sure what I want. Definitely *not* to get smashed. But something. Maybe to scream.'

'I'd say you're seriously in need of some excellent jazz.'

At a narrow doorway in a Soho side street Bernard was let inside, Elizabeth following down steps into a dark cavern, warm and crowded, bursting with sound, raw, wild notes now sharp, now cool, tender as snow, now woven into haunting melody. Two grey-bearded black saxophonists stood spotlit, masters of their craft, backed by drums and piano. Reflections from the brass instruments glinted across black and white faces, men and women around tables and tiered seats, heads and shoulders in motion. To his surprise Elizabeth took Bernard's hand and kissed it, held it against her face. 'Thank you for bringing me. Come back to my place after.'

———

ALEX

Born May 1975, Stratford, London E15

1

F rom Elm Park station they strode into a raw November dusk, gloves on, jackets zipped and scarves wrapped. Elizabeth had judged this the moment for her mother and Bernard to meet. Suddenly it could wait no longer. Wintry cloud hung low, its misty fingers moistening the roofs and treetops. The chill stung Elizabeth's cheeks. They walked quickly and crossed into the council estate.

Elizabeth had briefed Bernard not to argue with Maud, nor discuss anything. Bitter campaigning was under way for the second general election of the year. 'Don't talk about *that*. Ask about her record collection.' There were a dozen topics to avoid at all costs: the three-day week, the power cuts and blackouts, the miners, unions, strikes…

'What happens if she mentions it first?'

'Oh, she will. "We have to work by candlelight in the shop", all that. Don't be drawn.'

What, he asked, might they agree upon? IRA bombs, she said, as long as he did not actually discuss Ireland. 'Condemn blowing up working men in pubs.' He agreed he could condemn that, without exploring the background. 'And the price rises. She'll tell you every time she buys a loaf of bread or a pint of milk it costs more than last time.' He readily agreed to condemn that, or at least lament it. 'After all, it's true for us, too.'

As they walked a melody was drifting in the damp air, a trumpet solo backed by brass, coming, it seemed, from every house. 'Coronation Street,' Elizabeth explained.

'Is that what it is?' Bernard was secretly terrified of such unanimity, of crowds with one mind. 'You can hear what everyone's watching!' he laughed.

They sat by the cosy gas fire with cups of tea and slices of Maud's Dundee cake. He called her Mrs Blake. They discussed the year's unusual weather. After the hottest summer it was now the wettest autumn.

Maud wondered what Len, that imposing, taciturn man, would have made of Lizzie's insubstantial boyfriend. Liz had told her this beardie young chatterer was a clever solicitor making a name for himself. A solicitor! No doubt Len would have been secretly proud. No doubt she was secretly proud herself.

Bernard remarked blandly, 'Liz tells me you have a good record collection.'

'Just a few from the old days. 78s, mostly. Not your sort of thing, I shouldn't think. Traditional jazz. You know, Dixieland. A bit of blues. Jazz piano. Big bands and that.'

'Oh, wow! That's what I especially like. May I have a look?'

'Course you can.' She gestured to a rack loaded with Fats Waller albums, Django Reinhardt, an Acker Bilk, a Ray Charles, a Dizzy Gillespie.

'Can I put on this Fats Waller?'

'Course you can. Careful with it, you can't buy that now. There's more behind the settee.' As the music played Bernard pulled the sofa away from the wall and there found a row of record cases filled with old LPs and 78s of Duke Ellington, Count Basie, Jimmy Dorsey, Benny Goodman, Jelly Roll Morton, Stéphane Grappelli. 'This is fantastic,' he exclaimed, 'incredible!'.

'There's more under my bed,' she added.

'Liz tells me you play the piano very well.'

Elizabeth suggested she give them a tune, but Maud laughed, scorning herself. 'Nah! I'm no good anymore. It's the arthritis in my hands, look,' and she insisted on showing Bernard that her finger joints had become disfigured by the disease. 'More cake?'

'No, thank you, Mrs Blake. Are your hands painful?'

She shrugged with resignation. 'What can you do?'

'Still play for the Keep Fit though, don't you?' interjected Elizabeth. She turned to explain, 'Mum does a little piano-playing job for a ladies' evening class, don't you, Mum? They sort of dance to keep fit.'

'I'll have to give it up if my hands go on like this. What about a biscuit? Help yourself to a biscuit.' A plate of shortbread and digestives was pushed closer. 'Where exactly is it you work, Bernard?'

'Oh, thank you!' He took a shortbread biscuit and ate it with sips of tea. He said that his practice was in Romford Road, near the County

Court at Stratford.'

'Oh, blimey. It's all coloureds round there now, isn't it? Mosques and that. So I been told.'

Elizabeth gave Bernard a warning stare: *Taboo topic ahead!* He could not hold back a slight laugh. 'Yeah, it's a mix round there, people from all over. There's a couple of prayer halls in the area. Our office is above an Indian grocers. It's a good spot for us. And there's a terrific little caff next door run by a Greek guy, does a great fry-up.'

Maud grimaced. Her secret pride was a little dented. 'You want to get yourself a nice office in a good area, that's what I say. D'you want another biscuit? I've got rich tea and garibaldi in the kitchen.'

When Bernard left the room, Maud turned to Elizabeth. 'You do know he's Jewish, don't you?'

'Of course, Mum! I've got nothing against Jews.'

'Oh, me neither! They were *very* good to my mum and me. Lovely dancers, Jewish fellers,' Maud chuckled at the memory. 'I was always glad when a Jewish boy asked me to dance. Thing is though, his parents won't want him involved with a shiksa – that means a non-Jewish girl, and it's no compliment. They worry where it might lead.'

'Where might it lead?' – 'Grandchildren who aren't Jewish, that's where.'

'Oh, I don't think Bernard's parents care about that.' – 'You ever met them?'

'Yes. They're nice. They like musicals and go on cruises.' – 'Aha, I know the sort. They definitely won't want him marrying a shiksa.'

Elizabeth chuckled. 'They don't have to worry, then. We've got no intention of marrying.'

'Oh, so it's not serious, then?'

'Yes, it is, very! We're living together. Didn't I say? I've moved in with Bernard.'

Maud turned her face as if slapped. She writhed as if physically in pain. 'No, you *didn't* say. Living in sin with a shiksa! No, they *definitely* won't like that.'

Elizabeth snorted, amused by the phrase. 'Well, bad luck for them.'

Maud did not know how to respond. 'Do his parents know you're living together?' she demanded unhappily. Without waiting for an answer she said, 'I suppose it makes no difference unless you have a baby. Not planning a baby, are you?'

'Well, Mum, as it happens, that's why I've brought Bernard to meet you. I'm twelve weeks gone. I am pregnant.'

*

The latest scare for women was thrombosis. The risk was caused by oestrogen in the pill. The evidence had convinced even Elizabeth. Almost as soon as she switched to using a diaphragm, she had missed a period. Apparently, she was assured, it was not unusual in women who gave up the contraceptive pill. There were no home pregnancy tests then, so she waited anxiously until a second period failed to occur before accepting the dreadful fact. Although it was 'an accident', Bernard was thrilled. He loved the child even when it was little more than an idea. In fact, she realised, for a man "having a baby" could only ever be an idea until it looks him in the face.

Elizabeth told him candidly that she was not happy. She wanted neither the physical toll of pregnancy nor a maternity break from work. She had reached a crucial point in her career, winning several appeals thanks to forensic science unavailable in the original trials. *This* is what she found exciting, not the prospect of motherhood! Past convictions were being disinterred and exposed to the light. Officers who took bribes, planted evidence, had a share of the loot were named. These men were still in post. The media was taking notice. The Commissioner of the Metropolitan Police set up an anti-corruption unit to unmask dishonest CID officers.

Bernard said, 'Having a baby is important too.'

Whatever her view of it, the day came, the hour, and the first waves of clenching pain. There were no thoughts now of her career, only a pleading that everything should stop or they let her die. The breathing routine she had learned became an impossible irrelevance. It was not soon over. She and Bernard were alone together in a windowless room as she sweated. A day and a night passed, the final stage of labour exceptionally long.

It was to Bernard that the midwife handed the slippery red body. Elizabeth, with a strange ethereal smile, lay too weakened by drugs and exhaustion to hold her newborn. She was, though, suffused with tearful joy as she heard its cry. Bernard raised the baby to show her.

'Greetings, Alexandra Harriet Blake Kassin!' he announced. 'Welcome, belovèd!' The tiny girl stared at him transfixed as if listening carefully for the source of the sound. Elizabeth whispered, 'Let me touch her.' Outside the hospital, the first light of a midsummer morning coloured the sky.

Bernard's parents were the first to visit. Eve and Morris Kassin embraced baby Alex with noisy kisses and caresses and cries of delight. They did not show the slightest disappointment that this granddaughter – and Bernard's girlfriend – were not Jewish. Maud was not wrong, though: these were regrets expressed privately between themselves. Eve and Morris were wise enough to make themselves content with the situation. They wanted to love Bernard's partner, and consoled themselves that Bernard had two sisters whose children inevitably would be Jewish. Besides, they felt this girl Elizabeth had made their argumentative son a happier man and were grateful to her for that. Then, there was always the possibility that she would convert. The baby, too, could be converted – if Elizabeth would agree. They did not, of course, mention these hopes out loud.

'You must come to us,' said Eve. 'On Friday night,' added Morris. He meant, for Shabbat dinner.

Until now Elizabeth had not thought much about Bernard's family. She did know he was Jewish. That much was obvious. He had mentioned two sisters, and that his parents had built up a thriving children's clothing business.

She had not prepared for the discovery that her sweet life with him in their little house beside Victoria Park was on the edge of a larger galaxy. Now she brushed against its magnetic field and from a distance of light-years felt it tugging. She both resisted and succumbed, willing and unwilling to approach. However, she could not escape the fact that Bernard's family *was* his family. Just as Bernard made an effort with her mother, so Elizabeth steeled herself to make an effort with Eve and Morris.

She had no experience of such people. It was true they adored musicals and cruises, but they also talked in loud, disputatious voices about Russian ballet, French films and German composers, sometimes confessing unashamed ignorance of the subject in hand. They adored opera in an absurdly sentimental fashion, openly singing along. Elizabeth lent Eve a hand preparing the Friday night meal, and so learned the rules of a kosher kitchen and listened to blessings chanted.

She did not utter *amens*, standing in awkward silence. Elizabeth had conflicting feelings about the family's antique traditions (as she considered them). Religion – and all else that places a wedge between peoples – she deplored as a trap, dismissed it as preposterous. About that she was sure. Or had been. She did not dismiss the mystique of an ancient identity. There was something about that which she must respect. But also something about it she did not like, tribalism, particularism. She was unclear about old customs; the love of them. She read the improbable translations of mealtime benedictions and asked innocently, 'These things it says here, *King of the Universe* and all that – is that what Jews believe in?'

Eve roared with laughter. 'What a question! Course not, my dear. Come along to shul with us and find out what it's all about.'

Elizabeth was determined not to be drawn in. She must stand her ground and remain true to herself. She valued secularism and rationality and universality of mind, erasing differences and hierarchies, to bring all together. She knew Bernard passionately shared this with her. Yet Bernard himself seemed quite at ease with age-old rituals. Rituals! The very word had a distasteful element.

During the night hours of exhausted wakefulness with baby Alex, she would sit – or walk up and down, soothing the fretful infant – determined to 'be herself' and 'go so far and no further'. As if having a child, 'starting a family', were not a sufficient revolution! What troubled her was that starting a family apparently also meant joining one.

In the synagogue hall, after the Sabbath morning service, the congregation gathered for the wine blessing, familiar snacks, amiable shmoozing and exchange of news. Elizabeth, standing with Eve among the cheerful crowd, was introduced to the rabbi. She asked him by way of conversation if baby Alex could in theory become Jewish even if she herself did not. She was merely chatting.

The rabbi asked matter-of-factly whether Alex would be brought up keeping Shabbat and Jewish festivals in a kosher home. 'I suppose that would be the idea,' smiled Elizabeth. She assumed the rabbi knew that in reality Bernard would make no such commitment.

Not being Jewish herself would present difficulties, the rabbi pointed out. 'This isn't the time or place to discuss these things! Call me during the week and we'll fix something up to talk some more, both you and Bernard.'

To Bernard, Elizabeth said, 'Obviously we can't keep a kosher home, not in the sense he means. I'm not religious, never will be.'

'Oh, I know,' he replied nonchalantly, 'me neither, obviously. Being Jewish isn't about that. Really nice of him to invite us. It'll be interesting to hear what he has to say.'

She pulled a face. 'I don't mind going. But I don't see myself converting to anything. I am what I am.'

'Oh, same here. Everyone is what they are,' he replied cheerfully.

The meeting at the rabbi's home was amiable. Coffee was brought out. 'We need to be satisfied that Alex will have a Jewish upbringing. You know it would be no bed of roses, being Jewish,' he warned. 'Alex might not thank you. Who'd want to be Jewish? From time to time she'll face hostility, even hatred. Or even, God forbid, violence. These are dangerous times for Jews. Are you sure that's what you want?'

They made no reply. Elizabeth frowned, unable to say that it was what she wanted, nor that it wasn't. She was surprised by the rabbi trying to dissuade her. Most emphatically she did not want Alex to face hatred; nor Bernard.

Elizabeth replied, 'If Bernard and Alex are to face hostility, I'm on their side.' Bernard shot her a surprised glance.

'Good,' responded the rabbi. 'Let's deal with Alex first. One thing at a time. For you to convert, Elizabeth, would be quite different. It depends on your motives. And it would require a considerable period of study and of course, keeping the mitzvot. And the mitzvot – the commandments, laws if you will – can be onerous if you're not used to them. What religion do you follow now?'

She shook her head with a smile. 'I believe my mother is under the impression that we are C of E. I have never actually been to a church service.'

Bernard interjected eagerly, 'It's not *just* about mitzvot, though, is it? To join the Jewish people,' he said, 'is to take your part in a dramatic story reaching back into earliest times, an immense adventure, a great destiny.'

The rabbi and Elizabeth were startled by this effusive contribution. The rabbi listened uneasy with Bernard's romantic view of Yiddishkeit. Elizabeth stared astonished. This did not sound like Bernard at all. The vision he conjured up had something of Cecil B. DeMille about it. However, it appealed to her. She did wonder, though, what exactly is meant by *destiny*.

She said, 'The other day Bernard described being Jewish as belonging to a community, and I thought – what community do I belong to? I'm just a demographic.'

The rabbi smiled slightly. 'If you were on our conversion course, Alex could be converted. It's quite simple for a baby. She would go in the mikveh. At batmitzvah age, she will either renounce her conversion or confirm it.'

Somehow, Elizabeth found herself agreeing to that arrangement. 'I must be mad,' she declared, back at home. Yet she found herself looking forward to learning something new. Bernard said eagerly that he would be interested to join her in study, and promised that the very next day he would attach a mezuzah beside the front door.

'Don't tell anyone just yet,' she implored him, 'let's see how it goes.' She could guess what her colleagues at chambers would think!

'Mum,' she said during an ad break. 'I'm doing a course to become Jewish.' – 'Sorry, what was that, dear?'

Elizabeth quietened the TV. 'I'm going to become Jewish. Convert, you know. To Judaism.'

There was so little reaction, Elizabeth wondered if her mother had heard and understood. 'You don't mind?'

Maud turned to look. 'Free country. Not as if we're church-goers, is it? I knew this would happen – bound to, wasn't it? It's fate. At least you won't be a shiksa anymore! What about little Alex?'

'She's been done already. Alex is Jewish now. I didn't want to mention it before. I thought you might be unhappy.'

'Not a bit of it! Don't you worry about that.' Maud leaned back in her armchair and gazed blankly at figures moving on the screen. 'You do as you want. You'll still be you, in your bones. You can never change what you are.'

'True enough.'

'I mean, don't be surprised if nothing's different afterwards.'

'Yeah, I've been wondering about that.'

Maud stared at the television screen. 'I wonder if people will call you a Yid. What synagogue will you belong to?'

Elizabeth was not expecting her mother to know about 'belonging' to a synagogue. She answered, 'You know the one near Forest Gate station? Bernard and his family are members there.'

'Heh, heh!' Maud shook her head at the strangeness of life. 'And what about Christmas?'

'Oh, we'll come over for Christmas dinner, don't worry about that! I'll do it kosher for you.'

'What *would* Dad have said?' Maud chuckled. 'I *must* let Yitzy know! He'll appreciate the joke.'

'How so, Mum?' But the ad break was over.

'You watching this, love? Let's see what's on the other side.' Maud switched channels. 'Only if it wasn't for him and his family none of this would've happened, that's all.'

*

Alex was three years old before Maud met Eve and Morris. A wedding would have brought both sides of the family together. Without any occasion at all to force the encounter, nothing was arranged and the months passed, and then the years. However it came into Maud's mind that to celebrate her seventieth birthday, she would like everyone to get together. She wanted a little family tea party with Elizabeth and Bernard, Alexandra, and Bernard's parents. Nothing could be more suitable for a seventieth birthday.

Maud was quite out of the habit of inviting guests. She had long ago given up the Christmas parties and hardly knew the new people in the street. Besides, going to neighbours' houses wasn't done anymore. For the first time in years, the folding dining table was opened up in the living room, and laid with her best damask cloth and best china tea set. Elizabeth baked and iced a cake and prepared plates of sandwiches.

Morris and Eve Kassin arrived by taxi, bringing a card and a huge bouquet. 'Happy seventieth birthday!' they cried out like old friends. Their warmth and energy caught Maud by surprise. Morris took her hands and exclaimed what a pleasure it was to meet her at last. They apologised for not getting together sooner. Maud almost recoiled in astonishment when Eve pecked her cheek. Tea was poured and smiling remarks exchanged.

Candles on the cake were lit and blown out, *Happy Birthday* sung and generous slices cut. Maud was indulged. More tea was poured.

'It appears we know someone in common, Maud,' remarked Eve, a piece of cake teetering genteelly on her fork. 'Isaac Zuckerman.'

'Oh, that's right! Small world! Of course, he's Yitzy to me, not Isaac. I knew him when we were nippers in Barking. Then we lived near them in Spitalfields. That's where I learned my bit of Yiddish.' Each of these revelations was met with amazement. 'Later on, Yitzy and me played in a little jazz combo together.'

'Isaac played in a jazz band? That's incredible. I never knew,' responded Morris.

'Oh yes! It was his own band. Yitz on clarinet, me on the joanner. We played all round Whitechapel. We had a regular gig at a pub in Aldgate. And we did Jewish events, simchas.'

'*You* did? Incredible! Want to give us a few bars, then?'

Maud made the usual apology that her hands were too stiff. Nevertheless, she took her seat at the keyboard and began to play her old favourites with verve, shoulders turning with the beat. Alex stood beside her at the piano, closely watching. Morris and Eve, delighted, were out of their chairs as soon as she struck up. They danced wildly on the fitted carpet as joyous tunes filled the room. Though he did not know the steps, Bernard jumped up, swaying and moving to the rhythm. Even Elizabeth had to abandon her reserve as he grabbed her hands and pulled her to join him.

With a plaintive, 'Ooh, my hands!' Maud came to an abrupt stop. She called Eve and Morris to examine the swelling knuckles. The base of her thumb was grotesque. Morris said, 'Here, rest your poor fingers,' and suggested stacking records on the gramophone instead. Even more surprising, despite a brief protest that she was crippled by arthritis in her hips and knees and feet as well, Maud then danced with Morris as if both were young again, laughing and merry. With Morris's careless arm around Maud's waist, the pair of them quickstepping around the living room to the Victor Silvester Orchestra, she was vivacious, her eyes sparkled.

Elizabeth watched with a bemused smile, and remembered *'I was always glad when a Jewish boy asked me to dance.'* She wondered how long it was since her mother had been in such a happy mood. Bernard had never seen anything like that in Maud until today. Her dyed, permed hair and polyester floral dress he noticed anew as having a certain chic, the height of elderly-widow fashion. The thought crossed Bernard's mind that his father and Elizabeth's mother would have made a great couple if they had met in the old days.

Alex stood and stared as though she had never seen anyone dance before. When the record ended, the little girl went to the piano and ran her fingertips gently over the keys. With careful attention she picked out *Happy Birthday* from beginning to end, left hand and right hand. Maud, Morris and Eve, Elizabeth and Bernard stopped moving and listened in awestruck silence.

'Well, I'll be blowed, you clever little sweetie. Thank you!' Maud put her arms around the bashful toddler, who smiled shyly. Elizabeth and Bernard cuddled her. Bernard began to speak, 'That was...' – it was hard to know what to say – '...unbelievable.'

Morris also fumbled for words. 'My God,' he declared at last, 'she's got a ruddy gift! No, I mean – hasn't she? A proper one, a talent.'

'Gran,' whispered Alex, 'show me.' Her eyes turned towards the keyboard.

'If Mummy and Daddy bring you more often, I'll teach you.'

Elizabeth and Bernard laughed awkwardly. They certainly did not want to visit Elm Park more often.

Besides, as soon as they returned home there was something more pressing to concern them that drove Alex's piano-playing out of their minds.

*

The news they returned to was that City of London police officers had been involved in a payroll robbery at the Daily Mirror a few weeks before. A security guard had been shot dead during the raid. It was only a few months since the commander of the Robbery Squad had himself been jailed for corruption. A dozen other officers had lately been convicted. Now this!

Police from far-away Dorset were called in to investigate the City of London police. Some in the criminal world could easily name the officers who had taken part, but preferred to protect their contacts inside the force. The investigation was to be called Operation Countryman.

The Countryman team made contact with criminal defence lawyers to discuss in confidence what they knew about collusion between criminal gangs and City police. Elizabeth was drawn into the investigation. She had made something of a speciality of police dishonesty. She knew that even men from criminal families had been accepted into the force. The justification for it seemed to be, *set a thief to catch a thief.*

The rural officers soon discovered that the rot extended well beyond the City. The investigation spiralled to include the entire London region, and was obstructed on every side. Hundreds of Metropolitan Police officers were questioned, of all ranks from bottom to top. Yet there was little progress.

This did not surprise Elizabeth. She and Bernard knew well that within the police was an *omertà*, a code of silence and loyalty as powerful as within any underworld fraternity. She said, 'You've heard the expression, *the police family*. People lie for their family, don't they? Cover up for them, forgive them, just as the police do for their brother officers. That's how they get away with stealing, lying, even murder. Countryman is a once-only opportunity. If Countryman fails, if criminality in the police is not rooted out now,' she predicted ferociously, 'then it never will be.'

2

U sually Alex spent the day with a child minder. But she would not shut up about the promised piano lessons. Like it or not Elizabeth felt she must take the little mite to her grandmother's. Whenever she was appearing at Snaresbrook Crown Court in East London, which was frequently, or one of the Essex courts, she would drop Alex at Maud's.

With Alex brightly smiling on her lap or beside her on the piano stool, Maud began at the beginning with scales and keys, and carefully taught her granddaughter how to get the sound she wanted, whether dancey, sing-along, comic or moody. She noticed with what strange intensity Alex focused on the keyboard, with what astonishing quickness she understood. Maud knew nothing of music theory. Like her mother, she saw music scores as mere dots tossed over lined paper. Her granddaughter, she was sure, must one day learn from some other teacher to read music, master this instrument and fulfil Maud's own dream of being the young lady on the stage, turning to smile at her audience.

She concentrated at first on teaching her public-house and music-hall repertoire, starting with an old favourite, *Yes Sir, That's My Baby*. Alex copied exactly, impeded only by the small span of her fingers. The extraordinary little girl had no difficulty remembering. 'You aren't half good at this!' chuckled Maud.

Court sittings rose for the day at around four o'clock. Travelling home and back was difficult during the strikes, so if trials were to resume in the morning Elizabeth returned to her mother's house and spent the night there.

After Alex had been put to bed, Elizabeth and Maud would sit together for a while.

'Everything all right, Lizzie?' asked Maud. 'You look worried.'

Countryman was indeed worrying Elizabeth. She replied, 'Oh, it's nothing, just work.'

She did not want to sit in silence. Topics to be avoided had increased with the fraught political situation. As the 'Winter of Discontent' ground on, they talked in sweet voices only of the garden, the doings of neighbours, TV shows.

Maud let slip a comment about the heaps of uncollected rubbish rotting in the streets, hospital workers on strike, buses not running. She was nearly ecstatic at the prospect of a woman prime minister. Not just any woman, but someone who would 'get rid of this Socialist shambles.'

Unable to hold back a retort, Elizabeth blurted out that a Tory victory would be a catastrophe for the working class – especially working-class women. She was torn, regretful that this was her opinion. She thought it might benefit women to see a woman in power. She shared the general fascination to know if a woman prime minister would be different from a man.

Maud retorted, 'It was Tories gave working class women the vote. The Socialists opposed it. You know why? They thought women would vote Tory. Well, they were right, here's one. *And* the unions opposed equal pay. They think only a man is a proper breadwinner, see? That's Socialists for you.'

'That's rubbish, Mum. Harold Wilson brought in equal pay.'

'Pah! You know why? It was the women's strike at Ford's! My neighbour down the road was in the strike, she'll tell you. The ruddy union was dead against them – protecting men's jobs, weren't they? Barbara Castle – a *woman* MP – *forced* Labour to change their tune; she *made* Wilson support equal pay. Only because she wanted to get more women voting Labour! Even *then* they didn't get equal pay. Oh, no, not under Labour! Labour have always been against women. The first woman in Parliament was a Tory, I remember it well. Socialists think they own the so-called working class. They think they can keep us buttoned up in their pocket. Well, we don't belong to them. And don't say it's rubbish. If you can't be polite, go up to bed.'

'I'm sorry, Mum.' Elizabeth was not sure of her ground. Taken aback at being defeated by someone like her mother, she resolved to look into the history of equal pay.

Maud said kindly, 'We shouldn't argue, darling.' She stood up and shuffled in her slippers over to Elizabeth. She leaned to kiss her daughter's head. 'Now you see why me and Dad never discussed politics. Where does it get you? He was a union man.'

'I know. Can I make you a cup of tea, Mum?'

'Come on then, let's have a nice cup of tea. There's cake in the tin.'

Operation Countryman was worrying because police officers under suspicion seemed to know exactly who was providing evidence against them. Perhaps witnesses had been bribed or bugged, or colleagues close to the Countryman team were tipping them off. The more the investigation uncovered, the more Elizabeth became afraid. Soon her fears were realised.

It happened in the park on a Sunday morning. Elizabeth hardly noticed the two men until they stopped on the path in front of her, agreeable-looking, casually but respectably dressed. Could be father and son out for a stroll, both rather tall, the older man's face much creased, the younger smooth-skinned. Alexandra looked up at them uncertainly from her pushchair. 'What a nice little girl! So pretty,' remarked the older of the two amiably.

'Thank you,' Elizabeth replied.

'Shame if anything was to happen to her,' he said.

'What?'

'Just saying. You want to keep away from country bumpkins poking their noses, asking questions. Could be dangerous for you and your family, Mrs Kassin – sorry, I mean, Miss Blake.'

She said, 'Do we know each other?' She tried to appear in command of herself.

'Well, we know you, love. A word of friendly advice: be careful who you talk to. Not a dickie bird to no swede-bashers. You're too fucking gabby. Shut it. Just saying. No one wants a pretty girl to lose her good looks. Anything could happen.'

'What?' Her mouth was painfully dry and her heartbeat racing. She was not at all in command of herself. She saw how vulnerable Alex was, reclining innocently in the pushchair. Someone could throw acid in her face. There came a darkness around her vision. She began to feel that she urgently needed the toilet.

'No more talking to the wrong people, all right? Be careful. Anyway, good luck, Miss Blake. Bye bye, Alex.' He gave a friendly wave and the two passed on their way. She noticed that the younger man had said nothing.

Elizabeth almost sprinted Alex back to the house. She knew Bernard would not be there. He went for a cycle ride on Sundays. There was no way to contact him – of course. Who could advise her? She must call the police – no, no, of course not! Jake or Abi would know what to do – no, they would not know. She picked up the phone. 'Hello, Mum.'

In haste she wrote Bernard a note and had Alex in the car within minutes. The route she took was a nightmare of congestion and delays, with countless stops and turn-offs to check whether she was being followed.

Maud put the kettle on the stove. In the front hall Elizabeth closed all doors to keep her phone call private. Bernard was back at home. She explained, 'They told me not to talk to "country bumpkins".'

'Was it just... I don't know, a joke, a couple of idiots?'

'It was deadly serious. They knew my name, and Alex's. They knew I live with you. They threatened to harm her, Bernard. They said she would lose her good looks. They said I shouldn't talk so much.'

'D'you want to stop helping the investigation?'

'This is why it's important to carry on. Except there's Alex to think of.'

'Will you tell your mother?'

'Yes, I'd better.'

They sat in the kitchen. Maud listened with grim attention to Elizabeth's frightening account. 'Who were these men? Were they police or...what? Who sent them?'

'I assume it's to do with a case, a witness, a suspect. I can't think what it's about.' She could hardly tell her mother about Operation Countryman.

Maud said, 'I'm not so green as I'm cabbage-looking, love. Didn't you tell me you win cases by proving people were framed? The police won't like that. Be careful, Liz. I happen to know there's no limit to what coppers can get away with. I've got a feeling you know who's behind this. Who is it?'

Elizabeth replied in a low voice, 'All right, one name does come up a lot.' She gave the name. 'He's a real crooked bastard, excuse my language, Mum, but he is.' As if the kitchen table were a kind of confessional, her voice became ever softer. She did not want to say outright that she was involved in gathering evidence against corrupt officers. 'He's an inspector. I came up against him on my very first big case and several times since. I think he's working some kind of protection racket, framing men who don't pay, gets them sent down. He doesn't like the work I'm doing. Whatever you do, Mum, don't tell anyone what I've said. Not a soul. It's confidential.'

Maud was also quiet. 'Don't go home till this is sorted, love. You and Alex must stay here. We'll do whatever it takes to keep you safe. Leave it to me.'

'To *you*, Mum?'

'You've given me an idea.' She would say no more.

As soon as Elizabeth left in the morning for court, Maud dialled the number. 'Well, I never,' came the answer, 'it's Mrs Blake! I thought you wanted to draw a line,' cackled Dora in mocking delight, 'ain't that what you said?'

'I do want to, only it seems I can't. Your husband promised if anyone gives us grief he would deal with it. Well, I want to find out where we stand with that.'

'My husband's dead, and he made that promise to your husband, not you.'

'No, he repeated it to my face at my husband's funeral. He came specially to tell me. He said it was for the rest of my days. Well, someone has sent two bully boys threatening me and my daughter and my baby granddaughter.' This was not, of course, completely true, as Maud herself had not been threatened.

'I couldn't care tuppence, Missis. Far's I'm concerned, that promise died with Micky. I don't get mixed up in nothing. Who is this someone, anyway? What does he want?'

'He's a copper. A vicious bastard bent as a nine-bob note, I'm not kidding. He's a high up, and been putting innocent men inside for years.' For that is what Elizabeth had told her.

'How d'you know that?'

*

Frankie Scallop's villa, in a handsome development of white houses and blue swimming pools cut into the rocky slopes above old Mijas, was a joy to him, exquisitely airy with wide doors and windows folded open, the views thrilling of mountains behind and the Mediterranean in front. Fragrant oleander and hibiscus flourished alongside a paved sun terrace around the pool. Vivid purple bougainvillea draped the arcaded veranda. On most evenings Scallop slowly swam two lengths as daylight faded, and sat on the terrace with an icy beer before going indoors to shower, eat and dress. A taxi arrived and drove him down a steep, serpentine road to the hectic seafront.

Detective-Inspector Frankie Scallop enjoyed a good time. On the face of it he did not look like a hedonist. A large walrus-like creature, his weighty muscularity heavily padded with flesh, he had the bullish air of one who knows how to have his own way. The hair, sparse at the crown, was thick enough at the sides for a comb-over. He had changed little since giving evidence in the trial of Ray Meldew, but here the man was off duty and at ease. His character was more clearly on view. He had always been popular among his crowd – for he was better as a friend than an enemy. In a neatly pressed dress uniform back in London he made an impressive figure. Here, stepping with his companions out of the Scorpion Club into the balmy waterside night of Cala de Mijas, comfortable in a light suit and open-necked shirt, he looked almost the playboy or a playboy's minder.

The club offered music, drink, dancing and go-go girls. Yet it was not all play for Frankie Scallop. With the end of the extradition agreement, Spain's Coast of the Sun had become for Scallop and his coterie (and many like them) the ideal bolthole, a place beyond the scrutiny of home in which to make deals and do business while living as well as any man could wish. At the end of the evening, after a few last minutes of banter and backslapping, Scallop got into the waiting taxi to be driven at speed back up to the Urbanizacion and the gates of his villa.

Twenty kilometres away in a modest self-catering apartment at Marbella, two young cousins spent the afternoon and evening discussing tactics. It was clear that Trish Winslow, who had trained as a nurse to obtain drugs for the family business, knew what she was talking about. She showed her cousin Josie Renvoize the sachets, yellow capsules and tiny bottle of liquid she had brought.

'That's amytal, that's seconal and that's pentobarbital. You can swallow it or inject it or put it in a drink. Anyway it's all just barbiturates. Inject is the quick way; only that leaves a needle mark, obviously.'

They reflected. Josie said, 'Better start with the one you put in a drink. If he don't drink it, we'll try something else.'

They had made trial runs to Scallop's villa. They knew he was in residence. At two in the morning the pair wrapped scarves around their faces and buttoned their gloves, helmets, jeans and leather jackets, for it would be cold on the hill road. They were armed with needle-sharp hairdressing scissors, ready either to stab or to cut. It was Josie's usual custom, if a weapon were needed, to take a knife from the kitchen of a house she entered. That would not be done this time. Everything for the job was in a backpack. They settled themselves astride the rented scooter and started out for Mijas. Josie drove and Trish rode pillion, clinging on as they sped into the starry darkness.

At the villa they swiftly climbed over the garden wall, dropping onto the terrace and crossing behind the flowering bushes. They knew there was no CCTV. This they had already checked. They guessed Scallop had alarms only on the outer doors. They watched as a security light clicked on and off with the passing of a tomcat in the night.

From the backpack the cousins pulled plastic overshoes and surgical gloves. Over her shoulders Josie draped the length of rope, already looped and tied. She knew from experience that with Scallop at home the alarm system would likely be switched off, but she did not take chances. Josie was an expert burglar. She said these new chalet villas with their shallow roofs, patio doors and entry on two levels – the rear generally being on higher ground than the front – was a 'fucking doddle.' On the reconnoitres they had noticed rear windows locked slightly ajar. Tonight there was a light on inside one of them. There were no shadows on the glass, no movement inside. She planned to climb through that window, make her way to the man's bedroom and find him asleep in his bed.

They could not know that Scallop cared nothing for security devices. He believed himself capable of handling any two men at once, and slept with a loaded revolver in the bedside cabinet.

The cousins were in their early thirties. After three decades of fighting and stealing, Josie was fit, agile and quick. Through the window in seconds, she reached down to help Trish scramble in. As she supposed, the room was a bathroom. Josie had learned that there was a logic, a common sense, to the arrangement of rooms in a house. There was a predictability about human beings that made thieving easy. She went about her work without fuss or sound. One of the bedroom doors was fully closed. She pointed.

She swung the door open and her torchlight shone. The man's bed was there, but the man himself was not in it. 'Sh! He's in another fucking room.'

Trish's torch beam came to rest on the bedside cabinet. She pulled the drawer. 'Fuck me,' she whispered, 'have a butcher's at this, Jose.'

'Bloody hell, Trish. D'you know how to use it? Just point an' pull, right?'

'Pretty much. Keep it steady, aim straight. 'Cept we'd wake the whole frigging neighbourhood.'

'How d'you tell if it's loaded?'

Trish picked up the weapon. 'It is. I'll take it. Could be handy.'

The villa floors were laid with smooth terracotta tiles, hard and silent. From a spacious upstairs landing half a dozen wide paved steps led down to a front hallway. Glass doors ahead were closed and black. To one side an archway opened into darkness, which turned out to be a kitchen. Trish shone her light around at cupboards and drawers. The beam fell upon a notebook and a red pen on the kitchen table. They had hoped to find pen and paper in the house: Josie tore out a page, took the pen. There was no sign of life, no sound; except perhaps, hardly more than a breath, merely a sense of human presence.

Josie peeked through another arched opening and stepped away sharply. For he was there, the big man. He sat resting on a sofa, leaning back, apparently watching television. The screen was dark: television had closed down for the night. On a small table beside him stood a bottle of whisky and a glass half full.

Now they understood. Frankie Scallop had fallen asleep, still in his suit and polished shoes. Trish breathed deeply to control her nerves, inspired by the calmness of her companion. Josie was not unfamiliar with situations like this. As for the size and bulk of the great creature dozing on the sofa, she had known such men all her life. Her own father was cast from the same mould.

Josie pointed, gestured, and Trish understood. From her pocket she took the soluble powder and darted forward to empty it into the glass. Josie moved swiftly. She was deft with the rope, pulling hard on the slip-knot. Even as he woke, Scallop's feet were already tied together. 'What the fuck?' In roaring rage and shock, he raised himself and lashed out with a heavy forearm.

But the twin points of her long, slender scissors were sharp at his throat. 'Shut up, mate, an' sit still.' He drew back. Now in the gloom he saw Trish armed with his own pistol, aimed at his chest.

'Wha'd'you want?' he growled.

'Why, what you got?' sneered Josie.

'You looking for dosh?'

'We ain't come for dosh. We come for an apology.'

'*Apology?* What for? Do I know you?'

'You know my dad, Gary Renvoize. You fitted him up an' he's on a fifteen-year stretch in Strangeways.'

'Well, fuck him then, an' fuck you. He had it coming.'

'That don't sound quite like the words we want to hear, mate. Either we get to work with these scissors, an' leave you a lesser man than you already was, or you write a note for my mum.' She placed the pen and paper on the table. 'That's what she wants, my mum.'

'A note! Is it a joke?'

'Mum said make the slimy fucking shitface write down that he's sorry. If he don't, cut him to shreds, pet. *Make* him sorry. Those was her very words.'

'All right, I'm sorry,' he jeered. 'Happy now?' She lowered the scissors and he shook his head at their idiocy.

'Good. Write it down, then, so we can show her. Write it big.'

He took the pen and scrawled *Sorry* in large letters. 'That's it? You literally come in here just for that? Now put that fucking shooter down.'

'Yeah, that's right. I think we'll hang on to the pistol. Let's have a splash o' that Scotch while we're here, if you don't mind, then we'll scarper. One for the road. Where d'you keep the glasses? Want one, Trish? What about you, Inspector, top up?'

'Couple of nutters.' Again he shook his head. Trish continued to point the pistol as Josie poured. She raised her glass. 'Well, Mum'll be pleased. Bottoms up! Come on, Inspector, be friendly, chin-chin.'

Scallop emptied his in two gulps. 'Now fuck off,' he said, 'daft bitches.'

'No, we'll stay for a bit,' said Trish. 'Make sure it's worked.'

'Worked?'

She sat in an armchair and rested the gun in her lap.

As Frankie Scallop slipped rapidly into oblivion, Josie and Trish looked around the house. They discovered a small safe fixed into a wall, but had to ignore it. This must not look like burglary. In a drawer were bundles of British and Spanish banknotes. These they pocketed. 'If there's this much in a drawer, think what there must be in the fucking safe.'

On the kitchen table the lined notebook lay open. 'Oi, Jose, come an' look. What the fuck is this?' They studied the strange lists of names, arranged year by year, month by month, columns of amounts due, amounts received.

It seemed those who paid were crossed out, those who owed were not. Some who owed were marked with enigmatic letters, CC, FG, CL that Trish surmised might be a code. She turned through the pages. 'Hey! Jose, look at this one. See this name – it's your dad, ain' it?'

'Fucking Christ, look at that! You know what this is, Trish?'

'Yeah, who owes what. A fucking account book, is what it is. The bugger was going through his accounts! Look at the numbers – a grand an' a half every time. This is the whole fucking racket, right here.'

The lifeless Detective Inspector Frankie Scallop lay like a large slab of concrete amongst his sofa cushions. The cousins were surprised by how indifferent they were to the sight. Josie untied his legs, smoothed his clothes and pressed his fingertips to the empty amytal sachets. These she set down beside the pen, bottle and glass, together with the sheet of paper with its single word scrawled: *Sorry*. Carefully she placed the pistol in his hand, as if he had contemplated shooting himself.

They left the house as they had come, through the rear window. Gloves, overshoes, drinking glasses and everything else they had used was gathered in a rubbish bag to take away. The account book and the banknotes were buttoned into Josie's inside pockets.

The scooter moved along the old hill road, its keening the only sound in the night. A string of lights twinkled below them against the black seafront. Mountains rising inland were blacker still. When they reached Marbella a few bars and clubs remained open. In a street near the beach Trish leaned from her pillion to empty the rubbish bag into a large municipal garbage bin. At a telephone kiosk they paused for Josie to make an international call.

'Auntie? Sorry to wake you. Job's done. We found something very important to show you.'

*

What, Dora asked herself, was she to do with this dangerous, incriminating account book that Josie Renvoize and Trish Winslow had brought back? It was like being given a gift of radioactive rock. She wore cotton gloves to handle the thing. She recognised several of the names listed, and knew what their fate had been. Gary Renvoize, her own nephew, was one of them. The book appeared to prove what they all suspected, that there was a connection between Gary and DI Scallop *before* Gary's arrest. It had not been mentioned during his trial. According to the girls, Scallop said that Gary had it coming. That in itself was an admission of sorts.

Dora realised straight away that the enigmatic 'code' letters were merely abbreviations. *CC* obviously meant Charing Cross Police Station, *FG* was Forest Gate, *CL* City of London, *HPS* Holborn Police Station, *WEC* West End Central. Indeed the abbreviations were pencilled on the inside cover, each followed by further letters that she guessed might be initials.

She could see what had gone on here: Scallop offered 'protection' to villains. But they did not know who they were dealing with. Scallop had other men do the face-to-face work. If the villains didn't cough up, he had officers at London police stations charge them and fit them up. The officers must have had a good cut. In that way Scallop himself was always out of the picture. It was clever, she thought, fiendishly clever. She half-chuckled at the wicked brilliance of it. *If the law ran crime, that really would be the way to make it pay.*

Dora was no intellectual. She never gave a moment's thought to morality or ethics. She was not concerned with right and wrong beyond how she herself was treated. But surely it was one thing, she reasoned, to give a copper a drink to keep him sweet. That had always gone on. It was only natural. She and Micky had done plenty of it, going right back to the old Well Smack days. Without that they'd never have made a start in life. But it was another thing, wasn't it, for coppers to go *demanding* money off people for nothing, coming on with threats and extortion? The law was still supposed to be the actual law of the land – wasn't it?

How far and how high in the force, Dora wondered, did this spread? She paused to consider. Frankie Scallop was foolhardy. He must have known someone would catch up with him one of these days. Unless... he himself was being protected.

She could not send the book to the police. They would ensure it disappeared without trace. From what Maud Blake had said, ideally the Blake girl, Elizabeth, should have it. She could not hand it to her directly; that would require a lot of explaining. Nor could she send it to her chambers. Because not everyone in a barristers' chambers can be trusted.

Dora Sleet had become a kind of dowager. Her son Charles flew in a higher, golden orbit as Micky had desired and planned. Dora had the good sense to know that she must remain rooted in her native soil among her native people. There, respect for her husband lingered even among younger generations who had never known him. Everyone in the clan called her "Auntie", be they grand-nephews, second cousins or in-laws. The world had changed though, since Micky passed away, and was changing more. Foreign gangs were taking over London's rackets, spreading out of the West End to all parts of the city, including East London. They were savage, unfeeling, took hostages, routinely used the most terrible tortures. The old families were being driven out.

Dora wondered, were Scallop and his firm of coppers actually intending to take control of the rackets themselves? Were they working hand in glove with the new foreign gangs?

Detective Inspector Frankie Scallop, an East London lad himself, she reflected, knew well enough how this world works. He saw an opportunity and took it. He may have been right, thought Dora, that Gary Renvoize had it coming, but then, so did he.

*

'Hello, Mum. Everything all right? Sorry, can't chat right now, very busy.' Elizabeth wished her mother would not phone during the working day. She made an effort to be patient.

'Just to say, dear, the person who threatened you and Alex won't be a bother anymore.'

'What? Who did you hear that from?'

'Well, I can't actually swear it's true. But it is. I thought I'd tell you straight away.'

'Mum, who told you – how do they know?'

Now it was her mother who wanted to end the call. 'No one you know, love. I must go. I've got an appointment.'

'Who with?'

'Hairdresser. Anyway, you'll be fine. Nothing to worry about now.'

Later Elizabeth read the front page of the *Evening News* as she stood on a crowded tube train. A London police officer had been found dead at his luxury villa on the Costa del Sol. He left a simple one-word suicide note – *Sorry*. The dead man's name was given, and the information that he was under investigation for corruption. Senior officers in the Metropolitan Police declared that the Operation Countryman witch hunt should be shut down if it was driving such first-rate men to take their own lives.

People who knew Detective Inspector Scallop, it was reported, doubted that he had killed himself. He wasn't the type, they said. He wasn't the type to say *sorry*, either. One colleague, asked if the man had any enemies, replied 'That's all he had.' A Spanish police spokesman remarked that the brief note had been written on a page torn from an exercise book, but no such exercise book had been found in the house. Nothing was being ruled out.

3

I t was unnerving that her mother would not explain. Elizabeth feared that merely by mentioning the name of Scallop she had somehow caused a suicide or worse. Bewildered by the turn of events, she voiced her concern to Bernard, 'How did Mum find out before the newspapers what had happened to him? *Who told her?*'

'What does she say?'

'She says she can't remember.'

He scoffed, incredulous. 'So maybe one of her neighbours told her, you know, a friend on holiday in Spain?'

'She'd remember that, surely?'

'If she really *has* forgotten, I suppose we'll never know. I'd put it out of your mind if I were you,' responded Bernard, unhelpfully blithe. 'At least the bastard is dead. Personally I'm not sorry.'

When Bernard arrived at work an envelope lay on his desk. Inside was an exercise book and a typed, unsigned note: *PRIVATE + CONFIDENTIAL For Miss Blake, From Scallops place in Spain. Heres whats in his book...*

He read a few pages and picked up the phone. 'Liz, you got time to come over urgently to see something? It's actually addressed to you.' – 'What is?' – 'Rather not say. Just come over.'

Years had passed since Elizabeth last visited the offices of Kassin & Co. at Stratford. It was still in the same shabby upstairs premises above an Asian grocery. Condensation still ran down the steamy window of the caff next door. Most of the Bernard's staff – solicitors and support workers alike – were still radical-looking young women who gave not a nod either to femininity or fashion. The atmosphere was extremely informal and relaxed, more so than any other workplace she knew. On the walls were pinned women's liberation posters, the red fist clenched, others on prisoners' rights, miscarriages of justice and a *Disband the SPG* [Special Patrol Group].

In Bernard's room she sat with a mug of coffee. He brought out the handwritten account book and typed note. 'This was on my desk this morning. No one seems to have noticed who brought it. I've made a photocopy.'

Elizabeth studied some of the pages. She used the anonymous typed note to interpret the initials and abbreviations. 'This won't stand up,' she concluded. 'Evidence sent anonymously? It's speculation. We can't use it. We don't know how it was obtained. We'd need forensics even to confirm it's Scallop's.'

'Suppose the notebook itself can't be proved, but the information within it can?' said Bernard. 'You wanted Scallop's contacts. If the note is correct, the names are listed right there.' Then he noticed something. 'Oh look, a page has been torn out.'

She saw that it was true. 'I'm taking this to Countryman.'

*

After all these years she recognised the voice at once, loved the tone of it, the timbre, the unchanged accent of her schooldays.

'Chaz! This is a surprise!' – 'Know why I'm phoning?'

Since his wedding Elizabeth had remained in touch with Charles Sleet at the Christmas card level. There might be no contact from one festive season to the next, but they had each other's phone numbers. It was not a secret. When Bernard had asked her, as she asked him, about former lovers, she told him about Charles. On the seasonal card they scribbled their news, a whole year in two or three sentences. Elizabeth knew about Sleet Properties being floated on the Stock Exchange, the births of his two boys, Philip and Julian. He knew about her career, her husband, her little girl, her conversion, knew that she did not actually celebrate Christmas despite the card.

'No! Why?' – 'My mother hasn't been in touch, then?'

'Your mother! I don't even know your mother. I only met her once.' – 'She asked me for your address.'

'How strange!' – 'I didn't think you'd want to see her so I said I don't know where you live.'

'Why did she want my address?' – 'Said she had something to give you. I told her to send it to your solicitor, because he's also your husband.'

'Did she send me something?' – 'Well, I don't know. I suppose so.'

'I don't think she did. How are things, anyway?' – 'Pretty good. Are you free at all, darling?'

'Don't call me that anymore, Chaz.' – 'We're still us, Lizzie. It'll always be just us. You and me.'

Without warning, for an instant she could not draw breath. The sensation in her throat was as people describe it, a hard lump pressing. She covered the mouthpiece lest tears come. She fought them back.

'Just us.' – 'You free right now for lunch?'

She relieved her tension with a laugh. 'I'd love that!'

Charles was waiting outside Goodge Street station. He smiled happily as she came into view. 'Still a rebel deep down, I see,' he greeted her. – 'What? No! I play the super-straight now. Look at me!' She wore smart blue jeans, a white shirt, a light fitted jacket, a necklace of lapis lazuli set in silver filigree.

'You can't fool me! Something in the eyes.' He was in playful mood. 'So, *do* you have to balance a wig on your head?'

'When I'm in court, of course! I'm not in court today, as you see.'

Their lips touched. No carnal desire had brought her here, yet it thrilled her to see him in the flesh, embrace him once again and feel his kiss. The man was as beautiful as ever. How much bigger and stronger he was than Bernard! The face had matured, though there lingered something of boyish charm. The curious platinum hair was long, brushed back elegantly from a side parting. He had shaved off the ridiculous droopy moustache. He wore a pale grey suit, a turquoise shirt, pale pink tie and grey pointed shoes.

The longing she felt was covetousness, not lust; she knew him as others never would. He belonged to her. He was part of her box of treasures. She prized him, cherished him as something by rights already her own. In short, she loved him. She was elated in his presence.

She knew it was absurd. The man was an unscrupulous capitalist. It would have been idiotic to try to make a life with Charles instead of Bernard, she could see that. This she dare not think about.

He had not booked anything for lunch. They went into the Spaghetti House, round the corner. It was pleasantly busy and animated. Almost as soon as they sat down he sensed her stress. 'What's up, Liz – you all right? You and Bernard getting on all right?'

'Of course! I won't hear a word against him.'

'Oh, likewise. Nicola's a good partner.'

'Exactly.'

A waitress came with her notepad before they had looked at the menus. They ordered pizza and two glasses of house red.

'So what is it, Liz?'

'I've got up the noses of some bent coppers. I've been threatened. There's a gang of crooks working in the police. What they call the "firm within a firm". That British policeman in Spain, he was one of them. There are plenty more. He was part of a clique.'

'You think someone did for him over there?'

'Not sure. It wasn't me, anyway.'

'Tell me about this clique.'

'They meet at golf courses and Masonic lodges and nightclubs. Not a Freemason by any chance, are you?'

Charles chuckled. 'I am, as it happens.'

'Really? Which lodge?' Elizabeth was alert.

He told her. She said, 'My God, that could be useful, if you want to help me. Why are you a Mason?'

'Nic's dad put me up to it. It's useful. Didn't you say your dad was a union man? That's the same.'

'Not at all the same!' she retorted, indignant. 'That's silly, Charles. Trade unions aren't secretive! They're about collective bargaining, giving a bit of muscle to the working man.'

'No actually, it is the same. Closed shop, isn't it, the print? Everyone looks after their own. *And* I play golf, by the way.'

'*Do* you? That doesn't sound like you.'

He grinned. 'Yup. Eighteen handicap.'

'Chaz, does your wife know you're meeting me?'

'No. Nic has a full diary of her own. What about Bernard, does he know where you are?'

'No. I'll tell him we met, though, Charles. I hate deceiving him.'

'That's fine. Say it was for work.'

'Do you still have that flat?'

'Yes.'

In good humour and without haste they put their clothes back on,

Elizabeth buttoning her blouse with Charles's eye lingering upon her. 'We can come here anytime we like,' he said.

'I don't want it to be like that. It would feel furtive.'

'We've found each other again, Liz. I must keep seeing you.' He was in earnest. 'This is the perfect place.'

She shook her head, 'I don't want to be the secret mistress, or have a double life.'

'Listen then. Nic and me put on a lot of dos, garden parties in summer, concerts. We have a picnic at Glyndebourne. We invite guests for a day at Lord's, take a box at Ascot, that sort of thing. I can invite you and Bernard to join us now and then.'

'No, it would be terrible. We'd have to pretend. I'd be with Bernard!'

'We're good at pretending, Liz. At least we'd be together. And then... maybe we *can* come here sometimes.'

'Bernard's not interested in horses or cricket. Glyndebourne could be nice, though.'

'You'd meet useful people. You can find out what's going on behind the scenes. You'd be surprised who rubs shoulders at our parties.'

*

The weekly music lesson of the reception class at Park Gate Primary was fun for some, boring for others. The teacher hammered away at the piano, accompanied by the pupils' chaotic cacophony of tambourine, triangle and drum. With countless stops, corrections and repetitions she was teaching them to sing *Frères Jacques* as a round for an end-of-term performance. Among those who found it boring was the teacher herself. Another was Alexandra.

When the teacher was called to the door of the class by the headmistress, on an impulse Alexandra pushed back her chair and darted to the piano. To the awestruck horror of the other pupils, while standing at the keyboard she began to play *Frères Jacques* as a frenzied jazz piece. The room was loud with the sound.

The two women at the door turned. The music teacher raised her voice in outrage. 'Alexandra Kassin! Naughty girl!'

The headmistress grabbed her arm. 'No, listen! This is absolutely incredible.'

But Alex was already returning sheepish to her place. There was no punishment. Instead, Elizabeth and Bernard were invited to come in and chat to the headmistress. She proposed to arrange a private music lesson for Alex after school every day, if they agreed.

'She's not five years old yet,' protested Bernard.

'The music teacher feels that Alex is ready for lessons. Do you have a piano at home?'

'No. She plays my mother's when we go there,' said Elizabeth.

'In that case Alex may practise on the school piano during break.'

The school hall of Park Gate Primary was also the school gym, with an assortment of apparatus heaped against climbing frames at one end of the room, and a low platform or stage at the other. Between the platform and the stacked ropes, balls, mats and vaulting horses, several rows of chairs had been set out. Here, on the last day of the autumn term, parents filed into the hall and took their seats. Most were the children's mothers, their fathers being still at work. Bernard and Elizabeth, however, both made sure to be here.

The entertainment brimmed with the charm and naivete of any primary school performance. Every member of the audience relished joyous pride in their little star. The round of *Frères Jacques* was faultlessly executed by the reception class, Alex joining in with the rest.

It was the first time she had stood in front of an audience. She looked out at the staring faces, the peering eyes, and struggled to understand the part played by the platform. Were the children *just singing*, or by assembling on a platform were they *doing something else*? She thought of Gran watching variety acts on television, and men playing football, and cricket matches. *Some people are inside the game, while others watch from outside. Are the watchers also taking part? Would it be the same game without them?*

She looked into the hall and there spied Mummy and Daddy gazing directly at her. Next to Mummy was an empty chair. This, she decided, was Gran's seat, and in it she pictured Maud.

There followed an endearing show of the children's singing and reciting before the headmistress announced that the next act of the afternoon would be by a most remarkably talented pupil. Alex stepped from the chorus to take her seat at the piano. The other children gathered together staring at this singular individual who had been pulled from amongst them.

From the audience a murmur could be heard. Alex was aware that she must stop thinking. She did not want to see the faces or hear the murmuring. She must concentrate instead on the white and black keys in their orderly parallels, each one unique, with its own sound and personality. As if deciding for themselves when to start, her hands suddenly moved forward and began to play the notes of *Für Elise*.

A collective breath of astonishment came from the adults in their chairs. Someone tittered in disbelief, one or two clapped after just a few seconds. The room was filled with the familiar tune, presented with uncanny precision and delicacy. The parents fell into awestruck silence, watching the little girl as if she were a comet in the night sky, a spectacle from the Universe unknown.

Until this moment Alex had never associated music with her own physical body. Music had been something in the ear and in the mind. But these people were not *listening* to a piano being played, they were *watching* it being played.

Her questions were answered, her uncertainty dispersed. The children had *not* been 'just singing'. And she understood; the centre of attention is the performer, not the performance.

Bernard was having similar thoughts. So was Elizabeth. She whispered into his ear: 'This was a mistake.'

He nodded grimly in return. He whispered, 'Poor little thing, like a circus animal doing tricks. We shouldn't have allowed it.' Nevertheless he proudly took a photo.

As applause and cheers rang out, Alex made a modest bow and smiled sweetly. She looked at the empty chair and there imagined Maud, her lined old face looking up in delight and praise. Elizabeth gave a wave and Bernard took another photo. He murmured, 'She's a natural though, isn't she?'

*

There had been no more threats. Perhaps that was because after the mysterious death of Detective Inspector Frank Scallop it became known to the "firm within a firm" that Elizabeth Kassin and her husband now belonged to Charles Sleet's circle of powerful and influential friends.

With Alex progressing and time passing (as Bernard insisted it was), they decided it was a good moment to 'try for' a second child. This one was no accident. Before the end of the next school year, Ruth had been born and a cot was placed in Elizabeth and Bernard's tiny shared study (the original study had become Alex's bedroom). It became impossible to work in there.

Elizabeth and Bernard followed Jake and Abigail out of East London, from Wanstead Flats to Hampstead Heath, from Victoria Park to Golders Hill Park. There they found a spacious, high-ceilinged pre-War semi-detached of dark old red brick. Jake and Abi were not five minutes' drive away. They even joined the same synagogue.

Straight away Alex gained a place at a music school in Hertfordshire. She was to be a boarder, coming home at weekends if she wanted. Naturally everyone expressed their doubts about 'sending her away' at such a young age (she was eight). Bernard and Elizabeth insisted, 'This is what she wants. It's one of the most famous music schools in the country.'

Maud could hardly be persuaded to come and see the new place. For Maud, London had become a continent. There used to be a time when she went on the bus along Romford Road to tend her parents' grave and lay a posy on Len's plaque. That was long ago. Longer ago still Len's sister Audrey had sold the Blake family home and quit the area. Maud didn't blame her. Who'd want to live in Manor Park now?

It was ages since she last went. She was afraid of the new people. It worried her to see 'KBW' – *Keep Britain White* – scrawled in white paint on the red-brick walls. The angry graffiti threatened a new disorder. She reasoned with herself that these 'coloureds' were no more strange than the Yiddish-speaking Jews she had once lived among. Maud recalled how they too were pestered and hated. She had never forgotten the contemptible strutting Mosleyites. She bore no ill-will towards the exotic newcomers. She felt only that she must abandon the area to them. They could have it. She had no need anymore of these pinched streets, no need of Romford Road which flowed now like a torrent of unfamiliar humanity fit to burst its banks.

She preferred not to think of it at all.

Dagenham was a frontier to her now. The little Roding was a Styx. Her youth lay beyond it, Up West, at dances long ago. As for the River Thames, Maud knew as much about South London as she did about the South Seas. Hampstead, away to the north-west, was unthinkably remote, a highland of dreams and songs, funfairs and bank holiday outings, a legendary Shangri-La.

Elizabeth had to drive over to fetch her. It made a tedious journey in those days, before the North Circular Road, there and back on zig-zag rat-runs across North London. Nevertheless, Maud was eventually delivered to the door of their new home. Half-a-dozen shrubs in majestic glazed pots stood either side of a deep porch. The front garden was laid with fine old paving. Neat flowerbeds decorated the perimeter.

'Oh, this is nice.' Maud was frankly impressed. Her daughter's new home was positively grand.

Elizabeth felt as if she were proudly showing off, and was a little ashamed of the feeling. The rooms were large, with high ceilings and pleasingly proportioned. At the back, french windows opened onto a handsome garden. 'I made some scones,' she said. Elizabeth's scones were always good.

They sat awkwardly with cups of tea. Maud felt she must be on her best behaviour in such a place. Framed paintings hung on ivory-coloured walls. On one side of the room, tall shelves were filled with a Bernard's huge collection of LPs. Beside them was a baby grand.

'Lovely piano,' observed Maud. Clearly she was rather shocked by it.

'Alex practises a lot when she's at home,' Bernard explained. 'Actually,' he confessed with unaccustomed bashfulness, '...I'm having piano lessons myself.'

Maud responded dryly, 'Are you?' in a *you-must-have-money-to-burn* tone. It almost seemed that she disapproved.

Elizabeth wondered how to put her at her ease. She said that Bernard had opened a second office near the High Court, devoted solely to major crime. 'It's close to my chambers, which is very handy.' The office at Stratford, she said, was now staffed mainly with specialists in immigration, employment and housing law.

Maud pulled a face. 'Still in Stratford? I been telling you for years, get a smart office in Mayfair, Bernard.'

Bernard smiled. 'No, well, our clients mostly live in East London, not the West End. Do you fancy a go on the piano?' he suggested gently.

'I can't. It's my hands. My fingers won't move.'

'Don't tell me you can't play the piano anymore?' He was truly dismayed. The poor woman had few enough pleasures.

Elizabeth had thought she was up to date with her mother's ailments. 'What about the Keep Fit job?'

'Oh, I had to give that up. I can't go on with my gardening neither. It's too much for me.' There was wry resignation.

'Oh no! I didn't realise, Mum!'

'Maud, that's terrible,' exclaimed Bernard. 'We'll get you some help. What about the housework, the cleaning? Can we get someone to do that for you?'

'Oh, no, I manage that all right. I don't want a stranger in the house.' Bernard was apparently unaware that on every visit to her mother, Elizabeth had to 'quickly' vacuum the floors and 'go around with a duster'.

'Well, what about a gardener, at least?'

A shake of the head. 'Thanks all the same, love, but there's no need. I don't want anyone.' She was faintly amused. No one in her street, probably no one on the estate, no one she had ever known, employed a gardener. She supposed, though, on reflection, that there might be one or two local men who worked as jobbing gardeners. Maybe, somehow... but the thought was pre-empted by Bernard: 'We'll do it for you,' he said, 'We'll come more often and keep the garden nice.' This Maud considered a far happier, more normal, very sensible suggestion even if (as she suspected) nothing much came of it. Bernard, she guessed, could not prune a rose to save his life. He might be able to mow the lawn though.

Shortly afterwards, Elizabeth drove her home. 'Sometimes,' Maud mused strangely as they turned into the crescent, 'I feel as if I'm already dead.'

'Why d'you say that? You've got years ahead of you.'

'Died and gone to heaven. The world's going on without me.' She was glad to get back into her own home and went straight to bed.

*

Elizabeth ignored the doorbell. She could not face anyone. Operation Countryman, on which she had worked for so long and in such danger, had been hastily wound up and the investigators sent back to Dorset. Having struggled to protect their evidence from the Metropolitan Police whom they had been investigating, the Countryman team had now been ordered to hand over their confidential dossiers to that very force under its new Commissioner. This was the last straw and a humiliating, impotent end to the operation.

On a further long ring Elizabeth thought it must be the postman or a delivery. She went down in her dressing gown and bare feet.

Jake Zuckerman stood on the step, uninvited, very casual, hair tousled, gazing straight into her eyes. He was holding his bicycle.

'Oh! Jake! What... a surprise! Is everything all right?'

'I've just come over to see if you're OK.' She could not understand his expression. There was humour and concern.

'OK? Of course I'm OK! Oh God, sorry I'm not dressed yet!'

Jake's voice was calm and gentle. 'Ask me in. Where can I put my bike?'

She offered him a coffee. 'I'm working from home today. Truly I am OK, Jake. What makes you think I'm not?'

'Well, not dressed at lunchtime, for a start. That's not like you. Not at chambers, not in court, not anywhere. Never free to come round. Answering machine on all the time. I know what this is, Liz. I can see it in your face.'

She said not a single word as she spooned coffee, poured water, set out cups. She opened a cupboard and peered inside as if she had forgotten what she was looking for. 'Oh God, I must look a fright.' A reluctant, almost embarrassed, admission: 'You're right, I'm not OK.'

'Tell me.'

She sighed with tremendous weariness. 'I feel... what do I feel? Oh God! I don't know. Purposeless.'

'Does Bernard know you're like this?'

'Well,' and she sighed deeply. 'Thing is, he's really preoccupied. Bernard has a lot to think about. He's busy at work and writing his book on common law in the evening. I don't want to be a problem for him! When we're together I make an effort. I go to bed early. He's always nice, considerate.'

'Surely you've discussed it with him?'

In answer Elizabeth merely looked down, as if helpless and defeated.

Jake asked, 'Where's Ruth?'

'Childminder picks her up.'

He shook his head, questioning. 'You stopped coming to shul, Liz. You said you liked it. You meet people.'

'No, no, I don't want to meet people. I can hardly even call my mother.'

He nodded. 'There's us. You can call Abi anytime.'

'I know that, Jake, I know – and thank you. I don't think Abi can help me with this.'

'Come for a walk.'

'Thanks, Jake, but no, I'm too tired, honestly. I can't just be cheered up with a walk. It isn't like that.'

'Come on. It's nice out.'

'That's what you said the last time. Remember, at UCL?'

'That's how we got to know each other. We need to do that again.'

She stared in the mirror as she washed her face and brushed her hair. She did not recognise herself.

They left the house on foot, walking the uneven pavements where great spreading plane trees had shed sheets of pale bark and huge leathery green leaves. Large Victorian houses, handsome and individual, stood well back behind clipped hedges and driveways harbouring expensive cars.

Elizabeth said, 'It actually *is* a nice day, isn't it?'

'How's Alex?' Jake asked. He knew there had been friction, but that was normal whether or not one's child was a musical prodigy.

'She stays with her friends at the weekends. We never see her.'

'Is that getting you down?'

She shrugged helplessly. It was difficult to talk in any case as they weaved around wheeled bins on the pavement. They crossed at last onto the Heath and continued one behind the other between trees, the earth moist and soft underfoot. Tangled branches above were alive with chattering songbirds, abruptly muted by an occasional fly-past of screeching parakeets.

Ahead, raised on red brick walls, the elegant white pillars of the Heath's pergola emerged from the woods like a fairytale domain. At the wall. Jake pushed an iron gate. Up a flight of steps they climbed to walkways of pale stone. Elizabeth looked around in wonder. 'How come I never found this place before?'

Not another person did they see in any direction. Slowly they passed between white columns and twining foliage, jasmine abandoned and unkempt, coils of wisteria grasping, ivy creeping uninvited, vines laden with surreal fruit, some of the pillars concealed altogether within tangled threads and stems. Unpruned roses stretched across wooden crossbeams sculpted by rot.

Jake tenderly repeated his question. 'What's getting you down, Liz?'

Now they could talk. 'I spent years becoming a barrister,' she reflected, 'don't laugh, but it was a big struggle.'

'Yes, I know.'

'I did it for many reasons, but most especially I wanted to expose dishonesty in the police. Turns out it was a waste of time and money. That battle is lost. I can't bear what's happened. Operation Countryman has been shut down. The crooks won. They got away with it.' She knew that Jake, through his work as a government policy adviser, was fully aware of the investigation.

He said, 'A chief inspector jailed for three years and a sergeant for two, that's a result.'

'A couple of scapegoats, Jake! There were scores under investigation, dozens suspected of crime, eleven officers charged with serious offences, and in the end just *two* paid a price. For the others it's back to business.'

Reaching a bench, they sat beside one another with a wide view over treetops. 'What does Bernard think?' asked Jake.

'You know how he makes light of things. He's upset about Countryman, but he says dishonesty is the human condition and without it there would be less work for lawyers.'

Jake snorted. 'He's right there. Don't worry, Liz, everyone agrees the police can't go on as they are. It's not just the corruption – we've been looking at racism, misogyny, bullying, the whole gamut. They can't sack the entire police force, so Mrs T asked for new procedures. The Royal Commission on Criminal Procedure is reporting shortly.

What's proposed is: no police interviews without a solicitor present, prosecution to be completely separate from the police, and new police vetting procedures. In a year or so there will be a bill before Parliament, the Police and Criminal Evidence Bill. It will change a lot of things. If Countryman contributed to that, it wasn't a failure.'

'We'll see. If it becomes law, the police will find ways around it.'

'If they do, couldn't officers be pursued through the civil courts?'

'Yes.' Elizabeth replied quietly, 'they could. Lovely here, isn't it? I'll walk up here every day till I get my head together.'

4

A lex opened a window to enter more closely into the fathomless realm. She saw a slender curve of bright pearl, set low. Exquisite paleness to the east had begun to sweep away stars, the heavens a palette of lapis, azure, violet. What struck her then, with mountain air fresh on her face, was the ineffable stillness. *How quiet! Not a sound!* She listened intently. Not a peep, not a rustle, no distant motor.

She learned years before that she had a condition (and was surprised to be told it was abnormal) known as synaesthesia – she visualised sound as well as hearing it. However, the reverse was not true: a sight did not conjure sound. Yet the dawn before her, more delicate than fine translucent china, seemed the very picture of utter silence.

Later this morning would be the last stage of the International Piano Competition. She made a wish upon the moon to achieve something as lovely as this. She closed the window and returned to bed.

Propped up against pillows, the duvet pulled high, she went over the scores in her mind note by note then dozed a little. Waking again, she flicked through the pages of a brochure about the contestants and the works they would play. Turning a page it startled her to confront her own photograph and biography. *Alexandra Harriet Blake Kassin. Born 1975 in East London*, she read. She hated the photo. It had been chosen by her mother. It was an old one. She looked hardly more than a child in this picture, and was (she considered) too dark, too high-browed, smiling foolishly. She regretted her hairstyle, which looked excruciatingly dated now. She could hardly believe that such an idiotic bouffant had ever existed. *Classical and jazz piano*, she read. *Also saxophone and cello. By the age of 13 Alexandra had achieved Grade 8 Distinction on all three instruments. At 15 she... She has studied with ... played with ... attends...* followed by a list of the successes of her teenage years, Young Musician of the Year, national and international competitions.

This would be her fifth and most important piano competition.

Apart from the honour of a top ranking, the first prize amounted to thirty thousand Swiss francs. She dozed a little more, then rose again from the bed. It was time to face the music.

The finalists were each to play entirely from memory a programme of eighty minutes, with full orchestra, in the town's grand and gilded old theatre before an international audience of discerning connoisseurs. She had chosen Brahms' *Sonata in E minor, Op.38*, for piano and cello, followed by a modern piece, Bernstein's second symphony, *The Age of Anxiety*. Between the two came a short compulsory work, Scarlatti's *Sonata in E Major*. She had practised hours every day for months; and not only these pieces, for the contestants had to prepare two different programmes, the judges deciding which should be played. That uncertainty was one of the most difficult elements in the competition.

*

Her triumph was rewarded with an ovation, cries of *brava*, handshakes, endless hugs and kisses – and a holiday, probably the last she would ever spend with her parents. She was almost dazed with relief, yet the constant praise and the cornucopia of the prize made her uneasy, as if walking on a frozen river. Elizabeth and Bernard felt that after the great pressure she had been under, their beloved daughter deserved peace and quiet and a chance to unwind. Alex did not see it like that. She longed to get back to her friends. The last thing she wanted was to be cooped up with her excruciatingly dull, foolish mum and dad, listening to their fretting and prattling.

Nevertheless she humoured them. Together they wandered in the town, wonderful with frescoes, murals, cobbled squares and lanes, flower-covered bridges and balconies, sun glinting on the water, the entire place watched over by white peaks. At a table by the lakeside they raised icy glasses to her success. The hotel Elizabeth and Bernard had chosen was high in a grand old Edwardian mountain resort not far away. There was edelweiss in the grounds and a heated swimming pool in which Alex decided to spend as much time as she could.

In the night a giant storm arose, lightning in the next valley making the mountains into colossal shadows, immense silhouettes against a purple, livid sky. Mad cathartic drumrolls of thunder pounded, fireballs flashing over the peaks. Not a drop of rain fell. Afterwards she slept in a dream of Brahms and Scarlatti, bending her body to reach into a foliage of notes with slender cutting wire, pruning the staves with miniature blades.

Waking, she remembered the applause. She had nothing to do today. It was a morning of sweet sun, and pretty clouds cast across the blue like white petals.

*

From a heavy cream envelope Bernard pulled a heavy cream card. He had been expecting it. Every few months such an invitation would arrive from the Sleets. However, this occasion was to be quite different from any other.

In a gala celebration of being bestowed with a knighthood for services to the housing industry, announced the gold lettering, the newly ennobled Sir Charles and Lady Sleet invited Bernard and Elizabeth to a fund-raising youth concert on behalf of Diamonds, the children's charity founded by his father of which Charles was now chairman.

Bernard felt he had nothing in common with Charles, still less with Nicola. Charles Sleet, well known as a hard-headed, down to earth and ruthlessly successful business magnate, was in Bernard's eyes merely a big, brash, boorish egotist, a crass ignoramus, hedonist and philistine. As for Nicola...!

However, despite Elizabeth's early forebodings, Bernard invariably enjoyed Charles and Nicola's events. He found them surprisingly sophisticated, knowing affairs. Nicola had developed the knack of ensuring guests came not to meet herself or her husband but to meet each other. Indeed it was possible to meet every type of person of influence. Interesting conversations over champagne and smoked salmon could turn into valuable contacts and understandings, sometimes promises and deals.

On this special occasion Miss Alexandra Kassin would entertain with a piano recital and a chamber orchestra of talented young musicians. The programme was to include passages from her recent prize-winning triumph at the prestigious International Piano

Competition in Switzerland. The Sleets' own son, Julian, would perform as first violinist.

Among the guests, Charles had assured them, would be artistes' agents, musicians' managers and record company talent scouts. Bernard admitted it was remarkably generous of the Sleets to help the youngsters in this way.

Alex pulled together a small group of players she admired at school. They were all girls. However, Julian Sleet was forced on them as part of the deal. He came along for an audition and to meet the others. The general view of him turned out to be favourable after all. This boy had an appealing, confident manner. He was rather nice looking, with thick flowing hair almost milky in colour. As for his musical ability, Alex and her friends abandoned their scepticism as soon as he took the violin into his hands. Julian was clearly at home with the instrument.

She decided they should perform only the *Allegretto quasi Menuetto* from the Brahms, and from the Bernstein only the *Masque* and *Epiloque*. She decided against the Scarlatti piano solo altogether. Instead she would solo with Liszt's *Hungarian Rhapsody number 6* from the alternative pieces that the Swiss judges had not asked her to play. Altogether it made a program which would, Alex hoped, impress Sir Charles's not-too-demanding audience of philanthropists. She had an idea to finish on something jazzy.

As the little orchestra of teenagers filed onto the stage and began to tune up, Bernard declared to Charles, 'Human beings are amazing. The relationship between the musician and the instrument – that's the human mind at work!'

Charles frowned at yet another of Bernard's whimsical observations. He replied. 'I used to have a skiffle group myself. Played washboard and drums.' At which he rose abruptly and stepped up to the stage, calling the audience to order. He declared that he was 'incredibly proud' to have been honoured, revealing that the Sleets were always a noble family. 'I've been told we're descended from Slede, the first Saxon King of Essex.' Finally he introduced 'the phenomenal Alexandra Kassin and her youth orchestra.'

Bernard leaned across to whisper to Elizabeth. 'Is that true about the skiffle group?'

'Yeah. His dad put a stop to it.' But the concert had started. From the first notes of the Brahms, Alex's mastery was beyond doubt. The switch to Bernstein stirred exhilaration around the room. The whole audience held its breath as Alex slowly began a further change of mood with a keyboard arrangement they recognised with excitement as a Bruce Springsteen top-ten single. Alex's poignant, heartrending notes were like words softly murmured. She whispered just one line into the microphone, *There's something happening somewhere, baby I just know there is.*

'I'll finish,' she said, 'with a dance number. If you know the charleston, ladies and gentlemen, or better still, the black bottom, now's your chance. This is dedicated to my grandmother, Maud Blake, my teacher, my mentor, my inspiration, and a great dancer, by the way. For you, Gran, the first piece you ever taught me. *Yes Sir, That's My Baby.*'

She and the little orchestra, miraculously transformed by saxophones into a hot jazz band, sprang into a ragtime that sent foot-tapping joy through the audience. In mid-play Alex rose from the keyboard and casually swapped instruments with a saxophonist, who took her place at the piano. Bernard covered his eyes with his hand, hiding tears. That Alex could weave Brahms, Springsteen, Liszt and Donaldson's 1920s hit into a single cohesive performance, the pieces linked like a symphony in four emotions, was too wonderful for him to bear. Elizabeth leaned across, 'She's better than we thought.' He kissed her. 'Who is this amazing person that we created?'

It was over. Waiters appeared carrying large trays of canapés and wine. Agents, managers and recording companies were in discussion in another room. As the crowd mingled, Charles approached Elizabeth. He squeezed her hand.

'Thank you, Chaz. Shame my mother couldn't see this.'

'It's all on film. Alex will get a copy to show people.'

Alex turned up on the doorstep wearing a tight red sweater, white trousers, red shoes and black-framed glasses. Her dark hair had been cut short. By a perverse instinct Maud could not show how thrilled she was to see her beloved granddaughter. She greeted her matter-of-factly. Alex rarely visited nowadays, never during term time. Indeed it had been many months, perhaps a year (Maud dared not work it out) since the last time. Yet here the girl was, grinning happily, unannounced! Maud said calmly, 'Hello, darling! You look great. Come in. Well done winning in Switzerland.'

Alex noticed that the once-deft, magical, musical fingers had become stiff and disfigured, seemingly pushed out of position by the arthritis, some of them curled into the shape of a bird's claws, as it appeared to Alex. It was a horrifying doom that she could not allow herself to consider for a second. Nevertheless she bent forward to kiss her grandmother's wracked hands. 'Do they hurt?'

A slight nod and raised eyebrows confirmed that her hands were in constant pain. 'I have to take a load of paracetamol. It's not just my hands. I've got it all over. I'm eighty-three. Getting old is like being in a war you can't win. Every year you get more injuries and lose more ground.'

'I've come to tell you I'll carry on the fight for you, Gran. Me and some friends started a group, seven of us,' she explained eagerly, 'an ensemble It's all girls except one.'

'Classical, I suppose, is it?' For she knew about Alex's previous competition successes.

'Not really. Jazz-rock classical, our own arrangements. We named the band after you.'

'After *me*?' Maud responded with amused disbelief. 'You're pulling my leg.'

'No, Gran. We're called *Blake's Fusion*.'

'Ha ha, you really calling it that? Course, that would be naming it after my husband, not me. If he only knew!'

'Oh! What's your name then, Gran?'

'I'm Maud Cotter, as was.'

'How about Cotter's Fusion, then?'

With a shrug Maud wrinkled her nose. 'Up to you. Makes no difference. A woman doesn't have a family name of her own. It's always a father or husband's name. Cotter is my dad.'

'Well, then, let's stick with Blake's Fusion! We gave a concert for a charity do. I've brought a video to show you.'

Maud clapped with delight. Alex set up the projector, ready to cast the film onto the wallpaper above the living room sofa. She turned her grandmother's armchair to face the wall.

The first thing Maud remarked upon was the ethnic mix. 'That girl on cello, what is she, Chinese?' – 'Korean.' – '*Korean?* Blimey. And those black girls, where are they from?' – 'Hackney.'

'What was the charity?' – 'Dunno.'

'My God, you're terrific,' Maud exclaimed as she watched. When *Yes Sir* began, she swung her hands and moved her feet as if dancing in her chair. 'This is special,' she said. 'You could earn money doing this.'

Alex replied eagerly, 'We are, Gran! We're making a recording with Parlophone.' She was thrilled by Maud's approval. She felt that visually and musically Blake's Fusion had a brilliant, compelling presence.

'What, you *already* got signed? How did you do that?'

'The studios sent people to hear the concert. One of our dads arranged it.'

'That's lucky. He gave someone a bung, then.'

Alex laughed. 'No, honestly I doubt it, Gran. Well,' she reflected, 'maybe he did! He's mega-rich.'

'Who's the boy on fiddle?' Maud asked. There was something about him that perturbed her.

'That's my boyfriend, Julian. He's good, isn't he? He's the one whose dad helped us.'

'Julian…?'

'Sleet.'

Yes, it's unmistakeable. Looks like Billy. 'Who d'you say his father was?'

'Sir Charles Sleet. He's from round here. Comes from Romford.'

How did Alex get mixed up with that family of crooks? How did someone like Julian emerge from such a family?

'He and Mum are good friends from way back,' added Alex.

'Are they now? Well, well.'

5

Alex and Julian were serious about each other. When they started living together, Elizabeth and Charles understood that their own 'special relationship' must end. 'It would seem almost incestuous otherwise,' Elizabeth said.

Charles agreed. 'Let their love be ours.'

'Just this once, Charles, can we go away, you and me, and be alone together? Before it's too late.'

He answered unhappily. 'How? I can't be out of touch. And everything I spend is put through the books.'

'Surely you can take a day off? Just say you can't be contacted. You must have some money of your own, don't you?'

To Bernard, Elizabeth announced that she and Katie were thinking of spending a couple of days away. He said it was a good idea. He loved it that from time to time the two childhood friends – they had always kept in touch – would meet up. Katie was happy to cover for her. She promised to tell Bernard anything Elizabeth wanted.

To Nicola, Charles said he had to visit Portsmouth for a couple of days to look at development sites. He was also interested in buying a motor cruiser and would call on some yacht brokers while he was there. Did she want to come along? He knew it was the sort of thing she hated. Nicola said she did not want to come.

Charles had his office book him a night at a hotel in Portsmouth. On the day, he actually did drive to Portsmouth, checked in at the hotel and told reception he was on no account to be disturbed. He even went to his room and had a shower before continuing his journey. Approaching Chichester, he used a map to find his way among lanes beside the great harbour.

Elizabeth was already waiting at the holiday let when he arrived. She had found a house set back from the untamed shore, too modern for her taste but wonderfully private and luxurious. A frontage of glass faced across the spectacular ebb and flow of tide that swept at a running pace across the acres of shining mud flats. In vast airy spaces above the silvery expanse, hundreds of water-loving birds swooped and circled. Along the harbour's weedy rim hundreds more, homelier species, chattered, scurried and foraged.

She held Charles and kissed him. 'Did you bring the wine?'

He had brought wine, and flowers too.

In the morning, Elizabeth stretched in bliss between white cotton sheets, pressed her head dreamily into soft white pillows, watching as the naked Charles walked comfortably between bedroom and bathroom. There was about him a compelling vigour, his pale muscled physique nearly hairless, in every particular unlike Bernard.

She looked out idly at the pearly morning sky. She felt somehow that Bernard was not deceived. And Nicola, she guessed, understood her own situation perfectly. Alex and Julian would be horrified, sickened, if *they* knew. She supposed (correctly) that this was the last time she and Charles would ever have sex.

They made breakfast, a mountain of buttery scrambled eggs and a pot of coffee. They were very happy, not daring to think beyond the moment. Elizabeth wondered aloud, 'Is this just some squalid affair, or is it something else?'

'Maybe there's no difference between this and an affair. It's in the eye of the beholder, I guess.'

'There is a difference. Love is never squalid. But it's the lying.'

'Oh, white lies between friends!' he smiled, unconcerned.

'Might it have worked for us,' she asked, 'if our parents hadn't come between us?'

'Darling, it has worked. We've had a wonderful life together. It will always be just us. Always and always, just us.'

*

To get to Alex and Julian's place, you would drive around the city of Montpellier to Route Nationale 109. Hardly ten minutes out of town this old drovers' way to the plateaux country was already climbing, the slopes to either side roughly dressed with wild Mediterranean scrub of bristling dryness. The road skirted massive boulders with the look and feel of pumice. A crest was reached and a curve, and at last ahead opened Languedoc's majestic amphitheatre filled with light and vines. Along a distant horizon lay a low jagged line of heat-shimmering hills.

Back then, after the success of Alex's third album, the Languedoc plain in southern France was known, if at all, for little more than raw red wine, inexpensive and plentiful. The historic drove road has since become an autoroute and some of the wine *domaines* and *caves*, to be sure, deserve compliments. Yet Alex was no connoisseur of wine. It was the air and light, the sound and fragrance that she loved, savouring the place with all the mind's senses.

She drove thirty miles into that luminous, scented terrain before turning off the main road. Steep narrow byways took her into the dense cover of dark evergreen *garrigue*, matted thyme, thistles, rock rose and broom. In places clearings afforded a wide vista across the tapestry of vines below. She would pull onto a verge to take in the view, the wheels of the car crushing roadside tufts that released fountains of scent, aromas that she knew but did not know – wild oregano, perhaps; or wild sage.

Alex's 'tower house', as she called it, grew from a dream, for she had first pictured it while sleeping. The spacious ground floor was laid out as a hexagon to fill with friends and guests, the smaller upstairs a square of private rooms, and from here a tiny stairway spiralled to the circular tower with its keyboard raised above the tops of the *chêne vert*. In this secretive domain there was freedom to move and to think, and a heady sense that days were endless and the diary empty.

Yet her diary was not empty. No longer a 'child prodigy' but a grown-up star, at the tower house she prepared for a relentless regime of concerts. And from each tour she returned through the dry hills to her little room among the tree tops.

The London base could hardly be more different, a large brick studio on the "Bow Backs", as they were called, the meandering back rivers off the River Lea. The building was one of the centuries-old tide mills north of Stratford High Street, defunct yet sound, refashioned as modern studios in which to live, work and play. There was space for the whole band to rehearse, and no neighbours to annoy.

Even the ravaged terrain of abandoned, despoiled waterways had a strange fascination. Alex found it oddly inspiring to look out in the early morning at the ghostly desolation of former workplaces and murky canals. Plucky vegetation found footholds between fences, railings and concrete. From brickwork and bridges trailed tangled foliage and branches, green weedy bittercress and agrimony, pondweeds, ragged water plantain and feral garden blooms. Resolute tufts thrust roots into ancient rotting timbers.

There was wildlife, too. Rats, cats and foxes knew the place well. In the insalubrious waters peaceful ducks swam innocent of the discarded tyres and waste. Exquisite dragonflies and damsels, butterflies and hoverflies inhabited the air. Flocks of pigeons flew down in elegant arcs to forage jerkily on grassy towpath strips.

Despite these beauties, Alex and Julian came here solely to work. Alex bought a scooter, a nippy Vespa, to dash around town. In the traffic it was faster than a car. Being hidden away in Stratford had advantages. For one thing, they were not known or recognised. Around here, in this uneasy minestrone of cultures and nations, no one took any notice of anyone.

Hers was certainly not a familiar face to the immigrant communities. Being a classical and jazz pianist did not make her a household name in this neighbourhood. Most, she guessed, had never heard a note of Scott Joplin, Thelonious Monk or Charlie Mingus, nor Vladimir Ashkenazy or Daniel Barenboim or Martha Argerich – let alone Alexandra Kassin. Quite a few, she suspected, had never even heard of Mozart or Gershwin. They knew what they knew. They had other concerns, other music and other heroes.

*

Maud made her way from room to room with a duster and cloth. She would need to rest afterwards, even have a little nap. She rather liked to sit in the armchair after some housework, with a cup of tea and her Daily Mail, and fall into a doze. With the arthritis, and having no reason to go out, Maud did not often leave the house. She kept the radio on low during the day. Its voices, barely audible, did provide a sort of companionship.

From the upstairs window Maud observed her neighbours. What she observed was that the estate had changed. There were now cars parked where the front gardens used to be. A few people, she realised, did keep an eye out for her, the kind, noticing ones. Nowadays, though, such people could be dangerous. Instead of knocking on the door to offer help, today's 'do-gooders' call social services. She did not want that! Pried into, interfered with, taken away.

There was something oddly enjoyable about getting washed and dressed and putting on proper shoes and her coat and hat for the weekly outing to 'the shops'. She went no further than the parade where she used to work. These days walking on the flat felt like walking up a steep hill. It was slow, but Maud preferred not to use a stick. Her hips and feet hurt too, walking. But she was not infirm. She could manage. She wanted people to see that.

She hoped not to encounter any youngsters en route. She was friendly if she met any. The lads and lasses these days, you had to be careful, you never knew what they would do.

Of course, no one at the Co-op knew her any more. It was hardly surprising after so long. Aching and weary, she returned to the house with a carrier bag that seemed to pull first one arm, then the other, half out of its socket. It was worth it. She put everything in its place, made a cup of tea and told herself she had thoroughly enjoyed taking the air and meeting people. The television was switched on and replaced the radio as her companion for the rest of the day.

Perhaps she was dozing slightly in front of the television. The sound was immense, a bang that overwhelmed her. Bewildered and afraid, Maud could not understand what had happened, or was happening, and in the same instant glass shattered beside her. The front window! Her heart rattled trembling against her ribs, breath gasping, arms and legs immovable heavy as lead. But she must not remain sitting and vulnerable. She forced herself to her feet, standing in a terror such as she had not felt since the awful day Micky Sleet set fire to their home. Now, in the madness of fear, she believed Micky Sleet had come once again. Inside her skull a rhythmic tympanum began to pound, for a few seconds there was a whirling dizziness and shifting darkness. Her legs were trembling, her hands shaking. She held the chair for balance.

But Micky was long dead, she recalled. She tried to make sense of things. It was past ten o'clock. There was a guffaw outside, two or three men's voices laughing, and a woman cackling too. For two brief seconds Maud returned in vivid memory to the sounds of a childhood night when coloured slivers from the pub's breaking windows crashed down into the saloon bar. Maud braced herself for a confrontation, perhaps torment or torture. She supposed she would probably put up resistance, though her body was as feeble and fragile as a twig. Would it be wiser, she wondered, not to resist? She damned her cowardice. She remembered the bravery of other women, her own mother among them. That old pistol of Dad's was packed away upstairs somewhere.

She switched off the light and the television and peeked between the curtains. She was afraid to reveal herself. In the window was a large hole. Shards and splinters and countless tiny specks of glass clung to the curtain, the sill and the fitted carpet beneath. For a moment she began picking them out of the curtain fabric, then stopped. There were too many. She could not face dealing with it.

Through the window she saw no one. The street was empty. From the houses opposite, no face looked out curiously. The laughter had stopped. Raucous voices were moving swiftly into the distance. She looked again at the jagged opening in the window, thinking perhaps to cover it. The shape was uneven; she did not know where to begin.

The object itself, Maud saw now, the missile thrown at her house, was a can of beer. She pushed it with her foot. It was unopened. 'Who would do that? Why?' she asked aloud. 'Waste a can of beer like that?'

The sound of her own voice restored a sort of normality to the room. She pulled the curtains together. She felt nauseous, her whole body shivering. Maud picked up the phone, but stopped herself. It was too late to call Elizabeth. What could Elizabeth do, in any case, at this hour? It would just worry her.

She went upstairs, step by step. In the bedroom she lay clothed on the bed intending at all costs to remain alert and watchful but fell at once into fretful unconsciousness. At two-thirty in the morning she awoke terribly thirsty, mouth like sand, and was disgusted that she had not undressed nor cleaned her teeth. Cautiously she looked out of the window. All was dark and quiet.

Maud waited before phoning Elizabeth in the morning. It would be embarrassing to seem panicked. Nor did she want to appear pathetic and helpless, or admit to being petrified with fear. She tried to speak lightly. 'You'll never believe it, love, someone threw a can of beer through the living room window last night. Ha ha! Frightened me half out of my wits! Made a terrible mess.'

'A can of *beer*? Was the window open?' Elizabeth's tone suggested her mother might be confused or mistaken. 'You don't mean it broke the window?' She asked three times for a fuller account, eventually arriving at 'Oh, no! How absolutely horrid!' Even then she struggled to grasp the enormity of what had occurred. 'So is the window actually broken, right now? Is there glass everywhere?' The answer to both was Yes. 'Did you see who did it?' The answer was No.

'Are you hurt?' – 'I'm fine.'

'Have you told the police?' – 'The police! What good would that do? Surprised at you.'

'I'll come over after work.'

Elizabeth let herself in. She was shocked by her mother's appearance. Old and feeble as Maud was, at this moment she looked older still, haggard, dazed after her wretched night. In the face and eyes was a weary incomprehension. She looked terribly afraid.

Maud, for her part, was equally startled by Elizabeth's appearance. Because as she waited anxiously Maud had fallen into daydreaming of family life, the three of them, her bright little girl so shy and clever. It made her jump to see a trim, severe woman in her late forties, smart in a pale shirt and dark trousers and well-fitted jacket. The straight hair was neatly cut with a touch of grey. At that moment she did not recognise her own daughter.

'Oh, Mum, you poor thing!' Turning to look at the damage, Elizabeth said, 'Don't worry, I'll take care of it.'

She immediately set to work, brushed and gathered the broken fragments, vacuumed the carpet and the curtains. 'Probably wouldn't have happened if you had double glazing,' she remarked. 'Probably would've bounced off. These old estates *desperately* need modernising.' Her mother did not respond.

Elizabeth covered the broken pane with cardboard. 'I'll stay over and see what can be done tomorrow.'

'Would you? That's nice. You know, what really worries me,' said Maud, 'is why they threw it. Was it personal?'

'Why would it be?'

'Revenge.'

'Revenge! For what?'

'I don't know. Things years ago.'

Elizabeth smiled. 'What things? It was just idiots having a laugh –

what *they* call a laugh. You were unlucky, that's all.'

'This estate has become so rough.'

The next morning Elizabeth made a quick outing to the hardware shop in the parade. She saw nothing rough or threatening at all. *But then, I'm not frail and elderly*. The shopkeeper cut a piece of glass to size and sold her a tin of putty. She told him what had happened. 'Mum says the estate is getting rougher.'

'Oh blimey, she's right there,' he agreed grimly.

Before lunchtime, Elizabeth had removed all the broken shards and replaced the window pane. She washed her hands and put on her jacket. Maud hugged her with feeble arms. 'D'you have to go so soon, dear? Stay awhile. I bought a bit of fish we could have for lunch.'

'Sorry, Mum. I've got work to get on with.'

Maud watched from the door as her daughter walked briskly away, along the curve of the street and out of view.

It occurred to Elizabeth before she reached the station that she had made a serious mistake. She had come to help her mother. Instead she had seen only a broken window and repaired it. There was more to this than a pane of glass. It was the human being that had been shattered. She had come all this way and *not* helped her mother. It might almost have been better to forget the window and pay more attention to the woman. She chided herself: she lacked warmth and understanding. She could at least have stayed for lunch. Well, it was done now. And she really did have work to get on with.

Maud steeled herself to dial Dora Sleet's number. Surely *she* could deal with whoever did this. That old promise to Len still stood! She hesitated. No doubt Dora would say nothing can be done about a few louts in the street. On the other hand, she might be able to find out who they were. And if she found out, she would deal with it. Maud dialled the number and the phone was answered. Dora Sleet, she learned, died in a care home at Leigh-on-Sea three years ago.

Died in a care home! And her so young! Maud sat back in her armchair. Truly she felt alone in the world.

She was mistaken. She was not alone. One of the 'do-gooders' she dreaded had been observing poor Mrs Blake. She had noticed the broken window and the daughter's hasty overnight visit. She had been in touch, not with social services but with Age Concern. That very afternoon one of the charity's volunteers called on Maud. She was a pleasant, kindly, down-to-earth woman in her late thirties, wearing a generous amount of mascara and lipstick. She said her name was Renée ("Reenie"). 'We heard you need some help. I'll do what I can.'

'Who sent you, Reen? Not council are you?' Maud was suspicious.

Renée showed her identification and explained. She lived on the estate, a short drive away. Her two children were at the junior school. Her husband, a bricklayer, ran a small building firm. 'I do his books,' said Renée. 'I'm happy to give you a hand two or three days a week.'

'Why, Reen, why should you?'

'Do with a bit of help managing things, couldn't you? And a bit of company? Well, then. It's no trouble.'

'D'you want a cup of tea?'

'Sit tight, I'll do it,' said Renée.

'Fancy a piece of cake?' suggested Maud. 'Go on, don't let it go to waste after the ruddy struggle I had making it!' With a rueful chuckle Maud explained her difficulty lifting a bowl of cake mix.

Renée drove her to a 'proper supermarket' for some shopping, brought her home and made 'a nice bit of supper'. Renée seemed like a real daughter, the sort of daughter Maud sometimes wished she had, an ordinary woman with an ordinary husband. They chatted about family and TV shows and the doings of the neighbourhood. They shared their sadness about Princess Diana. They agreed about politics: 'That bloke Major, honestly!' – 'The Tories had it coming. Never should've got rid of Maggie!' – 'The poll tax was what did for her. She lost her touch.'

At the supermarket Renée persuaded Maud to buy ready-made cake in future. 'Just as good and keeps for ages. It's the easy way, Maud. Do things the easy way.'

Despite Renée's friendly companionship, Maud would never again leave the house unaccompanied. She remained always alert, listening. Her sleep was worse, bad dreams more frequent, her digestion affected. She settled into a routine of dread, wondering who was watching, pondering who was responsible. Sometimes she stood in her bedroom with the light out, peering through a narrow gap in the curtains at the empty street.

6

E lizabeth walked to the library to read the law reports. About an hour later she returned to chambers. On her desk lay a message from the clerk: *Call at once, very urgent.* It was her mother's phone number.

But it was not her mother who answered the phone. She heard a stranger's voice. 'You Maud's daughter? I'm from over the road. The ambulance has took your mum to Oldchurch Hospital in Romford. You need to get over there quick.'

'I'm at work. What's the matter? Is she ill?'

'I saw her front door was stood open and her lying on the floor. So I've come over to see what's happened. I rang 999.'

'On the floor?'

'Yeah, on the mat. Shall I shut her door – you got a key?'

'Yes. I'll come straight away. Thank you so much for helping her.'

It was past six when Elizabeth arrived at the hospital. As soon as she asked after Mrs Blake, a nurse led her to a windowless side room.

'I'm sorry,' said the nurse, 'I'm afraid we couldn't save her. It was a coronary thrombosis. A heart attack.'

Elizabeth's first thought was that presumably they bring you into this room in case you have hysterics. She did not have hysterics. She was aware of no emotion whatever. 'Are you saying... my mother is actually dead?' She had understood, yet wanted absolute clarity.

'I'm sorry.'

'Was she alone at the end?'

The nurse made an apologetic movement of the shoulder. 'She wouldn't have known anyway. She was already beyond help when the ambulance got to the house. We tried everything.'

In another room, a figure lay on a trolley, skeletal beneath a single sheet. At first sight it hardly seemed to be her mother at all. Indeed, the thought crossed Elizabeth's mind, *when your mother dies, is she still your mother?*

Staring at the lifeless creature, suddenly she felt the loss. Not only did she now recognise the drawn, stricken features as her own mother, but she felt engulfed by the pathos of every woman's and every man's wearisome struggle to make a good life. The futility of our efforts. This is what it comes to. Long years at work, private worries about health and money, all our hopes and disappointments, instants of abandon and joy and forgetfulness. As she stood by the body, she seemed to see a few treasured snapshots. Unconnected fragments filled her mind: Mum in the garden, making Dad's tea, Mum glancing up from the piano. Happy moments that passed unnoticed.

Why had she not had such thoughts when her father died? She did not know. Perhaps because she was younger then, perhaps because Dad was a man, perhaps because she never saw him laid out like this. Perhaps because she was angry with him.

Elizabeth knew of herself that she kept a tight rein on emotion. She always held down whatever inwardly stirred. Yet suddenly now weeping began, beyond her will or understanding, stinging her eyes and grasping her throat as she gazed without sound or movement into the dead face.

She brushed the permed hair back and bent to kiss the forehead. It was not cold. It seemed that the closed eyelids might open at the mere touch of a hand. 'Oh, Mum,' she said with gentle reproach, as if her mother had died by some pitiful carelessness. But the reproach was to herself. She knew with horrible veracity that she had not done enough for her mother, not been kind enough, not truly empathised with her, nor made her old age as good as it could be. Then, again without any will on her part, Elizabeth's tears ceased. *This is the way it is.*

At a call box by the hospital entrance, she phoned Bernard. 'I'm getting a taxi to Mum's house.' The words gave her a sickly, poignant sensation. *Is it Mum's house anymore? The dead have no home. Mum is no longer a council tenant. I must let them know.*

'Do you want me to come over?' he asked.

'Not really. I mean, yes, if you want to.'

In the living room nothing was unusual except the absence of Maud herself. Even so, she could be seen clearly. The cushions of the armchair were indented by the shape of her. A cup with cold dregs of tea stood on the little table beside, lip-marks on the rim. Her Daily

Mail had been dropped on the floor. The lid of the piano was open.

'I suppose she was playing it, as best she could with those painful fingers! Poor Mum!' Elizabeth spoke aloud to herself. 'This very day, she was sitting there! A living woman, making music! I wonder what was in her mind at that moment.' For the first time – too late – Elizabeth caught a glimpse into Maud's private existence. The solitude. 'I must sort out her things. Most of it's cheap rubbish,' she added with a note of bitterness, 'not worth keeping.' Next, contradicting herself, 'The piano and all her records. *They're* not rubbish. And the photo albums.'

The hall phone rang. It was Bernard. 'Shall I come over?' he asked.

'No need, really. 'I'll stay here until I've dealt with everything. All the formalities.'

'Well, I'll come anyway and be with you.'

'What must have happened,' Bernard keenly pieced together the evidence before him, 'was she got up from the piano, made herself a cup of tea, and sat in her armchair reading the paper while she drank it. She felt something seriously wrong, maybe a terrible pain in the chest. She managed to reach the front door and opened it to call out for help.'

'Or, she opened it so she could be seen. Otherwise no one would have found her until Reen's next visit. Maybe she realised what was happening to her.'

Bernard accepted this. 'And the instant she hit the floor, whatever it was Maud knew and never told us, whatever she feared, whatever she remembered, vanished from the world as if it had never been.'

'Not as if it had never been…' Elizabeth began. Then she saw what he meant: *The spell of the past is broken.*

*

A concert hall is a place of work, a concert is a product for sale and an after-concert party is a business meeting of sorts. Alex ate sparingly, drank little and paid close attention. The band were seated with their manager, the hall director and an American donor and promoter who had flown out to Tel Aviv to join them tonight. By the close of the evening an American tour was agreed in principle. There was mention of relocating to New York.

The reception finished at eleven-thirty. All emerged in good humour into a wide avenue where couples and families strolled on a pleasant tree-edged central walkway. Children here, it seemed, had no bedtime. Alex's next performance was not until Sunday; she was at leisure. The rest of the band, in high spirits, were heading up to a jazz club in the port area: 'Come with us.'

Alex called back, 'We'll come later, what's the club, where is it?'

Instead she and Julian returned to the seafront. There they sauntered hand in hand on the wide promenade. Bar tables on the beach were inviting under light bulbs precariously strung up. Thousands of people were out tonight in the balmy air, an exquisite warm breeze blowing in from the Mediterranean. Groups of friends sat chatting on plastic chairs. Middle-aged men were busking in string quartets, playing classical pieces. An elderly woman in a smart suit played a haunting tune on the violin, some sort of folk music. They put coins down for her. Across the beach, waves broke white under a black sky. Silhouettes of men and women could be made out at the water's edge, embracing in the dark.

Alex and Julian crossed the sandy beach to stand by the shifting darkness of the water, white spirals of surf just visible out to sea. Away from the streetlights and the bars the dome of the sky was full of stars.

When at last they returned to the hotel the receptionist handed Alex a message. *From Elizabeth Kassin. Darling, tried to reach you. So sorry, bad news. Gran died today from a heart attack. All love, Mum.*

Alex stepped back in dismay and sat down on a sofa at reception. 'Oh, poor old Gran!'

Julian put a consoling arm around her. 'What do you want to do? Go back home?'

'No, I can't cancel Sunday. She wouldn't have wanted me to. I'll go back for the funeral.'

*

Elizabeth notified the council that their model tenant for over forty years had passed away. There was no reply. She cancelled the television hire and the daily paper. For the death certificate, she gave her mother's occupation as "shop assistant and pianist."

She asked the rabbi, 'As mum wasn't Jewish, should I sit shiva?'

'Follow the customs of your mother's own community,' he advised. 'There's nothing to stop you lighting a shiva candle and mourning her as you wish in private.'

Bouquets and wreaths were brought to Maud's front garden and heaped upon the grass in their cellophane wrappings. That was certainly the custom of Maud's community. Bernard had never seen anything like it. The surprise for Elizabeth was just how many flowers and how much cellophane kept arriving until the little front lawn was covered entirely. Bunches were being delivered by the florists in the parade and placed straight on the pile without even a knock at the door. Every house in the street sent something. People at bus stops and in shops told each other, 'You know old Mrs Blake in the Crescent died? Ninety-something, she was. Lovely lady. She was one of them that come from East Ham after the War. Not many of 'em left.'

When the hearse pulled up outside, armfuls of flowers were gathered up and placed around the coffin. Sprays from Elizabeth and Bernard and from Alex were already on show. At a stately pace the vehicle set off for Manor Park crematorium, 'to join Len' as Maud had wished, followed by two limousines and a string of saloons and hatchbacks. Having been housebound for years, seen by few and forgotten by most, today Maud was in everyone's thoughts.

It was a long drive at an unseemly speed along the A13 and North Circular, slowing to a more funereal pace on reaching the traffic of Romford Road. There, pedestrians looked up blankly at the passing cortège. Elizabeth, Bernard and the others in their turn gazed out indifferent at colourful parades of Pakistani and Bangladeshi diners and mini-supermarkets, African hair salons, Halal take-aways. The ancient thoroughfare was as always a grimy unprosperous boulevard, a series of busy high streets edged with brick buildings Maud might have recognised. Most of the mourners had not been here in years. Some pointed out closed-down pubs they had known, disused churches and chapels.

After the ceremony the convoy repeated the voyage, and reaching the house all were given tea, cream cheese and cucumber sandwiches and cake. A smiling photograph of Maud hung over the mantelpiece. As such receptions can be when the deceased had reached 'a good age', it was a jolly occasion. Old acquaintances were met with smiles.

Elizabeth thanked the woman from across the road for calling the ambulance, and hugged Renée. Among the guests were those who recalled Len as well as Maud; what a fine chap he was, they said, capable and quiet. It pleased Elizabeth to listen to their reminiscences. Alex asked, 'Mum, can I play some of Gran's favourite tunes?' Elizabeth said, 'Yes, go on, then. She loved a party.'

Alex's tender version of *As Time Goes By* caused many to fall silent. It brought tears to the eyes of some in Maud's living room. Most knew that her grand-daughter became a concert musician, others did not, but all agreed she was a chip off the old block at the keyboard.

Elizabeth stayed another week at Maud's house, examining every object her mother had gathered and deciding its fate. Large plastic rubbish bags on the floor were the destiny of almost everything. There were puzzling discoveries, among them an extraordinarily beautiful purse or evening bag of tiny pink and pale blue enamel squares on a delicate silver net. It looked very precious, almost certainly antique. It was not the kind of thing her mother would own or could afford. Elizabeth was delighted; she certainly intended to keep it. Inside, another surprise, three crisp ten-pound notes. Oddly, one other small item had been set aside with a written instruction, an envelope inscribed in the wavering hand of Maud's last years, "For Alexandra and Julian when I have passed away."

For the rest, with curtains down, rugs rolled, the contents packed and her parents departed, Elizabeth hardly knew the place as her childhood home. The rooms looked much smaller than she remembered. It was as if she had never lived in this house.

Alex and Julian came to see. Elizabeth presented them with the envelope. 'I've no idea what it is.'

Alex peeled the paper open with care, unwilling to tear the precious handwriting. Inside was nothing but a curious trinket. It was a cheap-looking necklace, maybe even home-made, a square of smooth steel on a flimsy chain. From its centre a delicate heart shape had been cut.

'Wow, it's fantastic,' said Alex. 'I love that it's steel, not silver.'

'Well, that *is* a surprise!' cried Elizabeth, sincerely. 'It's not something I've ever seen.' It was incomprehensible. *Mum surely knew Julian was a Sleet.*

Alex said, 'If Gran wanted us to have it, I wonder why she never gave it before. What did it mean to her?'

Julian helped her put on the necklace, fastening the clasp behind.

'I can't imagine,' Elizabeth replied. She showed them her grandfather's old pistol and cosh. 'Look what else I found in Gran's wardrobe. A dealer is interested in them.'

'Blimey, what are they for?' queried Julian. 'That club looks vicious.'

'Ghastly, isn't it? Apparently my grandad needed it to keep order at his pub in Barking!' Elizabeth chuckled.

Julian did not understand. She explained. 'Maud was born in a pub in Barking, in a room over the bar. Her dad was the manager. Her piano,' she pointed at the instrument, 'used to be in the pub.'

'Really, that's amazing! My family had a pub in Barking,' Julian exclaimed. 'What was it called, the pub?'

'Oh, what was it – the Smack or something?' answered Elizabeth. 'I've never been there. I don't know Barking.'

'Wow, not the old Well Smack? That *is* the pub great-uncle George used to run!'

Alex was thrilled. '*Is* it? What a funny name, "Well Smack." Might our families have been friends, back then?'

Elizabeth felt dizzy with a disconcerting realisation, as if she had picked up a stray piece from a jigsaw but could not see where it fit. *Dad said I would be told when I was older. Well, I'm older and still haven't been told.* They destroyed her relationship with Charles because of it. Hadn't her mother mentioned "that man Sleet" appearing in bad dreams?

She said, 'I don't think they were actually friends. I believe my mother did have some dealings with the Sleet family. I was never told what it was about. I asked Yitzy once; you know, old Mr Zuckerman? Because he and Mum knew each other when they were kids. But he said he couldn't remember.'

Alex suggested eagerly, 'Julian, we must go and see this pub on the way back! We'll have a drink there, raise a glass to Gran in her memory. She would have loved that.'

Alex and Julian sat astride the Vespa and said farewell. 'Will you be staying in London for a while?' Elizabeth asked. – 'No, we're going back to France.' – 'When's America?'– 'That's not for a couple of months, Mum.' – 'Keep in touch, won't you, darling? Please.'

Alex promised she would. She revved the engine and drove along the Crescent, past the Co-op, the parade of shops, away from Elm Park estate, never to return. It took barely fifteen minutes to reach Barking. 'Look, it's still there.' She pulled up opposite the pub, which was now called simply The Well.

'Why was it called the Smack – was it to do with fighting?' wondered Alex. She laughed, 'Maybe that's why he had that cosh!'

Julian did not know. He pushed the door. Inside, the light was low, everyone was black, most were men. House music with a powerful bass pulsed and pressed the air. 'Wow, what is this?' Julian yelled into Alex's ear. 'A nightclub in the afternoon?'

'Listen!' she urged. 'Afrobeats. Drums in clave rhythm.' The very breath inside her lungs seemed to be vibrating.

He shook his head. 'I feel like an intruder. Still want to raise a glass to your gran?'

She smiled wickedly. 'Let's ask for a drink and see what happens.'

'Too loud. We can't talk in here.'

'No. And it's not the same place anymore. Not the place she knew.'

They turned instead towards a street market, its stalls strung with replica handbags, plastic sunglasses, women's wear improbably capacious and impossibly skimpy. The food barrows were piled with bulbous fruit and vegetables green or gold, brown or white, cassava and yams, pale garden egg, okro, bunches of fresh ewedu and oha leaves, heaped agbalumo.

'We could buy some,' suggested Alex. 'I wonder what you do with them. Let's ask.'

'What about a take-away?' Open-sided vans were serving suya, spicy skewered meats with jollof rice, and meat pies, grilled fish, yam and sauce and fried plantain. Alex and Julian asked uncertainly for jollof with fried plantain, and sugar and cinnamon bofrot to follow. They carried their meal to a bench by the ruins of old Barking Abbey.

'Whoa, spicy! So jollof is like biryani?' said Julian.

'No, biryani's creamier. It's different spices.'

After a couple of mouthfuls Julian commented, 'Rather have some pie 'n' mash 'n' liquor.'

Alex laughed. She had never known Julian eat pie and mash. She did not even know where the nearest eel and pie shop could be found.

From the Abbey they strolled along a riverside footway where once were the Roding's vanished quays and wharves. The path ended at a closed area where medieval workshops had lately been unearthed.

They set off towards the Stratford studio, Alex threading through the Romford Road traffic. Julian, clinging on behind, yelled, 'Pull over for a minute.'

'Why?'

'Need to ask you something.'

She turned up Rabbits Road and drew up beside the lake at Wanstead Flats. 'What's up?'

He said, 'Let's walk for a bit.'

They stood on the rough grass. He said, 'Alex, how do you feel about getting married?'

She grimaced. 'What, *us*?'

'Idiot! Of course I mean *us!*'

'Why?'

'So is that a "yes"?'

'Would I have to be Mrs Sleet?'

He smiled. 'Be anything you like.'

'OK then. Give us a kiss.'

Letting go his embrace, he gestured, 'Up that road there's a lovely bluebell wood. D'you want to see it?'

'Is this the right time for bluebells?'

'The perfect moment.'

---

www.ingramcontent.com/pod-product-compliance
Lightning Source LLC
Chambersburg PA
CBHW070021100426
42740CB00013B/2572